DINNER CHEZ MOI

LAURA CALDER

DINNER CHEZ MOI

THE FINE ART OF FEEDING FRIENDS

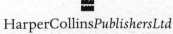

HarperCollins*Publishers*Ltd

Dinner Chez Moi
Text and hand-drawn illustrations copyright © 2011 by Laura Calder.
Photography copyright © 2011 by James Ingram.
All rights reserved.

Published by HarperCollins Publishers Ltd

First edition

HarperCollins books may be purchased for educational, business,
or sales promotional use through our Special Markets Department.

HarperCollins Publishers Ltd
2 Bloor Street East, 20th Floor
Toronto, Ontario, Canada
M4W 1A8

www.harpercollins.ca

Library and Archives Canada Cataloguing in Publication

Calder, Laura
Dinner chez moi : the fine art of feeding
friends / Laura Calder.

ISBN 978-1-55468-902-6

1. Entertaining. 2. Cooking. 3. Cookbooks. I. Title.
TX731.C28 2011   642'.4   C2011-903683-5

PP 9 8 7 6 5 4 3 2 1

Printed and bound in China

Food and props styling by Patti Hetherington

I dedicate this book,
with much love,
to my dear friend and the best host I ever met,

John Evans

as well as to "the pub group" (you know who you are),
with thanks beyond words for welcoming
me into your fold.

CONTENTS

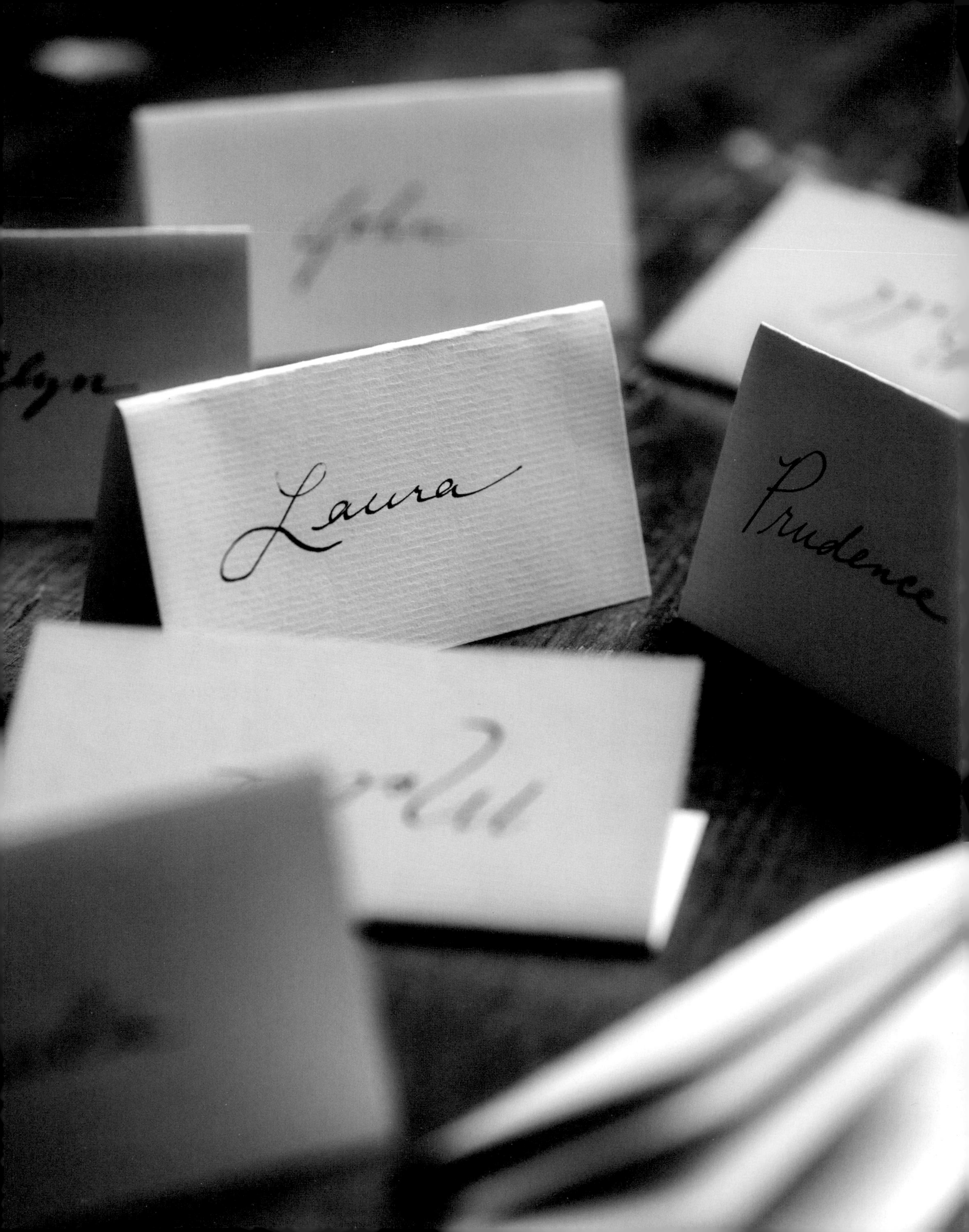
Laura
Prudence

Introduction

THE IRONY OF THIS BOOK'S TITLE, *DINNER CHEZ MOI*, IS THAT WHILE I WAS WRITING it I didn't have a *chez moi* to speak of, unless you counted my red suitcase on wheels. It was a turbulent couple of years, post-Paris, during which era I found myself moving several times, traveling incessantly, and ultimately staying at various friends' houses for long stretches, trying to figure out where I should end up.

Chez moi as a concept was therefore given a lot of thought. I did consider for a while changing the title (*Dinner Chez Everybody Except Moi?*), but in the end I kept it. I realized that feeding friends is about food that comes from the heart, not about what kitchen you happen to cook it in. In other words, *chez moi* is a place within that you give out to the world, and you can't help but take that with you wherever you go any more than a tortoise can his shell. At least that's how I've come to see it.

Another realization I had while writing this book is that in the run of an average day, dinner is often the likeliest candidate for being the highlight. That's an opportunity too good to pass up! It's all fine and dandy to rise to occasions in life, but we also have to take the initiative to create occasions to rise *to* when there don't seem to be any, which is most of the time. This is where dinner comes in with bells on: it's a chance every day to pull ourselves out of the mundane and give our lives a little polish and pizzazz.

None of this is to suggest that we have to get unreasonably fancy about the proceedings, a tendency from our more formal past that seems to have given the term "dinner party" a bad name. I'm aware of the stigma. For some people the very thought conjures up images of starched tablecloths and tomato aspics. In my world, "dinner party" simply means eating with others, so there's no reason not to keep it down to earth if we want to. Even if it's as basic as an omelet or a baked potato, if it's dinnertime and I'm not stuck eating it by myself, that's party enough for me. The menu suggestions in this book are not quite so minimalist, admittedly, but you can always scale them back—or elaborate—to suit your mood and the moment. Besides, setting the tone is a matter not so much of what you serve, but of how you serve it.

I created these menus from recipes I enjoyed with different friends in different places, which is why the mix is eclectic. Initially, I tried to adhere to a strict menu formula, but I quickly realized that food shares something in common with people: it resists being pigeon-holed. Every time I'd add a recipe to a menu, it would make me think of another recipe, sometimes two or three, which of course I couldn't resist including whether they fit or not. So, what you get are menus with occasional intruders (titles set in italics), with which you can do what you like. I like to think the collection has ended up more true to life that way. What we cook is so much a reflection of where we are at any given time and of who we have around us.

You can simply follow the menus as they are or create your own by picking and choosing recipes from throughout the book. I swap them around myself all the time, including dragging in recipes from entirely different cookbooks to keeps things personal and fresh. In any case, the menus take a bit of navigating, because with every recipe I wrote down came a torrent of thoughts and memories and I made no effort to dam the resulting flood. If you're trying to focus on chopping an onion and find that I suddenly veer off onto the subject of a long-ago holiday or the madness of men, now you know why. Perhaps you can think of my ramblings as the kind of chat we might have in the kitchen if we were cooking together, or as a conversation you might have over dinner with friends.

One last note: if you were looking for napkin-folding tricks, theme-party ideas, or dining etiquette and rules, I'm afraid you won't find them here. I did, once upon a time, consider discussing topics such as "how to draw up a guest list" and "how to set the table," but when I put pen to paper I found it all seemed silly and distracting. What's significant when it comes to feeding people is not whether we have impeccable fish-serving skills or the right number of matching silver dessert spoons, perfectly polished. What matters is gathering people we like around a metaphorical fire and sharing good food and a good time. That's the whole point of a dinner party. Seducing you into throwing them more often is the point of this book.

Happy hosting,

Laura

MOSTLY
WARM-WEATHER
MENUS

Cherry Crêpe Stack (p.8)

An Eclectic Lunch to Ward Off the Doldrums

HAVING BEEN A NOMAD ALL MY ADULT LIFE, I'VE REGRETTABLY NOT AMASSED AS MANY household possessions as I'd like. It occurs to me occasionally that if I'd chosen a home and stayed put the past twenty years, instead of trotting all over the planet, I might actually own an ironing board, not to mention a silver tea set, a few gravy boats, possibly a deep freeze . . .

Despite not owning much, I'm no minimalist. My taste is for a house full of all sorts of quirky collected bits: a zillion mismatched cushions on the sofa, piles of books spilling onto the floor, quantities of plants, portraits, mirrors, candlesticks, clocks . . . I'm at a friend's place right now, and trotting across his dining table is a silver rickshaw hauled by a boy and carrying as passengers a saltcellar, pepper shaker, and pot of mustard. How long does one have to live in a place, I wonder, before acquiring one of those?

One of the best parts about eating in other people's houses is seeing how they approach setting a table. The aesthetic is always delightfully revealing about the character of your host and his priorities in life. My friend Bill has the most exhaustive collection of discontinued Blue Willow china you've ever seen in your life. (Why, egg cups for the entire extended family, should he so choose!) My friend John is addicted to the Salvation Army. His kitchen cupboards sag under the weight of mismatched plates from bungalows gone by. Bridget on the East Coast has inherited the most gorgeous jade-green-rimmed china and another set of blue-and-brown floral-patterned soup plates, which I covet like a green-eyed monster. I myself have gargantuan German cutlery that you could row a boat with, but my plates *du jour* are boring white Limoges. As soon as I get them out of their storage boxes I may well dispense with them in one swift Frisbee tournament in the park. Then I can replace them with something more splendid.

What constitutes a nicely set table is, obviously, a very personal matter, but it does matter. After all, everything tastes better when it looks nice. No different from clothing style, food is more appealing when its presentation hints at something of the person behind it. That's why it makes me smile when John bakes his Key lime pie in that funny enamel plate he keeps in a drawer under the telephone. Anne and Ian have a marvelous wooden aperitifs tray, as long as a two-by-four but thin-lipped and which I think must be African. Meanwhile, nobody is better equipped for cupcake presentation than Dana; she has at least five frilly pedestal plates perched atop her fridge.

That reminds me of a platter I once desperately wanted at an auction. It was very old, and the porcelain was thick with painted figures and landscape etched onto it in an unusual plum-purple ink. The auctioneer's son was bidding against me (not exactly fair). Everyone else had dropped out of the bidding, and the son hiked it higher and higher until the price of that platter was as much as a plot of land and a title. The auctioneer's son got away with that one. Ever since, I've kept my eyes peeled for another like it, but I've never found one. Pity, because the halibut from this menu would have looked lovely on it, with the asparagus and mushrooms scattered pastorally beneath.

I suppose you could argue that all the menus in this book are eclectic (not to say eccentric), but this one in particular, perhaps because it's so motley, seems an especially good contender for doldrums eradication. The first and main courses are extremely easy, including the shopping, because ingredients are few. Make the soup first and get it out of the way, and then just heat it up. The main course you make at the last minute. Dessert is slightly more involved, but well worth the effort. If you don't have time for it, buy raspberries or strawberries and simply serve them with whipped cream and cookies such as Brown Sugar Shortbreads (p. 126).

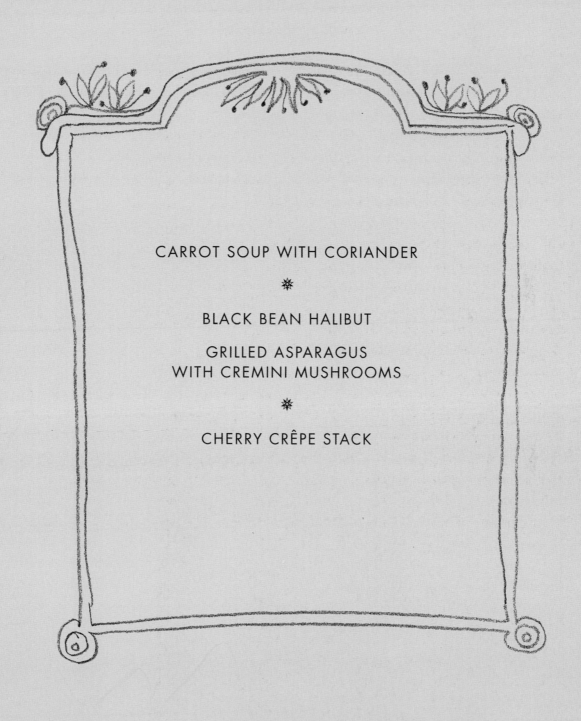

CARROT SOUP WITH CORIANDER

✳

BLACK BEAN HALIBUT

GRILLED ASPARAGUS
WITH CREMINI MUSHROOMS

✳

CHERRY CRÊPE STACK

CARROT SOUP WITH CORIANDER

MAKES: 6 TO 8 SERVINGS

My standards for carrots were set by the sweet ones in my grandfather's garden, which as children between swims in the river we would rip from the ground, wipe clean(ish) on our shirts, and crunch down like candy. What I wouldn't give to have some of those carrots right now! It may sound obvious, but carrot soup is fantastic when you start off with tasty carrots. You can do all sorts of variations on it, adding a bit of ginger or curry or orange juice, but when the carrots are top-notch to begin with, it's nice just to experience how wonderful things can taste when you let them be. Serve colorful bowls of this soup hot, at room temperature, or cold.

2 to 3 tablespoons (30 to 50 mL) butter

2 medium onions, thinly sliced

1 1/2 pounds (675 g) carrots, chopped or grated (about 8 medium)

3 garlic cloves, crushed

1 bay leaf

About 2 cups (500 mL) chicken stock

Salt and pepper

A few spoonfuls of sour cream

Paprika

A handful of fresh coriander leaves

Melt the butter in a large pot and gently sauté the onions until soft. Add the carrots, garlic, bay leaf, and the stock. It should be enough just to cover the vegetables. If not, add a splash more. Season with salt and pepper, bring to a boil, reduce the heat, and simmer until the carrots are very soft, about 15 minutes.

Cool slightly, then discard the bay leaf. Purée in a blender, in batches. If you're serving the soup hot, strain it back into the wiped-out pot and reheat. If you're serving it cold, strain it into a bowl, cool completely, then chill. Serve garnished with a spoonful of sour cream, a sprinkle of paprika, and a generous scattering of fresh coriander leaves.

Pea and Spinach Soup

MAKES: 4 SERVINGS

I once went to the countryside for a feast with friends in a lovely sprawling cottage right on a lake with no one else in sight. We cooked and fussed all day, then sat down to a marvelous meal, made all the better by first-rate storytelling. Our hostess, Donnalu, got the ball rolling early on by making everyone around the table tell a memorable food story. I told about the time I was walking to a birthday party in Paris and someone dropped a carton of tomato sauce on my head from a high-up balcony. I didn't know what had happened: disoriented, I looked down to discover I was covered in blood. . . Mentally, I prepared for the inevitable drop to the ground and my untimely exit from this plane of existence. Then I saw the tomato-sauce box and realized I'd been the target of a nasty prank. I took a taxi home, sobbing and demoralized, stepped fully clothed into the bathtub, and missed the birthday party. Don't feel sorry for me. Good stories are treasures, and it's quite amazing when they manage to fall, quite literally, into our laps. I've been dining out on that one for years! This soup was given to me by Donnalu; it's her favorite.

1/4 cup (55 g) butter
1 to 2 large onions, chopped
10 ounces (280 g) blanched spinach (about 1 packed cup/250 mL)
10 ounces (280 g) blanched peas (about 2 cups/500 mL)
3 cups (750 mL) chicken stock
20 large mint leaves, chopped
Salt and pepper
1/2 cup (125 mL) heavy cream, more as needed

Melt the butter in a soup pot and sauté the onions until very soft, about 20 minutes. Squeeze the spinach dry and chop. Add to the onions with the peas and stock. Bring to a boil, then reduce the heat and simmer for 10 minutes. Add the mint leaves and simmer 5 minutes longer. Purée. Season with salt and pepper. Add the cream and gently reheat. Serve.

BLACK BEAN HALIBUT

MAKES: AS MUCH AS YOU LIKE

An American cook taught me this recipe in a Canadian fishing village, which was good because I'm usually intimidated by exotic ingredients and might otherwise not have tried it. Served in that context of wooden piers, rubber boots, and blazing fireplaces, the dish took a comfortable seat in my brain and made itself at home. As a result, I've made it again and again. It's easy to memorize, but I must have worried I'd forget the details because I later found the recipe I'd scribbled on a piece of paper the night it was served to me. My note reads, "From Nancy, who picked rocks all afternoon and fell on a nail." (Sounds rather Edward Gorey . . .) Anyway, if my aim that night was to jot down recipe "details" I didn't exactly succeed, because all I have is a list of ingredients followed by the instruction, "7 minutes MAX!" Of course there's no temperature recorded . . .

The good news is that details are unnecessary, as I found out when I went to replicate it, so I'm giving you this recipe in a bit of a sketchy way. It's confidence-building, I think, to be reminded that sometimes sketchy is all you need, especially if you're one of those people who thinks your legs will collapse beneath you if you're not given exact quantities right down to the washing-up water, as the late Elizabeth David might have put it. If you happen to be in that fear-riddled category of cooks, please have faith: follow the method below and you'll see that you're quite wrong about needing a strict recipe to create something smashing, and only in a matter of minutes, too.

If you're against using commercial black bean paste, buy fermented black beans instead from a Chinatown near you. Measure a tablespoon of fermented beans per fish fillet, then, with a fork, mash with a drizzle of peanut oil. Scatter the result over the seasoned fish to replace the black bean sauce suggested below.

A piece of halibut per person, about 5 ounces (140 g)

Peanut oil

Salt and pepper

About 1 tablespoon (15 mL) black bean paste per piece of fish

Garlic, cut into paper-thin slices

Fresh ginger, peeled and cut into fine julienne

A few green onions, halved or quartered lengthwise

A splash of sake or white wine

Heat the oven to 400°F (200°C). Rub the fish all over with the oil, season with salt and pepper, and lay the pieces in a baking dish. Smear the top of each with a spoonful of black bean paste. Scatter over some sliced garlic and strands of julienned ginger. Lay a few artistic wands of green onion atop each, and pour around the sake. Bake "7 minutes MAX!," until the fish just flakes. Serve immediately with the mushrooms and asparagus (recipe follows).

GRILLED ASPARAGUS
WITH CREMINI MUSHROOMS

Sticking with the no-recipe theme since, anyway, I don't know how many are coming to dinner, here's what I can tell you: Bunches of asparagus, in markets near me, are about a pound (450 g) each. For 6 people, you'd want 2 of those, the fatter the better, because the skinny ones are like eating twigs. Trim the ends and place on a baking sheet. Clean 8 ounces (225 g) cremini mushrooms and quarter them. Toss with the asparagus and a little olive oil, and season with salt and pepper. Spread out the asparagus in a single layer (the mushrooms can be on top), and pop in the oven at 450°F (230°C) until the vegetables are slightly "shrinkled" (to use the word of a friend of mine describing the inevitability of her future self in old age) and the asparagus is starting to brown. This will take about 15 minutes, and I'd do it before the fish because they won't cool off that much while the fish cooks, and anyway, you could pop them back in for a minute when the fish comes out.

CHERRY CRÊPE STACK

MAKES: 6 TO 8 SERVINGS

The idea of this dessert is that you stack crêpes, which you've brushed with melted butter and sprinkled with sugar, with stewed cherries between the layers. Then you bake the crinkly-edged, sugar-topped stack, strew toasted almonds over top, and serve it in wedges with the sauce. It is extremely impressive, and the whole thing will get gobbled up and make you famous.

The crêpe part of this recipe yields 12 very thin 10-inch (25 cm) pancakes. If you have a crêpe pan of another size, don't worry, just increase or reduce the recipe, so long as you end up with 12 crêpes. You can cook the crêpes until they get some color and even get a bit crisp at the edges. I actually prefer their texture that way for this dessert.

If it happens to be winter (or you're stuck in a bunker) and you can't find in-season cherries, make no bones about using tinned instead. You'll need 3 tins, roughly 15 ounces (425 g) each. Use the juice from only 1 tin, however, and drain the 2 others.

Here's an alternative sauce to the one below if you're fond of caramel: Melt 1 cup (200 g) sugar to caramel. Carefully add 1/2 cup (125 mL) heavy cream, which will splatter and seize but then melt again on the heat. Finally add 1/4 cup (60 mL) brandy. Serve pourably warm. If you make it ahead, it will become firm, but will melt down again when reheated. If it's still too thick, whisk in a little boiling water or more cream.

FOR THE CRÊPES
2 cups (500 mL) milk
1 1/2 cups (185 g) flour, sifted
4 eggs
3 tablespoons (50 mL) sugar
3 tablespoons (50 mL) butter, melted
1/2 teaspoon (2 mL) vanilla
Pinch salt

FOR THE CHERRIES
2 1/2 to 3 pounds (1.1 to 1.3 kg) cherries, pitted
1/2 cup (95 g) sugar
3 strips lemon or orange peel
2 tablespoons (30 mL) cornstarch
Splash kirsch, Grand Marnier, or Cointreau
 (optional)

FOR ASSEMBLY
About 1/4 cup (55 g) butter, melted
About 1/4 cup (55 g) sugar

FOR THE SAUCE
2 cups (500 mL) heavy cream
3 tablespoons (50 mL) sugar
Pinch cinnamon

FOR THE GARNISH
Lightly toasted sliced almonds

First, make the crêpes. Pulse the crêpe ingredients in a food processor until smooth. (Alternatively, whisk together and strain.) Cover and refrigerate 2 hours.

Meanwhile, make the filling. Put the cherries, sugar, and peel in a saucepan and heat until the sugar melts. Simmer 5 minutes. With a slotted spoon, scoop the cherries into a bowl and boil the juices down to 1/2 cup (125 mL) syrup. In a small bowl, stir a spoonful of syrup into the cornstarch to dissolve, then add to the pot and cook until the mixture is thick, about a minute. Stir in the cherries, and add the kirsch (if using). Set aside to cool, so the cake will be easier to assemble.

Stir the crêpe batter, adding more liquid if necessary to bring it to the consistency of thin cream. Pour into a jug. Heat a 10-inch (25 cm) crêpe pan. Brush the surface with clarified butter, unless it's a nonstick pan. Holding the pan in one hand and the jug in the other, pour a little batter into the pan, turning it to coat thinly, and fry the crêpe, flipping once, until done. As the crêpes come off the pan, stack them on a plate and set aside.

To assemble the cake, brush a crêpe with some of the melted butter and sprinkle with sugar. Lay on the bottom of a springform pan just large enough to fit your crepes. Repeat with a second crêpe. Lay over a third (this one unadorned) and top with one-third of the cherry mixture. Repeat this sequence twice more. Finally, lay on the last three butter-brushed and sugar-strewn crêpes, perhaps with a bit of extra sugar on the top one.

For the sauce, put the cream, sugar, and cinnamon in a large saucepan and gently boil down to about 3/4 cup (175 mL), about 5 minutes, by which time it will be very lightly caramelized and thick. (If prepared ahead, the sauce will firm up slightly, but you can gently reheat before serving to thin it out again.)

Heat the oven to 350°F (180°C). If you haven't yet toasted the almonds, spread them on a baking sheet and do it now. They won't take 5 minutes. Set aside. Bake the torte until warmed through and the top is golden, about 15 minutes. Scatter the toasted almonds over the top. Bring the torte to the table warm or at room temperature, and cut into wedges. Serve with the warm sauce passed separately.

Key Lime Pie

I thought this was going to be a perfect end. Oddly enough, it is too close in texture to cooked halibut and therefore boring to serve on its heels. A friend of mine, having just finished said halibut, disagreed. "I don't care about texture similarities," he said. "I love this pie!" The reason I give the recipe, then, is because he said that, not because I'm recommending it in this menu. Also, I have been to Florida, Keys and all, where I ate Key lime pie upon Key lime pie in search of something worthy of the name, and I never found it. Every pie I bit into was dreadful. Where I did find a perfect specimen was *chez* John in his little house clinging by the skin of its teeth to the edge of the crashing Pacific.

Now, one word of warning: despite the exact measurements below, I find I always need to taste the filling before pouring it into the shell to make absolutely sure it's tart enough and limy enough, especially if I've used lime limes in place of Key limes. A sweet lime pie goes against its own nature.

4 teaspoons (20 mL) grated Key lime zest

1/2 cup (125 mL) strained Key lime juice

4 egg yolks

1 tin (10 ounces/300 mL) sweetened condensed milk

1 1/4 cups (150 g) graham cracker crumbs (about 11 crackers)

5 tablespoons (75 g) butter, melted

3 tablespoons (50 mL) sugar

Heat the oven to 325°F (160°C). Mix the zest, juice, and yolks. Beat in the condensed milk. Set aside. Mix the crumbs, melted butter, and sugar and press into a pie plate. Bake 15 minutes. Pour the filling into the shell and bake a further 15 minutes. Cool, then refrigerate at least 3 hours before serving.

AVOCADO WITH CITRUS DRESSING (P. 16)

An Unintimidating Dinner on a Reasonable Budget

N O ONE IN THE FOOD PROFESSION IS EVER GOING TO ADMIT THIS, SO ALLOW ME: COOKING dinner for people is hard work, time consuming, and it costs money, sometimes rather a lot. There. The cat's out of the bag. This may sound like a contradiction, given that I'm in favor of dinner parties being simple and honest, but the fact is that cooking from scratch always requires some effort, and even basic ingredients like butter and potatoes come at a price.

I'm not telling you this to turn you off. I spend nearly all my money feeding people and I don't worry about it because that's what I like to do. What can I say, some people fritter away their fortunes on electronic devices or shoes, I go bankrupt buying cheese. Also, although it takes time to cook and it *is* work, I enjoy the process and would rarely rather be doing anything else, so I can't complain. The trick is finding a balance that works.

In an article I once read about France and its gastronomy, the writer compared traditional French menu service to a funeral procession, yawning about the parade of one boringly delectable dish after the next and about the whole occasion lasting an excruciating number of hours. I'll bet that guy is a barrel of fun at a dinner party.

I can see the point being made about lengthy tasting menus. As far as I'm concerned, a twenty-course feast is a lost cause, because by about dish three your taste buds don't know what's hit them anymore, and besides, you're full, so you can't stay appreciative and excited through to the end. Worse is when home cooks try to replicate restaurant-style tasting menus themselves. Not only does total chaos ensue, but it's antisocial—you don't see your hosts all night because they're up to their elbows (and in way over their heads) in the kitchen the whole time.

All this is to defend the French menu format—at least the simple traditional design, which is *entrée, plat, dessert*—and I do so on the grounds that it is neither too long nor too short. In fact, it's perfect for making dinner a social event around the table (as opposed to just serving a bowl of soup, which is not so convivial because it's over with in a flash). At the same time, the structure prevents home cooks inclined to go overboard from doing too much and getting into a frazzle. (I'm reminded of the time I got myself in so much hot water with an elaborate dinner that my main course failed and I ended up serving boiled eggs in its place.)

You'll be happy to know that this menu is neither too expensive nor too time consuming, so no guests will have to walk away from dinner feeling unreasonably indebted. What's nice, too, is that although the ingredients are familiar supermarket fare, the result is quite chic, all in all a good example of how imposing a few boundaries for ourselves can be liberating rather than limiting. Here's how it goes: you whack up an avocado, roast a chicken, and stick a cake in the oven. That's way cheaper and less emotionally trying than a lot of hobbies, such as electronics and shoes.

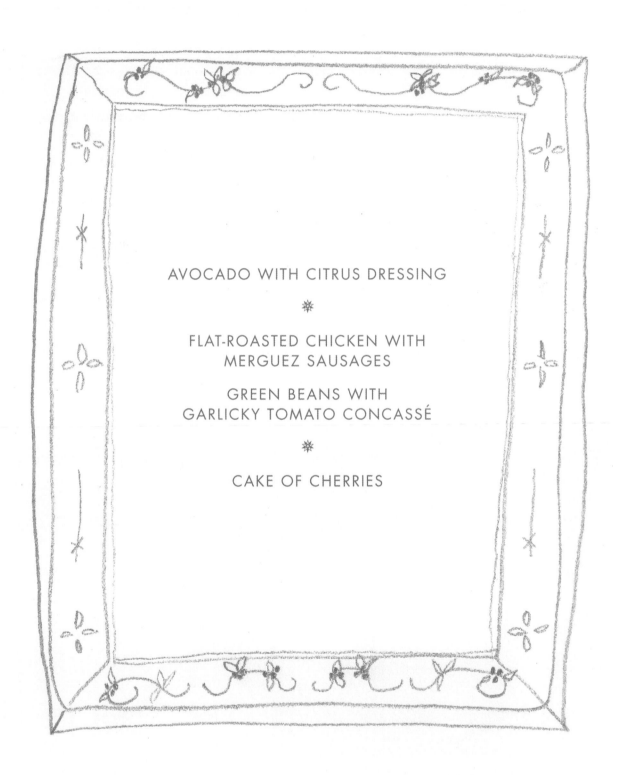

AVOCADO WITH CITRUS DRESSING

❋

FLAT-ROASTED CHICKEN WITH
MERGUEZ SAUSAGES

GREEN BEANS WITH
GARLICKY TOMATO CONCASSÉ

❋

CAKE OF CHERRIES

AVOCADO WITH CITRUS DRESSING

MAKES: 6 SERVINGS

If you're one who gets all in a twizzle over coming up with a first course, this idea is for you: soft, smooth, round-rumped avocado halves with a refreshing dressing of lime, lemon, and orange zests. The concept is inspired by something I used to eat when I briefly apprenticed at a Paris restaurant called Astrance. One of the first things on their menu was a starter of two thin slices of avocado with crab sandwiched between them, minced citrus zests on top, and a drizzle of almond oil. It was very simple, but excellent, and the dish became quite famous.

If you make the crab version, be aware that most almond oils are toasted, which is not ideal. Untoasted almond oil is very delicate and won't overwhelm the crab or the fruit, whereas the toasted varieties tend to take over, so use only a bit, mixed with olive oil, or use just olive oil. Sometimes I add a drop or two of soy or ponzu sauce (citrus soy sauce). You can mix up the dressing a little ahead of time, but the avocados must be cut at the last minute so they don't turn brown.

3 ripe avocados
About 1 tablespoon (15 mL) combined very finely minced or grated lemon, lime, and orange zests
About 3 tablespoons (50 mL) untoasted almond oil or olive oil
A squirt of lemon juice
Fleur de sel and freshly ground black pepper

Just before serving, halve the avocados and remove the pits by whacking a large knife into them and lifting them out. With a large spoon, neatly scoop the whole avocado halves out and set them round side up on 6 plates. Slice crosswise into roughly half-a-finger-width-thick slices, then fan them out a bit on the plates.

Stir the zests into the oil, adding a squirt of lemon. Spoon over the avocados. Season with fleur de sel and freshly ground black pepper. Serve immediately.

FLAT-ROASTED CHICKEN WITH MERGUEZ SAUSAGES

MAKES: 6 SERVINGS

I did think of putting a fancier chicken dish here, but when it comes down to it, nothing beats a well-roasted bird, and I found I kept coming back to this recipe. The meat is juicy, the skin is crisp and golden, and the sausages add a rich, meaty contrast to the mildness of the poultry. The combination is a friend's idea—and I'm in agreement with him in preferring chicken ever so slightly overdone and the sausages dark.

If you decide to roast the bird whole rather than flat, it'll take about 15 minutes longer. Start it on one side, then after 15 minutes flip it to the other side, then after another 15 minutes turn it breast side up, add the sausages to the pan, and continue roasting, basting the chicken occasionally, until the skin is deeply golden and crisp and the juices run clear at the leg when pierced with a fork. Total roasting time for the whole bird will be 1 1/4 to 1 1/2 hours.

If you crave potatoes alongside, see p. 303 for the crisp, oven-roasted kind, which you can put in the oven for the same length of time and at the same temperature as the bird.

1 chicken, about 3 pounds (1.3 kg)
Salt and pepper
1/2 cup (110 g) butter, at room temperature
2 handfuls of chopped fresh thyme leaves
6 merguez sausages, pricked all over

Heat the oven to 425°F (220°C). Pat the chicken dry. Split the bird by cutting down the back (but don't cut into the "oysters," those perfect oval morsels of meat on either side of the back roughly where the thigh bone joins), then cut slits in the skin of the front of the bird to pop the tips of the drumsticks through to hold them in place; the wings, meanwhile, can be folded behind like the arms of a happy sunbather. Season with salt and pepper. Mash the butter with the thyme leaves and smear it all over the bird in a roasting pan. Flip it over so it's breast side down and roast for 15 minutes. Turn it breast side up, add the sausages to the pan, and continue roasting everything, basting the bird occasionally, until the skin is very crisp and golden and the meat is done but still juicy, about 45 minutes longer.

Transfer the chicken to a cutting board and let it rest about 10 minutes before carving it. Serve on a warm platter with the sausages alongside and the thyme-butter juices poured over.

Spicy Chicken with Avocado Sauce

MAKES: 4 TO 6 SERVINGS

If you want to combine the first course and main course in a single dish, here's the answer. A room-mate from university days in Montreal used to make this avocado chicken all the time in our apartment at the corner of Guy and Sherbrooke Streets. Our kitchen and living room were all one room, and I remember she painted all the knobs on the cupboard doors turquoise and kept her cookbooks on a shelf behind one of them. I used to spend hours copying recipes out of her books when instead I should have been memorizing the antics of Greek gods or dissecting poetry. Oh well, surely every great recipe contains a measure of godliness and poetic license, so perhaps, despite the academic losses, something else back then was gained. If you're serving this variation, the green beans don't seem appropriate. Serve some lightly dressed watercress on the side instead.

FOR THE CHICKEN

1 chicken, about 3 pounds (1.3 kg), cut into 8

Salt and pepper

1 tablespoon (15 mL) olive oil

2 tablespoons (30 mL) paprika

1 tablespoon (15 mL) ground coriander

1 tablespoon (15 mL) ground cumin

1 teaspoon (5 mL) chili pepper flakes

About 1 tablespoon (15 mL) butter

FOR THE SAUCE

1 ripe avocado, peeled and cut into chunks

1 garlic clove, chopped

1 tablespoon (15 mL) chopped fresh coriander

1/4 cup (60 mL) yogurt

1/4 cup (60 mL) water

2 teaspoons (10 mL) lime or lemon juice

Salt

Heat the oven to 375°F (190°C). Season the chicken pieces with salt and pepper, place in a shallow roasting pan, and rub all over with the olive oil. Mix the dried spices and rub onto the chicken. Dot with the butter. Roast the chicken until the juices run clear and the skin is crisp, 45 minutes to an hour.

Meanwhile, in a food processor, whiz up the sauce ingredients and refrigerate until serving. Serve the chicken with the cooling sauce alongside.

GREEN BEANS WITH
GARLICKY TOMATO CONCASSÉ

MAKES: 6 SERVINGS

If you can't get nice ripe tomatoes, you can used tinned for this, but I don't have to tell you that for best results you want lovely fine beans and juicy ripe tomatoes at the height of summer. For an Asian twist, add a thumb of fresh ginger, peeled and minced, with the garlic, and garnish the whole dish with fresh coriander leaves.

4 large tomatoes

2 tablespoons (30 mL) olive oil

2 to 3 garlic cloves

1 teaspoon (5 mL) sugar

1/2 teaspoon (2 mL) balsamic vinegar

2 bay leaves

Salt and pepper

1 1/2 pounds (675 g) slim green beans, trimmed

Draw an X in the bottom of each tomato with the tip of a sharp knife and drop them into a large pot of boiling water for about 10 seconds until the skin loosens. With a slotted spoon, scoop out the tomatoes (reserving the water in the pot) and immediately cool in ice-cold water. Peel, seed, and chop the tomatoes to a pulp.

Heat the oil in a large frying pan over medium heat and gently cook the garlic without letting it color, no more than a minute. Add the tomato pulp, sugar, balsamic vinegar, and bay leaves, season with salt and pepper, and cook to a thick sauce, about 20 minutes. Discard the bay leaves.

Bring the tomato water back to a boil and salt it. Cook the green beans to al dente, about 5 minutes depending on their size. Drain, and plunge into ice-cold water to stop the cooking and preserve their color. Drain again.

Add the beans to the tomato concassé and toss to heat through.

CAKE OF CHERRIES

MAKES: 6 SERVINGS

This was cherry cake proper until I got hold of it. The original recipe was a fluffy deal with a smattering of red dots. It was okay, but not that interesting, so I peered into its soul and realized that deep down it wanted to have ground almonds instead of flour and a lot more cherries. Amazing how things blossom when they know they're understood. Suddenly this cake became an almost soufflé-like concoction with juicy summer cherries just held together by a light batter that rises up around them, creating a cloudy, pillowy effect. It doesn't need any ice cream or cream—it's great all on its own—but suit yourself. Incidentally, this dessert is very good for you: eggs, nuts, and fruit, and almost no sugar. You can remember that if there's a leftover piece eyeing you at breakfast time.

4 eggs, separated
1/2 teaspoon (2 mL) vanilla
1/2 cup (95 g) sugar
Zest of 1 lemon
Pinch salt
3/4 cup (100 g) ground almonds
1 tablespoon (15 mL) cherry brandy (optional)
A generous 3/4 pound (340 g) cherries, halved and pitted

Heat the oven to 350°F (180°C). Grease and flour a 9-inch (23 cm) springform pan.

In a large bowl, beat the yolks with the vanilla, half the sugar, and the lemon zest. In another bowl, beat the egg whites with the salt to soft peaks, then beat in the remaining sugar a spoonful at a time until whites are thick and glossy. Stir the almonds into the yolks, adding the cherry brandy if you're using it, then loosen the mixture by gently stirring in a spoonful of whites. Fold in the remaining whites and pour into the prepared pan. Scatter the cherries all over top (they'll sink during baking), and bake until a toothpick inserted in the center of the cake comes out clean, about 45 minutes.

Let cool for about 10 minutes before removing the sides of the pan. Serve warm or at room temperature.

Cherry Pound Cake for Christmas
MAKES: 1 LARGE TUBE CAKE OR LONG LOAF

The person who gave me this recipe swore me to secrecy, she having been sworn to secrecy herself. A long-distance acquaintance of hers was famous for it. "The best, but *the* best buttery, polka-dotted cherry pound cake going," my friend told me, "and *that woman* refused to share the recipe!" Luckily, my friend eventually talked *that woman* into letting her have it, but she agreed only if my friend promised never to tell anyone else, otherwise she'd get run over by a truck or something.

Eventually *that woman* passed away. I was sitting at my friend's kitchen table, pen in hand, listening to this tale. "Surely in the hereafter she's realizing how silly it was to hoard a good recipe all those years," said I. I pressed on, "You know, 'Lay not up for yourselves treasures on earth where moth and rust doth corrupt' and all that." Her eyes did a quick flick heavenward, vaguely tinged with doubt, then she slipped me the recipe. "But you must *never* . . . ," she insisted. "But of course not," I promised. "Mum's the word."

1 1/2 cups (335 g) butter, softened

2 cups (390 g) sugar

3 eggs

1 cup (250 mL) hot milk

2 teaspoons (10 mL) vanilla

3 1/2 cups (435 g) flour

1 1/2 teaspoons (7 mL) baking powder

Pinch salt

1 pound (450 g) candied cherries, halved

Heat the oven to 325°F (160°C). Line a 10-inch (25 cm) tube cake pan or 4 1/2 x 11-inch (12 x 28 cm) loaf pan with parchment paper. In a large bowl, cream the butter and sugar until pale and fluffy. Beat in the eggs 1 at a time. Stir together the milk and vanilla. Sift together the flour, baking powder, and salt. Add the milk mixture and dry ingredients in 3 stages to the butter mixture, beating well after each addition. Stir through the cherries and spoon into the prepared pan. Bake until a toothpick inserted in the center of the cake comes out clean, a generous hour. Cool on a rack.

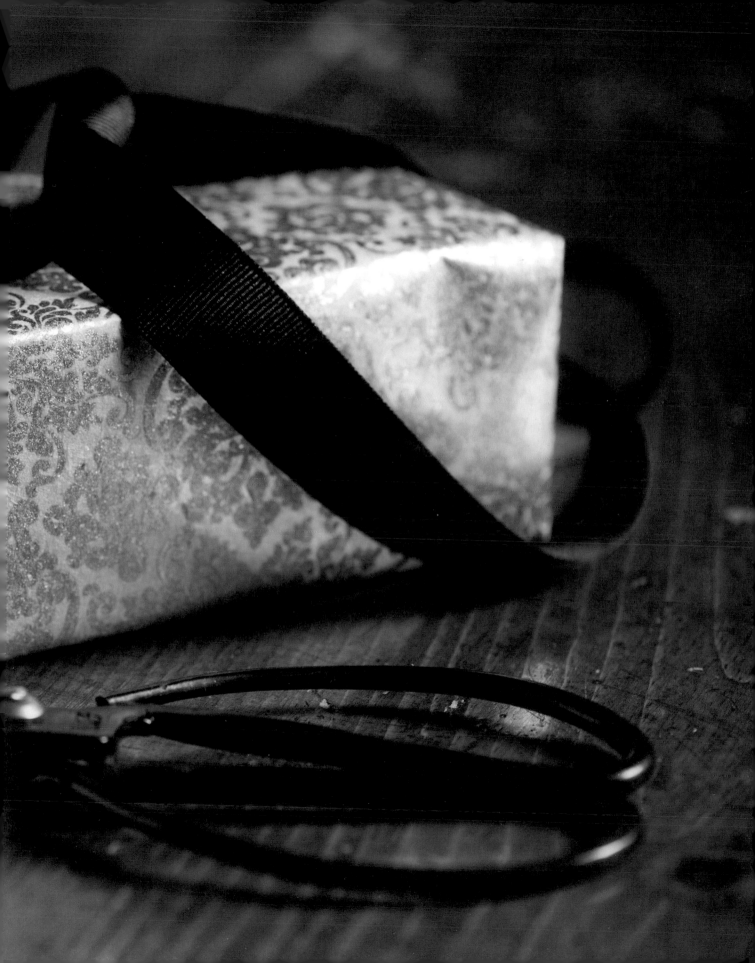

Pflaumenkuchen

MAKES: 12 SERVINGS

Moons ago, I think because of my classical music training in youth, I decided I needed to speak German. I took classes at university and later went to Germany, where I presented myself as an *au pair Mädchen,* the goal being to earn a few bucks taking care of children between my hours plodding through the minefields of *Dativ* and *Akkusativ.* I survived nine months of that in Munich. Before I got there, though, I somehow ended up near the Schwarzwald picking grapes. I stayed on a farm—friends of someone who knew someone who knew someone else—and for a few weeks I'd rise every morning and head out to the fields with a gaggle of Eastern European schoolteachers who were making more money on their grape-picking holiday than they could earn the rest of the year teaching back home. Such are the injustices of the universe.

I think I quite liked the work. We'd pick grapes for hours, which does keep a body strong, then, sitting at a picnic table amidst the vines, lunch on boiled potatoes and Quark, a fresh but relatively boring cheese. Every day we ate that. The experience was not overly interesting gastronomically, but I do remember marveling at the potato-eating method performed by my Eastern coworkers: they'd skewer a fat potato on the end of their fork, hold it up like a prize, then gently peel the skin away with a knife before returning it whole and bald to the plate to eat with the Quark. Attendance at these picnics was not unlike being trapped in a Van Gogh.

The Germans don't, alas, have a great reputation for cooking (neither have the English), but in the world of baking they shine. I have never eaten better breads anywhere in my life than in Germany, and the variety of *Kuchen* and *Torten* is magnificent. Enter a café in Deutschland in the early afternoon and it will be dead; go back around four and you'll find it busting at the seams with cake *Fressers.* You could eat cake every afternoon of the year and never eat the same one twice.

One in particular I remember eating a lot of was *Pflaumenkuchen,* also called *Zwetschgenkuchen.* At the end of summer, plum season swept the land and turned the fields and hillsides purple-black. I have a mental image of myself up a ladder in a Bavarian orchard, my head surrounded by hundreds of dangling, egg-sized bluish orbs, juicy yellow-pink on the inside. The tarts we made from them were on yeast pastry and not small: in fact, I remember them being as wide as a river, the plums fanned across the top like so many sails crammed cheek by jowl in a harbor.

The cake recipe here is similar, only it uses regular cake batter as the base, which I *think* I prefer. It makes a great breakfast or snack cake because it's not overly sweet. I put a nut and sugar streusel over top, but instead you could also strew-zle over *Hagelzucker,* or pearl sugar, which will make it look a bit as if a brief hailstorm had just passed through the kitchen. I'm not sure where to buy it outside Europe, but regular sugar rained over is just as tasty, so adapt to where you are at the moment, whether it be Deutschland or Timbuktu.

I am now tempted to tell you about how my German boss lived in a surprisingly *gemütlich* circus wagon in a Munich park, but for fear of testing your patience, I shall instead, at long last, give the recipe:

1/2 cup (110 g) butter, softened
3/4 cup (155 g) sugar
2 eggs
1 teaspoon (5 mL) vanilla
1 1/2 cups (185 g) flour
1 teaspoon (5 mL) baking powder
Pinch salt
1/3 cup (75 mL) milk, more as needed
Roughly 2 pounds (900 g) prune plums, halved and pitted
1/2 cup (50 g) walnuts
2 tablespoons (30 mL) brown sugar
1/4 teaspoon (1 mL) cinnamon

Heat the oven to 375°F (190°C). Grease a 10 1/2 x 15 1/2-inch (27 x 39 cm) jelly-roll pan.

In a large bowl, cream the butter and sugar until smooth. Beat in the eggs 1 at a time. Beat in the vanilla. Sift together the flour, baking powder, and salt, and beat in. Finally mix in the milk, adding more if necessary to loosen the batter to easy spoonability.

Spread the batter evenly in the prepared pan. Arrange the plums over top, cut side up, touching one another. Put the walnuts, brown sugar, and cinnamon in a food processor and pulse to crumbs. Sprinkle over the cake. Bake until a toothpick inserted into the cake comes out clean, about 30 minutes.

Chorizo Clams (p. 30)

A Cheerful Summer Supper

SOMETIMES EVEN NICER THAN A DINNER PARTY WHERE YOU ARRIVE TO FIND EVERY-thing all in order is spending an afternoon in the kitchen with someone while they cook. I love weekend parties for this reason. You hardly need any entertainment at all because the business of getting meals together (and walking them off afterward) covers it.

I'm also enthralled watching different people's cooking styles. My friend Chris Mooney, who is fearless in the kitchen (you should see him kill a bucket of crabs sometime), is a bit notorious for making the biggest mess of anyone you've ever known. He's not a wash-as-you-go kind of guy, so by the time dinner is on the table his kitchen looks as if a compost truck had just crashed off a cliff. Dreamy-tasting food, though.

My friend Camille has a way of cooking that's very sensual, better to watch than movies. When she has squeezed a lemon, for example, she bends over and grips the shell in her teeth to get the last squirts out. Garlic she grates on the tines of a fork, not in a crusher; herbs she washes and wraps softly in paper towel before zipping them into a plastic bag to keep in the fridge on stand-by.

A few idiosyncrasies of my own have been pointed out over the years. Rumor has it I have a terrible habit of slapping the wrong-sized lids onto pots (sometimes I even use another pot or frying pan as a lid). As I detest jarring noises, I tend to leave the stopper off the kettle so it won't whistle, and then I come along and *test* if the water is boiling by holding the stopper over the spout for a second until I hear the briefest tweet. I am incapable of loading a dishwasher (I have had the scene of how I do this re-enacted in front of me, and it was most embarrassing); however, I'm a whiz with a sink of soapy water and don't wear rubber gloves because I can't bear to have my hands cut off from the sudsy warmth. Anyway, they do add up, these little quirks, and we all have them. Surely some of them hint at our deeper characters, and so if you show up long enough before dinner to observe the actions of your host, who knows what you might find out.

It's only casual or spontaneous entertaining that allows for this peek into the intimacies of character, and perhaps this is why it's the kind of entertaining I love most. Dinner parties that are planned months in advance tend to be high pressure. Everyone has had their calendars blocked off and has planned what dress to wear, then arrives with a carload of high expectations . . . I admit I can get a bit rattled having to host one of those. But give me an impromptu dinner party any night of the week and I'll take it.

Of course, I'm about to tell you that this very menu was born thus. One summer's evening a bunch of us decided it would be cheerier to eat together than apart, so we each chose a dish to prepare and a place in the kitchen, and this is the dinner we ended up with. You can make everything ahead except the salad. Only the clams would need reheating, but not if you make that the dish you whip off dashingly last minute in front of your guests.

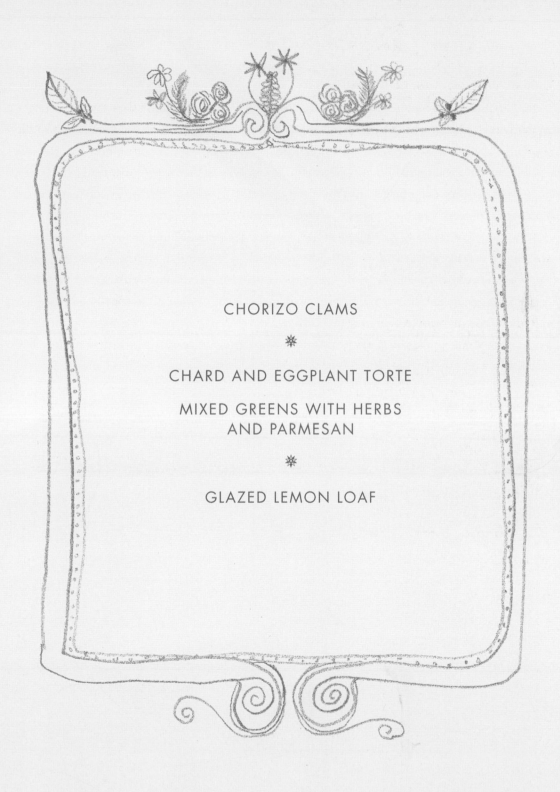

CHORIZO CLAMS

❋

CHARD AND EGGPLANT TORTE

MIXED GREENS WITH HERBS
AND PARMESAN

❋

GLAZED LEMON LOAF

CHORIZO CLAMS

MAKES: 8 SERVINGS

Living near perfectly fresh seafood is a marvelous thing, particularly when you're near it for only a short time. When you can have fresh seafood all the time, *hélas,* you can start to get bored eating the same thing, a bit like when you think that if your garden produces one more zucchini you're going to have the whole plot tilled and paved over. After several summer weeks on the Pacific coast, I thought I'd seen enough clams to do me out. Then word in the village came out that Kenny, the clam and oyster man, had 700 pounds more clams than he knew what to do with so could everyone please come buy. Argh!

I dragged out cookbooks and searched high and low for solutions, but apart from steaming in white wine or making *spaghetti alle vongole,* ideas were thin on the ground. Luckily, on the same night as the clams arrived, so too did my friend Mooney, whom I've been cooking with since my Paris days and who is amazingly inventive in the kitchen. I have never seen the man stressed, and I doubt he has ever encountered an ingredient he couldn't lead down the road to greatness. I plunked the bucket of clams into his hands, and not long afterward he plunked this fabulous, steaming dish onto the table: fresh clams in a punchy, hot, aromatic broth with tomatoes, parsley, and juicy chunks of chorizo.

4 fresh chorizo sausages

3 tablespoons (50 mL) butter

3 tablespoons (50 mL) olive oil

1 large onion, chopped

6 garlic cloves, minced

1 cup (250 mL) white wine

6 pounds (2.7 kg) fresh clams

4 large tomatoes, diced

A few large handfuls of finely chopped
    fresh parsley

Prick the sausages with the tip of a knife in 3 places each and lay in a large pot with 1/2 cup (125 mL) water. Bring to a boil, cover, and cook until tender, about 10 minutes. Remove the sausages, reserving any liquid, and slice them into thick rounds. Heat a tablespoon (15 mL) each of butter and oil in the pot and fry the chorizo pieces on both sides until slightly colored. Set aside.

Melt the remaining butter and oil in the pot. Cook the onions until soft, adding the garlic toward the end. Pour over the wine and any reserved liquid from cooking the chorizo. Add the clams and tomatoes. Cover and steam 5 minutes. Add the chorizo and half the parsley, cover again, and steam until the clams have all opened, about 5 minutes more. (Discard any that don't open.) Scatter over the remaining parsley.

Take the pot to the table with a ladle poking out and serve bowls of the clams and chorizo surrounded by the tomatoey broth. Spoons and fingers both are required to eat this dish. Don't forget to have a loaf of crusty white bread on the side as well.

Seafood Persillade

If you have access to fresh seafood such as prawns, scallops, and mussels, a quick and easy alternative is a speedy sauté. Seafood that needs peeling should be peeled and anything in a shell has to come out, so you'll have to steam clams or mussels (first discarding the open ones, which are dead) for a few minutes to open them, then take out the meat and discard the shells.

Heat some olive oil until spitting and sauté the seafood, seasoned with salt and pepper, just long enough to cook, 1 to 2 minutes. Remove the seafood to a platter. Add butter to the pan, and once it's foaming, toss in a finely minced garlic clove or two and a couple of handfuls of finely chopped parsley. Pour over the seafood and squeeze over lemon juice.

CHARD AND EGGPLANT TORTE

MAKES: 8 SERVINGS

This impressive dish is a barely modified Deborah Madison creation I have been making for years and delighting the masses with every time I set it on the table. I had a bit of an era with it, in fact, making it several times one summer in a Provençal château that had lovely pale blue shutters and a crunchy gravel driveway. The torte looks as if it must be hard to make, all neatly wrapped as it is in a perfect eggplant package, so don't let on how easy it was when people start raving about your genius.

The recipe calls for chard leaves only, but I usually use the stems too. Just separate them from the leaves and chop them, then add them to the onions once they're soft. Pour over a little water and cover the pan for about 10 minutes, then remove the lid and boil off any liquid before adding the leaves to wilt. This dish is meatless, so that makes it very congenial on any table. You can make it well in advance and serve it at room temperature with salad.

3 1/2 pounds (1.6 kg) large eggplant

Salt and pepper

Olive oil

1 onion, chopped

2 garlic cloves, minced

Leaves from 1 large bunch chard, chopped

2 generous handfuls of chopped fresh basil

1/3 cup (30 g) grated Gruyère cheese

3 ounces (85 g) goat cheese

1/4 cup (10 g) finely grated Parmesan cheese

3 eggs

Cut the eggplant lengthwise into 1/3-inch (8 mm) slices. Sprinkle the slices generously with salt and lay them on a rack over the sink for 30 minutes.

Heat the oven to 450°F (230°C). Rinse the eggplant and pat dry. Working in batches, brush both sides of the eggplant with olive oil and arrange on a baking sheet. Bake, turning once, until cooked and golden but still pliable, about 10 minutes per side. Do not let the eggplant get crisp.

While the eggplant bakes, fry the onions in 2 tablespoons (30 mL) olive oil until soft. Add the garlic and cook for a minute. Add the chard, season with salt and pepper, and cook until the chard is tender, adding a little water if needed. Remove from the heat and stir in the basil.

When the eggplant is done, reduce the oven temperature to 375°F (190°C). Lay a small slice of eggplant in the center of a 9-inch (23 cm) springform pan. Using that center slice as the hub of your wheel, arrange overlapping slices of eggplant in the pan, leading out from the hub like spokes and up the sides of the pan with a bit of overhang. Sprinkle in half the Gruyère, spoon in half the chard mixture, then sprinkle over half the goat cheese, in pinches, and finally sprinkle with half the Parmesan. Cover with a layer of eggplant. Repeat the layering with the remaining filling ingredients.

Lightly beat the eggs with a tablespoon (15 mL) of water. Season with salt and pepper and pour over the filling. Fold in the overhanging eggplant ends to cover the torte. Bake 40 minutes. Let cool 15 minutes before removing the sides of the pan and sliding the torte onto a serving platter.

MIXED GREENS WITH HERBS AND PARMESAN

MAKES: 8 SERVINGS

My little friend Sigovia (aged six) made us this delicious salad with her mom, Clara, and I think it's one of the nicest green salads I've ever had. I know there's already cheese in the torte, but the Parmesan is so good on this salad that I can't bear to leave it out. Siggy and I spent half a summer practicing headstands together, a good metaphor for how her salad will turn your world upside down.

8 large handfuls of mixed spring greens

4 large handfuls of arugula

A handful of fresh basil leaves, torn

A small handful of fresh dill, roughly chopped

1 garlic clove, minced

1/2 cup (20 g) finely grated Parmesan cheese

Salt and pepper

2 teaspoons (10 mL) white wine vinegar, more to taste

3 tablespoons (50 mL) olive oil, more to taste

Put all the ingredients in a large bowl and toss well just before serving. The dressing should just lightly coat the leaves.

GLAZED LEMON LOAF

MAKES: 1 LOAF

I have tried a zillion recipes for lemon loaf, but never found one I like as much as this one, which just happens to be my mother's. The lemon flavor is ultra-heightened because of the puckering lemon glaze that gets poured over top. I just slice it up and put a plate of it on the table to eat plain, but I recently learned that my mother always butters her slice. (She wot?!) With a heap of whipped cream and berries, surely that's not necessary, but to each his own!

FOR THE CAKE

1/3 cup (70 g) butter, softened

1 cup (200 g) sugar

2 eggs

1/2 cup (125 mL) milk

Zest of 1 large lemon

1 1/2 cups (185 g) flour

1 1/2 teaspoons (7 mL) baking powder

Pinch salt

FOR THE GLAZE

Strained juice of 1 large lemon

About 1/2 cup (95 g) sugar

Heat the oven to 325°F (160°C). Grease a loaf pan. In a large bowl, cream the butter and sugar until pale and fluffy. Beat in the eggs 1 at a time. Beat in the milk and lemon zest. (It's all right if the mixture looks curdled.) Sift together the flour, baking powder, and salt. Stir into the liquid ingredients. Pour into the prepared pan and bake until a toothpick inserted in the center comes out clean, about an hour.

While the loaf bakes, prepare the glaze by stirring the lemon juice and sugar together. If your lemon is on the small side, you'll need a little less sugar. You want the glaze to taste tangy, but not sour. As soon as the cake comes out of the oven, pour the glaze over the top, and cool completely in the pan before unmolding.

Fresh Berries and Cream

When I was growing up, we ate fresh berries in season and that was it (anything later in the year were those same berries, frozen, then thawed and added to ice cream or trifle). First came strawberries, and we'd eat those until we really didn't want to see another one for at least six months. Then came raspberries, then blueberries . . . same drill. Of course we made desserts from all of them, but often, especially at the beginning of the season when they still felt like such a treat, we'd just eat them fresh with pouring cream and sugar. It's an ideal dessert if you ask me, and totally stress-free for a cook. Strawberries I recommend cutting in half or quarters and sprinkling with a bit of brown or white sugar about half an hour before serving so the juices run. Raspberries don't need cutting but can get the same treatment with sugar. Blueberries you can simply leave alone, adding sugar at the last minute. With the red berries, these days I usually just serve slightly sweetened, vanilla-flavored whipped cream, although a faint whiff of rose water or orange-flower water is nice, too. Blueberries I like with brown sugar and pouring cream, thick and yellow from a jug, or topped with crème fraîche mixed with maple syrup or maple sugar.

Sinclair's Peppery Pasta (p. 43)

An Al Fresco Lunch, with Tone

"ELECTRICITY KILLS DARKNESS, CANDLELIGHT ILLUMINATES IT," THOREAU OBSERVED. I don't remember where I read that, but it was in the context of a discussion about the pros of allowing room in life for some things to remain a mystery.

You'd think, what with their great history of art, the Italians would understand this, but for some reason when it comes to restaurant lighting they lose their edge. Every time I've dined out in Italy I've felt as if someone were about to come along and give me a facial peel, so lab-like was the lighting. I'm not suggesting I want to poke around with my fork in the dark chasing obscured green peas across my plate, but I would rather not have 100 fluorescent watts aimed at my crow's-feet all night.

Never mind plastic surgery, the fastest way to take 10 years off a person is to turn the lights down and set a match to a few wicks. Instant gorgeousity and instant intrigue! (Or, as an old French expression had it, as I read in a Bill Bryson book recently, "By candle-light a goat is lady-like.") It's not only people who in the right light reveal more depth, but the very room itself takes on new dimensions. A space as familiar as your right hand becomes magically nebulous and full of wonder. All of this, of course, also makes food taste better and the experience of eating more enticing all round.

Not that I have any trouble with natural daylight, which, now that I'm feeling guilty for beating up on the Italians and their bright restaurant lighting, makes me want to give them special credit for excelling at. Nothing beats the color of Rome at sunset (that pink!). And what could be more heart melting than the golden glow on Tuscan hillsides on a late August afternoon? No wonder in Italy they're so mad about eating outdoors. Why not, then, follow suit and haul a table out onto the terrace for lunch and enjoy this menu with the sun on your back and a light, warm breeze fingering your wind chimes like an invisible harpist?

Prepare the semifreddo first, then the topping for the crostini. Peaches next, to have at the ready. If you roast your peppers ahead of time, you can make the crostini just before serving, with guests hanging around the kitchen. The duck you'll have to make between courses, but this is lunch and casual and it won't take long, so don't sweat it.

ROASTED PEPPER CROSTINI

*

FIGGY DUCK

*

PISTACHIO SEMIFREDDO WITH
POACHED PEACHES

ROASTED PEPPER CROSTINI

MAKES: ABOUT 24 CROSTINI

These bright-flavored bites, inspired by a Giuliano Bugialli salad recipe, disappear every time I make them. Make the topping well ahead and they're a snap to assemble right before serving.

A word about the toasted baguette slices: please do not over-toast them into paving stones. I once had to judge a cheffy competition, and I can't remember exactly what the spread was we were served, but the toasts to eat it off nearly left me toothless. I wanted to say, "You call yourself a chef and you can't even make toast?" It made me realize how important the little things are—and how so many of those little things are easily within the grasp of anyone who simply cares enough.

If you have a glut of heirloom tomatoes, you could make *tomato bruschetta* instead. Here's a version from a friend who learned her bruschetta recipe in Umbria, where I must say I have eaten some of the best food of my life. You seed and chop tomatoes and put them in a bowl with fleur de sel and let them sit half an hour. Then you rub garlic on toasted bread (preferably grilled over a fire), spoon some juice from the tomatoes over, then pile the tomatoes on top. The essence of simplicity, and with the best tomatoes I'll bet it's heaven indeed. If you want to add a little chopped red onion, shredded basil, and Parmesan cheese, I'm sure it would help bring lesser tomatoes up a notch.

4 colored peppers (red, orange, yellow, green)	2 tablespoons (30 mL) capers
Olive oil	A handful of chopped fresh mint
Salt and pepper	A handful of chopped fresh basil
1 medium tomato	A baguette, sliced into finger-width slices
1 garlic clove	

Heat the oven to 300°F (150°C). Halve the peppers, discarding the stems and seeds. Julienne the peppers and spread on a baking sheet. Douse with olive oil to coat, season with salt and pepper, and roast, stirring occasionally, until very soft, about 2 hours.

Purée the tomato and garlic in a blender and pour into a bowl. When the peppers emerge from the oven, add them to the bowl along with the capers and herbs. Check the seasonings, and add a little more olive oil if necessary to thin out the mixture. (If you're not using it soon, cool, cover and refrigerate, but bring to room temperature before using.)

To serve, heat the oven to 400°F (200°C). Lay the baguette slices on a baking sheet, brush with olive oil, and toast until lightly golden and crisp on the outside but still chewy in the center, just a matter of minutes. Top with the pepper mixture, arrange on a wooden board or platter, and serve.

Sinclair's Peppery Pasta

MAKES: 4 FIRST-COURSE SERVINGS

I'm not quite sure why I'm sliding this in here, but I had to put it somewhere. This is one of the most astonishing pasta dishes I've ever eaten. My friend Sinclair made it for me one night when I'd gone over to his place for some help figuring out the workings of the universe. I was losing my marbles that week, and when I saw him crushing handfuls of black peppercorns I thought he must be losing his, too. I was about to set a fire extinguisher on the table in case our mouths burst into flame mid-meal. Amazingly, though, the pepper didn't have that effect: it just gave brilliant sparks of heat at all the right times and to the right degree on the tongue, softened slightly by the cheese and more mildly peppery arugula. Life at its best should be just like this dish.

1/4 cup (40 g) black peppercorns
8 ounces (225 g) rigatoni
2 to 4 tablespoons (30 to 60 mL) olive oil
4 ounces (110 g) semi-hard sheep's cheese grated on a box grater (about 1 cup/250 mL)
About 4 ounces (110 g) arugula (a few generous handfuls)

Toast the peppercorns in a dry frying pan over medium-high heat until they start to crackle and jump, about 2 minutes. Pour into a mortar and pestle and coarsely crush. (Grinding them any finer will make the dish too hot, so stop at the "mignonette" stage.) Bring a large pot of water to a boil for the pasta. Salt it and add the pasta. Cook to al dente, then drain.

    Return the pasta to the pot, but don't put it back on the heat. Add the olive oil and crushed peppercorns, stirring to coat evenly. Add the cheese and stir so it melts and coats the pasta, then add the arugula, tossing to distribute evenly. Serve immediately.

Spaghetti with Aglio, Olio, and Peperoncino

MAKES: 6 FIRST-COURSE SERVINGS OR 2 GENEROUS MAIN-COURSE SERVINGS

I love this dish to the point that I could eat it almost every day. With the freshness of parsley (a Roman addition, I'm told), depth of garlic, and addictive heat of chili peppers all in my mouth at the same time, I can barely contain my excitement. I have an Italian friend, Annunciata, who crushes the cooked garlic with a fork in the pan and keeps cooking it until golden, before removing it. No grated Parmesan required or even desirable here, or so my friend Mooney informs me, he who blasphemously sneaks lemon zest into his.

1 pound (450 g) spaghetti

6 garlic cloves, peeled and halved

6 tablespoons (90 mL) olive oil

1 peperoncino, crushed (or 1/2 to 1 teaspoon/2 to 5 mL chili pepper flakes, to taste)

2 large handfuls of chopped fresh parsley

Freshly ground black pepper

Bring a large pot of water to a boil. Salt it and add the pasta, which will take about 10 minutes to cook.

While the pasta cooks, in a small pan gently heat the garlic cloves in the olive oil until the garlic is yellow, about 3 minutes. Add the peperoncino, and keep on low heat until the pasta is done. Remove the garlic halves.

When the pasta is ready, drain it, return it to the pot, and toss with the peperoncino oil and parsley. Grind on some black pepper and serve immediately.

FIGGY DUCK

MAKES: 4 SERVINGS

This is last thing you want to try to cook for a crowd. It may be the easiest duck dish on earth, not to mention practical for summer because it doesn't leave you slaving over a hot stove all day, but if you try to do it for too many people at the same time, your kitchen will turn into chaos and you might cry. Such is the case with most "à la minute" cooking, as restaurant cooks call it. For a small lunch, on the other hand, this duck is a marvelous, stress-free treat. The sweet-and-sour honey and rosemary sauce combined with roasted figs makes the dish seem much more complicated to make than it is. Since it's summertime, I'm not sure it needs a proper side dish. Usually, I just throw a fistful or two of watercress or arugula, lightly tossed in olive oil, in the vicinity of the duck to mop up the juices.

2 duck breasts, about 3/4 pound (340 g) each

Salt and pepper

4 fresh figs, halved

1/4 cup (60 mL) balsamic vinegar

1 tablespoon (15 mL) chopped fresh rosemary

1/4 cup (60 mL) honey

1 to 2 tablespoons (15 to 30 mL) butter

Heat the oven to 400°F (200°C). Season the duck with salt and pepper. Score the fat side with a knife in a crisscross pattern and lay the breasts, fat side down, in a cold sauté pan. Set on a burner turned to medium heat and let the fat render, 5 to 10 minutes. If the breasts are very fat, you'll have to pour off the melted fat every 3 minutes or so. If the breasts are not very fat, they may only take 5 minutes. What you want to do is to get rid of most of it, but not all, and have the fat side golden and crisp (but not burnt, so be on the watch for that too).

Once the fat has been dealt with, turn the duck over and lay the figs in the pan around it. Cook 2 minutes on the stovetop, then transfer to the oven to finish cooking, about 10 minutes longer. Transfer the duck and figs to a carving board, cover with foil, and let rest 10 minutes. (It's not that the figs also need resting, obviously; but it's nice to keep them warm.) Slide an oven mitt onto the pan handle and leave it there, otherwise you're bound to forget the thing's hot and do yourself an injury.

Five minutes before serving, reheat the pan and deglaze it with the vinegar, adding the rosemary at the same time. Boil 1 minute. Add the honey and continue gently boiling until the mixture reaches sauce consistency, another minute or two. Remove from the heat and whisk in the butter.

Slice the duck and arrange on a serving platter with the figs. Spoon the sauce over the duck, and serve with lightly dressed watercress or arugula.

PISTACHIO SEMIFREDDO WITH POACHED PEACHES

MAKES: 6 TO 8 SERVINGS

Creamier than ice cream, this soft, honey-scented, pistachio-studded slice of ice is absolute heaven on a spoon, and sunny poached peaches with fresh, fruity acidity are a perfect accompaniment. Another time, and for another menu, don't hesitate to make the semifreddo with pine nuts instead and to serve it with roasted figs. The honey, ideally, should be unpasteurized, and I wouldn't use one that's too dark: you want the honey to have presence, but not be bitterly overpowering.

FOR THE SEMIFREDDO

5 egg yolks

6 tablespoons (90 mL) honey

1 1/4 cups (300 mL) heavy cream

3 tablespoons (50 mL) sugar

1/4 cup (30 g) pistachios, roughly chopped

FOR THE PEACHES

1/2 cup (95 g) sugar

4 just-ripe peaches

Line a 4-cup (1 L) terrine mold with plastic wrap. Put the yolks and honey in a metal bowl and set over a pot of simmering water, without letting the bottom of the bowl touch the water. Using electric beaters, beat the mixture until very thick and ribbony, like cake batter. This will take a good 5 minutes. Remove the bowl from the heat and continue beating until cool, a few minutes more.

Now plunge the beaters into the cream and sugar in a large bowl and beat to stiff drifts. Fold the yolk mixture and the nuts gently but thoroughly into the cream. Pour the whole lot into the terrine, cover with plastic wrap, and freeze for at least 5 hours.

Meanwhile, prepare the peaches: Put the sugar and 2 cups (500 mL) water in a saucepan just large enough to accommodate the peaches in a single layer. Bring to a boil. Gently slash the tops of the peaches once with a knife, then add the peaches to the pot. Immediately reduce to a simmer. Simmer until tender, 5 to 15 minutes, depending on their ripeness. Drain, and as soon as you can handle them, peel, halve and pit, then cut the halves into quarters or thick slices.

To serve, unmold the semifreddo by setting the terrine in a pan of hot water for a few seconds, turning it out, and peeling away the plastic. Slice and serve with the peaches alongside.

Custard

MAKES: ABOUT 2 CUPS (500 ML)

There's nothing half-hearted about serving custard and fruit. For a big buffet party once, I made an enormous batch of custard. Then I poached a vast quantity of peaches, peeled and halved them, and lay them sunny-side up on a big platter. The peaches looked glorious, then even better once I'd sprinkled over handfuls of chopped emerald pistachios.

6 egg yolks
1/2 cup (95 g) sugar
2 cups (500 mL) whole milk
Either a vanilla bean or 1 teaspoon (5 mL) vanilla

In a medium bowl, whisk together the yolks and sugar until combined. Heat the milk in a heavy saucepan. If you're using a vanilla bean, split it in half and scrape the seeds into the milk, then drop the pod in. When the milk just reaches the boiling point, pull it off the heat, cover, and leave to infuse for 15 minutes. (Otherwise, heat the milk on its own.) Meanwhile, set a sieve over a metal bowl and have it at the ready.

When the milk is hot, whisk it gradually into the yolk mixture. Pour the mixture back into the pot and cook over medium heat, stirring constantly with the wooden spoon, to thicken. This will take at least 10 minutes, and you must be vigilant because, without starch in the mixture, if it gets too hot it will curdle and that's the end of it. At first, it will slosh in its milky way, but gradually it will thicken, and thicken some more until it sounds and feels as if you're stirring paint instead. This is your moment to go on red alert. Lift the wooden spoon and run your finger along the back of it. When it's ready it should make a clear line that doesn't run. Quick as a wink, pour the custard through the sieve into the metal bowl. (Stir in the vanilla now, if using extract.) Cool to room temperature, stirring occasionally (it will thicken some more), then transfer to a serving jug, cover, and chill until serving.

Lemon Mousse

MAKES: 8 SERVINGS

Someone I've never met, only heard about, is the origin of this recipe (sort of), a woman called Ina, who was apparently a hopeless cook. "She couldn't fill a pepper grinder!" someone who knew her confided. I thought, "Oh, that's a clever twist on 'So-and-so can't boil water.'" "I'm not being poetic!" that someone assured me. "I walked in on Ina once *actually* trying to fill a pepper grinder by shoving the peppercorns up the bottom. She couldn't figure out why it wasn't working."

Lemon mousse may well have been the only thing Ina could make, but she seems to have made her name on it because anyone who knew Ina remembers her signature dessert. I went to some lengths to get the recipe (a faraway niece provided it) and I made it. Twice. I hate to admit this, but . . . Ina's mousse didn't hold up. In fact, it slumped flat. It is therefore with apologies, Ina, that this is not your recipe, but it is close, and I include it in your memory, since in the minds of so many, you're still the lemon mousse lady of their dreams (and they say you had an exquisite voice, too).

Zest of 1 to 2 lemons

1/2 cup (125 mL) strained lemon juice (2 to 3 lemons)

4 eggs, separated

Pinch salt

1 cup (200 g) sugar

1 1/4 teaspoons (6 mL) gelatin

1 cup (250 mL) heavy cream

In a large metal bowl, combine the lemon zest, juice, egg yolks, salt, and half of the sugar; whisk to combine. Place the bowl over a pot of simmering water and cook, stirring, until thickened, about 10 minutes. (Do not boil.) Remove from the heat.

Meanwhile, in a small bowl, soak the gelatin in 1/4 cup (60 mL) cold water for 5 minutes. Set the bowl in a shallow pot of hot water to melt. Add the gelatin mixture to the yolks and stir to dissolve completely. Cool, but do not let stiffen.

Beat the whites until they're stiff, then beat in the remaining sugar, one spoonful at a time, to make a stiff meringue. In another bowl, whip the cream to firm peaks. Fold the whites and cream into the cooled lemon mixture. Pour into a cut-glass bowl, cover, and chill until serving.

CORN SOUP WITH CORIANDER (P. 54)

A Patchwork Menu of
Some Friends' Favorite Recipes

A NUMBER OF HOMES KEEP A VISITORS' BOOK SO THAT GUESTS WHO STAY THE WEEK-end can sign it and so that the hosts, years hence, can flip back through it nostalgically recalling their heyday of entertaining. It's a nice idea and I think I've had such a book once or twice myself, but usually about three pages into it I forget it in a drawer where it lies empty, a suggestion to amateur future anthropologists that there was an abrupt arrest in dinner parties *chez moi* for reasons unknown. Most misleading.

I had an autograph book in my youth and it met the same fate. Probably no more than 15 of its 200 pages got filled before I lost interest and accidentally on purpose forgot it on the school bus, or on a bench in the rain. I still remember one entry from it: "Yours 'til Chile eats Turkey in Greece," and I always thought that would make a great title for a travel book.

What pages I have never lost, however, are my recipe notebooks. I always have one on the go for collecting recipes and food ideas when I'm out and about. Eventually they wind up in a cookbook (this book, for example, is full of friends' recipes), but even before I was in the business professionally, I made cookbooks by hand. *The Calder Family Cookbook* was the biggie. I made four copies, one for my parents and one each for me and my brothers. We all still use them constantly, as they contain the family reci-pes, many of which hitherto had resided exclusively in my mother's head. I think I was in high school when it struck me that these precious formulas could easily go up in smoke if I didn't gather them and have backup copies around.

Most home-makers of bygone eras kept recipe notebooks. I have both grandmothers,' one great-grandmother's, and my own mother's, all so faded and worn you can barely read them. They are hand-written, of course, and precious possessions to pass on. If you don't have one, I highly recommend making one. All you need is a pen, a little book, and a few rainy Sunday afternoons.

This menu reminded me to bring that up because with every recipe here a friend's face pops into my head: Marinated Steak = Malcolm's barbecue, his tweed jackets, his kids racing around the back garden; Quinoa Tabbouleh = Sarah's wedding, where she wore the silvery-blue gown; Summer Pudding = Jennifer and Harald's terrace on a hot August night and the scent of a cigar . . . If I'd had a visitors' book this past decade it wouldn't have done much good because I was of no fixed address. But with my recipe-book equivalents, I'll be able to flip back through in my gray-haired years reading my personal history between the lines.

The summer pudding needs making a day ahead and at the same time you might as well marinate the steak. The soup you can make well in advance, and the quinoa for the salad you can cook ahead too. So really it's just the barbecuing that's last minute.

CORN SOUP WITH CORIANDER

❋

MARINATED SIRLOIN

QUINOA WITH SPINACH AND HAZELNUTS

❋

SUMMER PUDDING

CORN SOUP WITH CORIANDER

MAKES: 8 SERVINGS

This is a vibrant summery soup, full of sweet, fresh flavors swimming in a warm, jalapeño-heated broth. It's a nice change from traditional corn chowder, which I hasten to add I have nothing against as my mother's is magnificent, but this lively variation is better suited to summer. The recipe comes from the food column of a now defunct magazine for old people called *The Old Fart*. My friend JB used to edit it, which is how I got my hands on a few copies. I wish it were still around, because it was so brilliantly written and hilarious I could open to any page and be rolling on the floor in hysterics in no time (as I also was when I watched JB's *Old Fart Exercise Video,* in which he himself stars and had shot on the sly in the Toronto Zoo). There were leftovers of this soup last time I made it and I sent them to neighbors, who stirred in some cooked salmon and said it was spectacular. I'll bet it would be good with chorizo in it, too, although in that case the jalapeño pepper would be redundant.

6 ears of corn

3 tablespoons (50 mL) butter

2 large onions, minced

2 small red peppers, chopped

1/2 teaspoon (2 mL) chili pepper flakes,
   to taste

1 jalapeño pepper, seeded and finely chopped

2 medium tomatoes, seeded and chopped

4 cups (1 L) chicken stock

1 cup (250 mL) milk or light cream

Salt and black pepper

Leaves from a bunch of fresh coriander,
   roughly chopped

Shuck the corn, and with a small knife shave the kernels from the cobs. Melt the butter in a soup pot and sauté the onions until translucent. Add the corn, red peppers, and chili flakes and sauté 5 minutes. Add the jalapeño, tomatoes, and stock; simmer 15 minutes. Add the milk and heat through. Season with salt and black pepper. Stir through the chopped coriander leaves, and serve.

The Lovely Lady Pamela's Lobster Dip

MAKES: ABOUT 2 CUPS (500 ML)

Auntie Mame has long been a heroine of mine, so I was flabbergasted to meet her in the flesh, which is essentially what happened the day the glamorous Lady Pamela entered my life, rope of walnut-sized pearls around her long, Afghan-hound-elegant neck. We became fast friends, sharing a love of dry wit and irreverence. What we don't have in common is a love of the kitchen. "I can't cook," she says, flatly and unapologetically. "I make one thing."

That's true, as far as I know, but that one thing is absolutely dreamy. She brings it to dinner parties all the time and comes off like a culinary genius. I don't eat bought mayonnaise as a rule, but this recipe brought me to my knees. Serve with crackers and, of course, with flourish, which is the only way Pamelodious ever does anything.

1 tin (11.3 ounces/320 g) lobster meat, chopped if necessary
3/4 cup (175 mL) mayonnaise
1 teaspoon (5 mL) cayenne pepper, to taste

Drain the lobster in a sieve, pressing it to get rid of as much moisture as possible. Transfer the meat to a bowl and break it up with your fingers, removing any cartilage. Add the mayonnaise and cayenne, and using a fork, mix to a smooth paste. Scoop into an attractive bowl and serve with crackers.

MARINATED SIRLOIN

MAKES: 6 SERVINGS

"Trust me in all matters except cooking steak," a friend of mine once assured me, and then went off to prove there were a few other matters where I could reserve judgment as well. But this isn't his recipe anyway, it's my friend Malcolm's invention—he who when my last book came out walked into my house, tossed the book on the table with a sigh, and then slumped into a chair muttering, "Ah, Laura. Still trying to civilize everyone, are you?" What could he have meant by that, I wonder?

Anyway, it was at dinner *chez lui* that I was served this off the barbecue. It was extremely good . . . enough, *almost*, to make me wish I owned a barbecue myself. But as my father put it when I was living nowhere and had my eye on a new painting, "How about you first get *walls*?"

2 pounds (900 g) sirloin	2 garlic cloves, quartered
2 small dried hot peppers	Juice of 1 lime
2 tablespoons (30 mL) brown sugar	1 cup (250 mL) soy sauce
1 tablespoon (15 mL) cumin seeds, toasted and ground	1/2 cup (125 mL) olive oil
	Freshly ground black pepper
1 tablespoon (15 mL) dry mustard	A handful of chopped fresh parsley

Place the steak in a nonreactive dish. Mix together everything but the parsley and pour over the steak. Cover and refrigerate several hours (preferably overnight and all day), turning at least once.

Remove the meat from the refrigerator about an hour before cooking. Lift the meat from the marinade (the latter to be discarded) and grill on a very hot barbecue until done to your liking (for a 1-inch/2.5 cm steak, that's 5 to 7 minutes per side for medium-rare). Alternatively, sear on both sides in a very hot pan on the stovetop for the same amount of time. Set aside to rest a full 15 minutes. Slice very thinly against the grain, sprinkle with the parsley, and serve.

Apricot Ribs

I like these ribs for summer because you can eat them with your hands, which is a casual, cottagey thing to do. As it happens, though, I was introduced to the recipe in winter (only it was "marmalade" ribs that night). It was at cookbook author Anne Willan's house in California on Oscar night, when in a virtually unprecedented moment of informality she pulled the table out in front of the television and we ate the ribs with our fingers. I remember the best thing about the Academy Awards that year was Angelina Jolie's emeralds; remember them? Whenever I see a photograph of those earrings, I immediately think "marmalade ribs!" which is probably not quite the mind-association her jewelers were hoping for. Oh well. It brings ribs up a notch in my head at least.

4 racks spareribs
Salt and pepper
2 cups (500 mL) apricot jam or marmalade
2 tablespoons (30 mL) Worcestershire sauce
2 tablespoons (30 mL) lemon juice
2 scant tablespoons (25 mL) Dijon mustard

Heat the oven to 350°F (180°C). Season the ribs and lay them, bone side up, in a lightly oiled roasting pan. In a saucepan, mix the jam, Worcestershire sauce, lemon juice, and mustard. Stir in 1/2 cup (125 mL) water and heat, stirring occasionally, to melt the jam. Pour over the ribs. Bake 45 minutes. Turn the ribs meat side up, baste, and return to the oven for a further 45 minutes to an hour, basting every 15 minutes, until very tender. You may need to add water to the pan if the sauce gets too thick or starts to burn; add no more than 1/2 cup (125 mL) at a time. Cut the racks into individual ribs and serve.

QUINOA WITH SPINACH AND HAZELNUTS

MAKES: 8 SERVINGS

If this sounds too healthy to be interesting, prepare to be astounded. The combination of nuttiness and juicy sharp vinegar against the teensy, beady, earthy seeds makes this one of my latest favorite things to eat. Sometimes I even eat it as a lunch dish all on its own, perhaps with a bit of feta crumbled over and a few sliced sun-ripened tomatoes on the side. If you can't find hazelnuts, use pecans. If you can't find hazelnut oil, walnut oil is a good substitute, but you'll be missing something if you just use olive oil.

To toast the nuts, bake them on a baking sheet in a 350°F (180°C) oven for 10 minutes. Rub the nuts between the palms of your hands to remove some of the excess hazelnut skin (no need to get it *all* off).

2 1/2 cups (500 g) quinoa (preferably a mixture of red and white)

4 tomatoes, seeded and finely chopped

4 large handfuls of baby spinach (or use chopped cooked spinach)

6 radishes, sliced paper thin

1/2 cup (60 g) hazelnuts, lightly toasted and chopped

About 6 tablespoons (90 mL) hazelnut oil

2 teaspoons (10 mL) red wine or sherry vinegar, more to taste

Salt and pepper

Soak the quinoa in cold water 15 minutes. Rinse at least 3 times until the water runs clear. Drain. Heat a pot of water, salt it, and cook the quinoa until just tender, about 15 minutes. Drain well and squeeze dry in a towel. Mix with the remaining ingredients. Taste and adjust the seasonings, and serve.

Iceberg Lettuce with Green Goddess Dressing

When I asked a friend what, off the top of her head, she'd like to eat with the steak, she named this salad, so I include it with her craving in mind. Serve the iceberg cut into wedges and pour over this glamorous American dressing, which is also delicious when it very lightly dresses leaves of butter lettuce or hearts of romaine. To make 1 cup (250 mL) of dressing: In a blender, combine 1/2 cup (125 mL) mayonnaise, 1/2 cup (125 mL) sour cream, 1 ounce (30 g) rinsed anchovies, a big handful of fresh tarragon leaves, another of parsley, and a small one of chopped chives. Blend until smooth. Taste and add more of any of the herbs if you like, and blend again. Finally add either lemon juice or tarragon vinegar and salt and pepper to taste.

SUMMER PUDDING

MAKES: 8 SERVINGS

This gorgeous hot-pink pudding is very much a feature of English dinner tables in summer, and I can't figure out why it's not more popular here, because it's light, ultra-summery, easy to make, and spectacular to look at. I have made it before with equal quantities of raspberries and red currants, but found it too tart. I've also added black currants, but find they don't pop fast enough to cook with the rest of the fruit. Blackberries look nice, but again I'm not sure they really add their fair share to taste. So what's below, however simple sounding, to me is the *ne plus ultra*. It's a dazzling dessert; please try it.

2 pounds (900 g) fresh raspberries

8 ounces (225 g) red currants, stems removed

1 cup (200 g) sugar

8 to 10 slices firm white sandwich bread or egg bread, crusts removed

Put the fruit and sugar in a frying pan and cook very briefly to dissolve the sugar and make the red currants pop, 3 to 5 minutes (no longer or the fruit will fall apart). Drain, reserving the fruit and liquid separately.

Cut a round of bread to fit the bottom of a 6-cup (1.5 L) pudding bowl. Dip it in the juice and lay it in the bottom of the bowl, pink side down. Now arrange overlapping slices of bread around the edges, first dipping the out-facing side in juice, and pressing a bit to seal.

Fill with the fruit and all but about 1/2 cup (125 mL) juice, which you should reserve in the fridge. Cover the top of the pudding with bread. Place the bowl in a shallow dish to catch any juices, set a plate on top of the bread, and weight it down with a couple of tins of soup or beans. Refrigerate overnight.

Loosen the edges of the pudding with a thin knife, and turn out onto a serving platter. Pour over the reserved juice to cover any white spots. Serve with a bowl of slightly sweetened, vanilla-scented whipped cream on the side.

Blueberry Icebox Cake

MAKES: 6 TO 8 SERVINGS

What a marvelous surprise this was! You might think of it as an American take on summer pudding: a juicy blue-black terrine that slices nicely and makes the most of summer's blueberry bounty. Dessert doesn't get more fanciful, especially when everyone has had it up to the neck with buckles and crumbles.

4 cups (600 g) fresh blueberries
2/3 cup (140 g) sugar, more to taste
1 tablespoon (15 mL) lemon juice
Pinch salt
1 tablespoon (15 mL) cornstarch
About 10 slices boring white bread, crusts removed

Put the berries in a saucepan with 1/2 cup (125 mL) water. Bring to a simmer and stew 10 minutes. Strain, reserving the berries and returning the juice to the saucepan. Add the sugar, lemon juice, and salt; bring to a boil. Reduce to about 3/4 cup (175 mL). Scoop out a spoonful and mix with the cornstarch until smooth. Stir into the juice and cook until thickened. Stir the berries into the syrup.

Line a loaf pan with plastic wrap. Fit the bottom of the loaf pan with bread, trimming the bread if necessary. Spread a thick layer of berries over the bread. Repeat the layering until you've used up all the berries, ending with a layer of bread. Place the loaf pan in a shallow dish to catch any juices, cover with plastic wrap, set another loaf pan on top of the final bread layer, and inside it set a couple of tins to weight the pudding down. Refrigerate several hours until firm. Unmold, slice, and serve with cinnamon-scented whipped cream.

Mashed Potato Torte with Tomato and Mint (p. 66)

A Festive Feast to Celebrate Just About Anything

N EVER SAY NEVER, THEY SAY, BUT THERE ARE SOME THINGS I'M *NEVER* GOING TO WANT to do when it comes to making and serving dinner: I'm never going to want to look after drinks, I'm never going to barbecue, and I'll never want to carve. Please take note if you ever plan to marry me.

I don't know what it is about men, but they seem to have a gene that attracts them more than women to the details of sorting out wine and mixing cocktails. Thank goodness, because it really does bore me cross-eyed. (Fiddling with most corkscrews is alone enough to make me want to set off a bomb.) Anyway, I'm usually too busy cooking when guests arrive to stop and race about taking drinks orders. That task, therefore, gets signed off to the nearest member of the opposite sex, along with the job of making sure glasses are topped up throughout dinner. No one should ever have to start coughing manically to alert his host to the empty state of his glass. I knew of a woman in France who, whenever her wine glass sat empty too long, would place it on her head. That seemed to do the trick, although you'd probably want to know your audience fairly well to get away with it.

Barbecuing is another job I like to leave in a man's hands. I live in perpetual fear of being singed to cinders just by walking past a grilling machine, let alone lighting one. But, again, men—as if straight out of the cave—seem to like lighting fires and standing over them with a giant two-pronged fork. Fine by me!

Which brings me around to carving, one of the rare, rare skills among modern men, which I'm on the brink of starting a petition about in an attempt to revive. If you ask me, boys shouldn't be allowed out of school without decent knife skills and a sound handle on the anatomy of a turkey, but what can you do in an age when the world believes all that really counts is an ability to download. It was not always thus. I once read, I think in a Margaret Visser book, that the sure sign of a knight of any stature was when he could ride right up to the high table on horseback and, with his sword, carve roasts with exquisite precision—wait for it—without getting off the horse! Well, be still, my beating heart. I'm sure there are books out there about how to carve various meats, and how—this is important—to carve them thinly. If I were a man and knew I had a roast leg of lamb in my near future, I'd be rushing off to the bookshelf to look up techniques. Oh my, what a coincidence! A leg of lamb right here in this very menu . . . Doesn't opportunity know just when to knock.

I'd make the potato torte first, because I like it coldish, but even if you're serving it as a warm side dish with the lamb, I'd have it ready and just reheat it when the time comes. Make the green sauce and refrigerate. Bake the Pavlova base ahead, but don't dress it until just before serving. Save the lamb and vegetables for last.

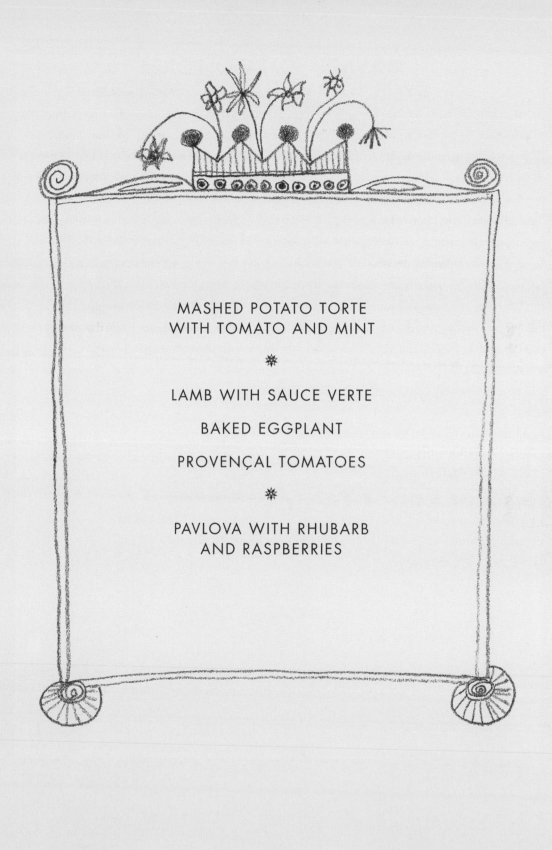

MASHED POTATO TORTE
WITH TOMATO AND MINT

❋

LAMB WITH SAUCE VERTE

BAKED EGGPLANT

PROVENÇAL TOMATOES

❋

PAVLOVA WITH RHUBARB
AND RASPBERRIES

MASHED POTATO TORTE
WITH TOMATO AND MINT

MAKES: 8 SERVINGS

I was reading Claudia Roden's mouthwatering classic on Italian food one day when I came across three recipes for potato torte-like deals, each of which sounded so delicious I wanted every one of them all at once. That, greedily, is more or less what happened: I set to work attempting to amalgamate them all in one pan. I promise one day I'll make each individually to see what they're like, but in the meantime the result of this holy trinity of potato cakes become One is absolutely divine *così*. I can't argue it's a great beauty, so a tuft of green salad on the side is a good distraction, but it is extremely tasty and leftovers in the fridge make a lovely snack. The best pan for this is a well-cured cast-iron frying pan (the best nonstick cookware you could ever want). For pan-curing instructions, see p. 122. I serve this at room temperature (or even on the cool side) as a first course because I find the mint taste more pronounced. If you'd rather it be a side dish to the lamb, then it's nicer warm. The photograph on p. 62 shows individual cakes, but usually I make the torte whole and serve it in wedges. For individual cakes, you may want to dip them into bread crumbs before frying.

1 pound (450 g) baking potatoes (about 2 large)

2 tablespoons (30 mL) butter

2 tablespoons (30 mL) olive oil

1 onion, minced

1 garlic clove, minced

1 medium tomato, chopped to pulp

1/4 cup (60 mL) white wine

A handful of chopped fresh mint

A handful of chopped fresh parsley

About 3 tablespoons (50 mL) finely grated
   Parmesan cheese

2 large eggs, lightly beaten

Salt and pepper

Peel the potatoes, cut them into a few even chunks, boil in salted water until very tender, drain, and mash. Set aside.

Heat half the butter and half the oil together in a cast-iron or nonstick frying pan and very gently cook the onions until soft, 10 to 12 minutes. Add the garlic and cook for 1 minute, then add the tomato and wine. Boil to evaporate the liquid completely and make a thick sauce, about 5 minutes. Remove from the heat and stir through the mint, parsley, and Parmesan. Stir the whole mixture into the potatoes and combine thoroughly. Quickly whisk in the eggs with a fork. Season the mixture with salt and pepper.

Heat the oven to 450°F (230°C). Heat the remaining butter and oil in the same frying pan (wiped clean) over medium-low heat. Add the potato mixture and cook, without disturbing, until set on the bottom, golden, and quite crisp, about 20 minutes. (At this point you can dot the top with a little more butter if you like.) Transfer to the oven and bake until the torte is completely set and the top golden, about 15 minutes. Serve straight from the pan or flip onto a large plate or cutting board. If anything stays behind in the pan, scrape it out and patch it back on. Nobody will notice. Serve in wedges.

Zucchini "Quiche"

MAKES: 8 SERVINGS

I was home for a sort of family reunion one summer and this "quiche" of my grandmother's (now my father's) appeared several times, suitable for everything from breakfast to lunch to aperitifs. It's called "quiche" in quotation marks because it's not custard in a crust, but sort of the two combined—in fact it's almost cakey, so it's easy to hold in the hand. You could also bake this in a shallow rectangular pan and then cut it into cubes to serve with drinks. In that event, to get snazzy, a dab of sour cream and a curl of smoked salmon on each square wouldn't hurt. This is a very practical recipe and a versatile one. Feel free to add a few handfuls of chopped fresh herbs, if you like. And if you change the cheese from Parmesan to Cheddar or Gruyère, use the cup measure, because the weight in grams will be different.

2 cups (250 g) flour

1 tablespoon (15 mL) baking powder

1/2 teaspoon (2 mL) salt

6 tablespoons (90 g) butter

6 slices bacon, cut into lardons

1 medium leek, sliced (or onion, chopped)

4 eggs, lightly beaten

3 cups (360 g) shredded zucchini (about 2 small)

1/2 cup (20 g) finely grated Parmesan cheese

1/2 cup (125 mL) peanut or grapeseed oil

1/2 to 1 teaspoon (2 to 5 mL) cayenne pepper, to taste

Salt and black pepper

Heat the oven to 350°F (180°C). Grease a 9-inch (23 cm) pie plate. Blend the flour, baking powder, salt, and butter to fine crumbs, either with your fingertips or in a food processor. Set aside in a large bowl. Fry the bacon gently until cooked but not crisp. Remove with a slotted spoon and add to the flour mixture. Fry the leek in the bacon fat (add a splash of oil if needed) until soft. Remove with a slotted spoon and add to the flour mixture along with the eggs, zucchini, cheese, oil, cayenne, salt, and black pepper. Stir to combine thoroughly and pour into the pie plate. Bake until set, about 40 minutes. Serve warm or at room temperature in wedges.

LAMB WITH SAUCE VERTE

MAKES: 8 SERVINGS

Sauce verte is a lively sauce with bright flavors that takes five minutes to make. If you can't find preserved lemons, here is a slight variation given to me by my friend Bob over the phone one day as he was driving across Arizona en route to a competition where he was going to try to win a world record for making the most table-sized Caesar salads in an hour. His sauce is *chimichurri*, from Argentina, and he says he dazzles his friends with it all summer long. *Chimichurri* is made exactly as below, only without the capers and lemon and with the addition of half a bunch of coriander, 1 shallot, and 1/2 teaspoon (2 mL) chili pepper flakes. (Bob won, by the way.)

1 bone-in leg of lamb (4 to 5 pounds/1.8 to 2.2 kg)

Salt and pepper

Olive oil

Leaves from 1 large bunch fresh parsley

2 heaping tablespoons (35 mL) capers, rinsed and drained

1 garlic clove

Peel of 1 preserved lemon, chopped

Zest of 1 lemon

2 teaspoons (10 mL) red wine vinegar

1/4 to 3/4 cup (60 to 175 mL) extra virgin olive oil

Heat the oven to 450°F (230°C). Season the lamb and rub it with oil. Roast 20 minutes, lower the heat to 350°F (180°C), and continue roasting until it reaches an internal temperature of 140°F (60°C), about an hour. Remove from the oven, wrap loosely in foil, and let rest 15 minutes before carving into thin (please, not thick) slices.

For the sauce, in a food processor combine the parsley, capers, garlic, lemon peel, zest, vinegar, and 1/4 cup (60 mL) oil; pulse until amalgamated and well chopped, like a coarse pesto (or, if you prefer smooth, whiz it smoother). Taste and adjust the seasonings, and add more oil if it needs thinning out and possibly a squirt of lemon juice.

BAKED EGGPLANT

MAKES: 8 SERVINGS

These don't need an introduction. They're plain but tasty, and just the right blank canvas for the sauce and lamb to play on.

Slice 2 largish eggplants crosswise about a lady's finger–width thick. Brush both sides of the rounds with olive oil, then season with salt and pepper. Lay in a single layer on a baking sheet and bake in a 425°F (220°C) oven until soft and golden, about 15 minutes per side. These can be served warm or at room temperature.

PROVENÇAL TOMATOES

MAKES: 8 SERVINGS

One summer I found myself making these several nights a week. They're fast and easy, but have in-built complexity: sweetness and acidity along with warm softness and golden crunch. A wonderful side dish for many things, not just lamb.

8 medium tomatoes, halved crosswise
Salt and pepper
6 tablespoons (20 g) fresh bread crumbs
6 tablespoons (15 g) chopped fresh parsley
6 tablespoons (15 g) finely grated Parmesan cheese
About 1/4 cup (60 mL) olive oil

Poke the seeds of the tomatoes with your finger, then turn the tomatoes upside down and tap them on the counter so the seeds fall out. Salt the tomatoes and leave upside down half an hour to lose some water. Heat the oven to 375°F (190°C).

Set the tomatoes cut side up on a baking sheet. Combine the bread crumbs, parsley, and cheese and mound on top. Season with pepper and drizzle with oil. Bake until the tops are golden brown and the tomatoes soft, about 20 minutes.

PAVLOVA WITH RHUBARB AND RASPBERRIES

MAKES: 8 SERVINGS

A proper Pavlova is a magnificent thing: high, not sunken, and porcelain creamy white, with thin, crisp sides enveloping a deep, soft, even marshmallowy pillow. My Australian-born friend, cookbook author Jennifer McLagan, enlightened me on Pavlova. I'd only ever seen pie-like types until I went to her house and was served one as tall as a birthday cake. A classic topping is passion fruit, but Jennifer's was decked instead with raspberries and bright pink inches of poached rhubarb. Gorgeous! I also like quartered strawberries (as long as they're very ripe, juicy, and in season), but you can't pile them all on top in a heap or you'll cause a collapse, so scatter only a few on top and serve the rest separately.

If you're interested in variations in the meringue itself, for *chocolate,* fold 2 to 3 tablespoons (30 to 50 mL) sifted cocoa powder in with the cornstarch; for *cinnamon,* add 1 teaspoon (5 mL) cinnamon with the cornstarch; for *nut,* fold in 2 ounces (60 g) ground nuts such as pistachio or hazelnut; for *coconut,* fold in some unsweetened coconut at the end. A *brown sugar* version can be made by using only 1/4 cup (55 g) white sugar and the rest dark brown sugar. To vary the cream topping, coffee, liqueur, or flower water can be used in place of vanilla. Or you could make a topping of half Greek yogurt and half whipped cream, slightly sweetened and flavored with vanilla. Or half Greek yogurt and half lemon curd . . . The options are countless as you can see, so go crazy.

FOR THE MERINGUE

4 large egg whites, at room temperature

Pinch salt

1/4 teaspoon (1 mL) cream of tartar (or 1 teaspoon/5 mL white vinegar or lemon juice)

1 cup (200 g) fruit sugar

1 tablespoon (15 mL) cornstarch

FOR THE TOPPING

3/4 pound (340 g) pink rhubarb

1/2 cup (95 g) + 2 teaspoons (10 mL) sugar

1 cup (250 mL) heavy cream

1/2 teaspoon (2 mL) vanilla

1 pint (330 g) raspberries

Heat the oven to 300°F (150°C). Line a baking sheet with parchment paper and draw a 7-inch (18 cm) circle on the paper.

For the meringue, put the whites in a clean bowl with the salt and beat to foam. Add the cream of tartar and continue to beat to pointed peaks. Add the sugar, 1 tablespoon (15 mL) at a time, beating very well after each addition. (Do not add the sugar too quickly or the meringue will fall.) Once all the sugar is added, continue beating until the meringue is very stiff and glossy (a whisk should stand straight up in it without falling over) and the sugar completely dissolved. (If in doubt, rub some of the mixture between your fingers; if it feels gritty, keep beating.) Finally, sift over the cornstarch and gently fold it in without losing any volume—do not beat it in or the meringue will fall.

Pile the meringue onto the parchment, staying within the circle. Shape it like a cake: smooth the top flat and smooth the sides. Pull a palette knife up the sides, going all around to create a fluted effect. This will help support the meringue and make it prettier. Put the Pavlova in the oven and immediately reduce the heat to 250°F (120°C). Bake for 1 hour. Turn off the oven, without opening the door, and leave the Pavlova in another hour to cool. Remove, peel off the parchment, and set the Pavlova on a serving plate.

For the topping, heat the oven to 350°F (180°C). Cut the rhubarb into 1-inch (2.5 cm) lengths and put them in a single layer in a baking dish. Scatter over 1/2 cup (95 g) of the sugar. Bake until just tender, 15 to 20 minutes. Carefully remove from the syrup to a plate and cool.

Just before serving, whip the cream with the remaining 2 teaspoons (10 mL) sugar and vanilla and pile on top of the Pavlova. (Some people like to scrunch the top down a little bit first with a light press of the palm of the hand.) Garnish with some of the rhubarb and raspberries, then serve with more rhubarb and raspberries passed separately.

Salade d'Everything (p. 87)

A Well-Tempered Table

SOME HOSTESSING BOOKS HAVE A BEE IN THEIR BONNET ABOUT SUCH MATTERS AS etiquette and table settings. I'm not sure it helps us overly much. Anyone with the slightest whiff of social intelligence will pick up on the norms of his particular peer group fairly quickly and conform to its rules, so usually everyone ends up fairly happy. As for the table, it can only be set with what you have at hand, so as long as you're not eating off plastic and paper I wouldn't get too hung up about it.

Once you get past the obvious rules of good manners, there are occasional idiosyncrasies to keep an eye out for. I have a friend, for example, who has a "no clinking" policy in his house. Boy, did I ever gaffle on to that one myself, clinking being one of my pet peeves. That makes me sound like a party pooper, perhaps, but there's something chaotic about orchestrating head-on collisions between every glass in the room before trying to get in a peaceful sip. Simply raising a glass to say "cheers" suffices for me. And when did ogling everyone in the eyeballs like a hypnotist at this juncture come into practice? I'm all for eye contact, but I like the idea of keeping eyeballs in their sockets during this brief communion.

Cell phones are another bugbear. I have gone so far as to erect a stool by the front door with a giant fishbowl on top of it and a sign, "Please leave your cell phones here." I recently read that this is common practice in British boarding schools, too: the "mobile basket" gets circulated before meals and again before bed. (May I never have to set the fishbowl at my bedroom door!) It is amazing to me how many people think it's okay to bring their electronic devices to the table and set them down at their right-hand side like a new fiancé. At one of my dinner parties, someone who knew way better actually got up from the table mid-meal and answered, "Hi, Dad!" Quite accidentally, she hasn't been back since.

In my Paris days, my roommate Camille and I actually kept a dinner-party book in which was included a "good guest" list, a "bad guest" list—and a blacklist. A philosopher called François was on the blacklist because once when he was supposed to bring dessert for a party of eight he showed up with a quarter of a prune flan, heavy as a wet life jacket, from the cheap bakery downstairs. A filmmaker called Michel from New York was on the "good guest" list because, unlike the types who show up contributing a 10 dollar headache-in-a-bottle and then drink your fine Burgundy, Michel always arrived with *two* bottles of exceptional wine, which he presented as "A good bottle of wine . . . and a better one." He was legendary, that guy.

Most of the time I've had good guests, because I only invite people to dine whom I like, or whom I expect to and want to like. These are the sorts of people who turn off their phones, who contribute to conversation, and who are open-minded enough that when you serve them a first course of romaine hearts to eat with the fingers, won't bat an eye.

Which brings me around to this menu (which, by the way, always behaves itself impeccably). The tart shell is the first order of business and your greatest challenge—albeit a challenge of the same caliber as making Play-Doh. Once that's out of the way and the tart assembled, make the lemon cream sauce and stick it in the fridge. The potato dish and the salmon happen in the hour before you eat.

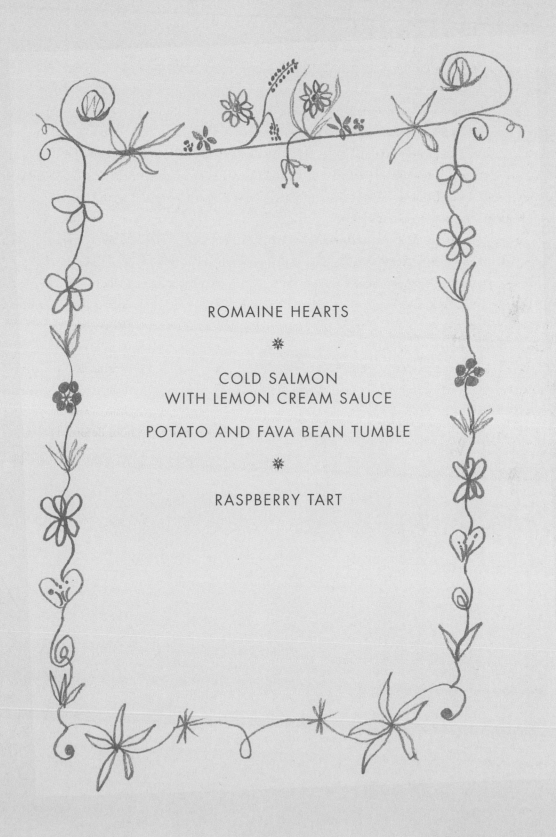

ROMAINE HEARTS

✳

COLD SALMON
WITH LEMON CREAM SAUCE

POTATO AND FAVA BEAN TUMBLE

✳

RASPBERRY TART

ROMAINE HEARTS

I've come to think of simplicity in cooking as a bit of an act of bravery, at least when it comes to entertaining. This dish, for example, I would have been terrified to pass off as a first course to guests, but my fearless cooking friend Chris Mooney did just that and so I've decided I too can get away with it. All you do is quarter hearts of romaine lettuce and arrange them on a platter. Drizzle over excellent olive oil (and I mean seriously excellent), squeeze over some lemon juice, grind over pepper, and scatter over fleur de sel. That's it, and it's great.

When Mooney made it, we ate the starter a bit like you do corn on the cob: picking up the salad by the tail and crunching in. M's children liked that approach, which doesn't surprise me because I remember one of my first childhood "recipes" being "lettuce rolls." I'd get soft lettuce leaves from the garden, lay each flat, sprinkle with salt, roll up, then eat. It was a wonderful thing, the rolling up being my magic touch. I couldn't have been more pleased with myself if I'd invented tournedos Rossini.

I had a nice lunch in a palatial hotel in Marrakech not long ago that put the romaine heart to good use. I wouldn't recommend it before the salmon, but you might consider it another time on another menu . . . or in a next life. Make a flat square of crabmeat on a plate, set a small half of romaine heart on top, dress with small crisp croutons, shaved Parmesan, and slivers of pink radish. Drizzle over dressing, such as Caesar or green goddess (p. 59), or even a lemon vinaigrette.

COLD SALMON WITH LEMON CREAM SAUCE

MAKES: *6 SERVINGS*

I spent the lion's share of one summer on Vancouver Island, where the village fishermen would haul in giant salmon that you'd be feasting on within the hour. It seems a miracle to taste something that fresh and wild in this day and age, which is why I lean toward this simple sauce for accompaniment; a really good fish doesn't need more. Indeed, you might argue that it doesn't need anything at all.

FOR THE SALMON

1 salmon fillet, about 2 pounds (900 g)

Salt and pepper

FOR THE SAUCE

1 egg yolk

1 teaspoon (5 mL) Dijon mustard

1 teaspoon (5 mL) white wine vinegar

3/4 cup (175 mL) grapeseed oil

Salt and pepper

Zest of 1 lemon and juice to taste

1/4 cup (60 mL) heavy cream, whipped

A handful of finely chopped fresh chives (optional)

Heat the oven to 325°F (160°C). Lightly oil a baking sheet and lay the salmon on it. Season with salt and pepper. Bake until just done, 15 to 20 minutes (less if you're cooking individual fillets). Remove from the oven and transfer to a serving platter. Cool to room temperature before serving.

For the sauce, whisk together the yolk, mustard, and vinegar. Whisk in the oil, drop by drop, until thick. Season with salt, pepper, and lemon juice. Add the zest and fold in the whipped cream. Taste and adjust the seasonings. Fold in the chives (if using) and refrigerate until serving.

Salmon Marinated in Whisky and Soy

MAKES: 8 SERVINGS

If salmon with creamy sauce is not your belly's desire, here's an alternative you can do on the barbecue. I know salmon recipes with soy and maple syrup abound, but this one is different. When you marinate the fish, it becomes almost mahogany, firm, and vaguely candied. A fisherman gave me the recipe and he swears by coho salmon, but use whatever you can get your hands on. This marinade is also good with steak.

8 skin-on salmon fillets, about 6 ounces (170 g) each
5 garlic cloves, minced
A 2-inch (5 cm) piece fresh ginger, peeled and minced
1 cup (250 mL) soy sauce
1 cup (250 mL) rye whiskey
1 cup (225 g) brown sugar
1/2 cup (125 mL) maple syrup
Freshly ground black pepper

Lay the fillets skin side up in a nonreactive dish just large enough to hold them in one layer. Mix the remaining ingredients and pour them over. Cover and refrigerate overnight. The next morning, flip the fillets over and return them to the fridge until you're ready to eat.

Heat the barbecue to a raging 500°F (260°C) and lay the fillets on the rack, skin side down. Close the lid and cook until the salmon is starting to flake but is still moist, 5 to 7 minutes, basting with a little marinade occasionally if you like. (Leftover marinade should be discarded.)

Salmon with Parsley Sauce

MAKES: 6 SERVINGS

I was positive, as I saw this dish being prepared, that I wasn't going to like it. I dismissed the parsley sauce as unnecessary, old-fashioned, and heavy, and I thought the fried parsley garnish sounded dull. Wrong! I really must stop being so presumptuous. This is the kind of dish my mother used to make, and I realize what I love about it: you can make it once every couple of weeks and never tire of it. The reason is that it's simple food, and I find that most of the time my body craves that, like it does after I've been to one of those restaurants that manage to use so many ingredients in one dish you feel as if you've got the entire United Nations on your plate.

FOR THE PARSLEY SAUCE

3 tablespoons (50 mL) butter

3 tablespoons (50 mL) flour

1 1/2 cups (375 mL) whole milk

2 handfuls of finely chopped fresh parsley

Lemon juice

Salt and pepper

FOR THE SALMON

6 skin-on salmon fillets, about 5 ounces (140 g) each

Salt and pepper

1/4 cup (55 g) butter

A very generous handful of chopped fresh parsley

For the sauce, melt the butter in a saucepan over medium heat. When it stops foaming, add the flour and whisk for 1 minute. Whisk in the milk, then switch to a wooden spoon and cook, stirring, until thick. Remove from the heat. Stir in the parsley and season to taste with lemon juice, salt, and pepper. Keep warm, and pour into a sauceboat just before serving.

Season the salmon with salt and pepper. In a frying pan, melt the butter over medium heat until foaming. Add the fish and cook on both sides until the salmon is starting to flake but is still moist, 5 to 7 minutes total. Remove the fish to a warm platter. Add the parsley to the pan and cook a few minutes, stirring, until it crispens slightly, then pour over the salmon. Serve immediately with the warm parsley sauce.

POTATO AND FAVA BEAN TUMBLE

MAKES: 6 SERVINGS

Fava beans must be among the top five most beautiful foods, bright jade and smooth as polished beach stones. Their soft, sweet bite against firm-fleshed new potatoes is a lovely combination, as much a treat for the eyes as for the tongue. I give mint as the herb here, but if you are ever serving this as a side dish to something else, tarragon or parsley are also good. If all this is too much, just serve some green beans with the salmon.

2 pounds (900 g) small new potatoes
2 pounds (900 g) fava beans, shelled
1/2 cup (125 mL) olive oil
1/4 cup (60 mL) chicken stock
3 to 4 tablespoons (50 to 60 mL) white wine vinegar, to taste
Salt and pepper
Chopped fresh mint, for garnish

Cook the potatoes in a pot of simmering salted water until tender, about 10 minutes depending on their size. At the same time, blanch the fava beans in simmering salted water for about 2 minutes. Drain the favas and plunge them immediately into ice water. Pop the beans out of their tough skins. Drain the potatoes, halve them, and place in a bowl. Toss with the oil, stock, and vinegar. Finally toss in the favas. Season with salt and pepper. Just before serving, toss with the chopped mint.

John's Minty Potatoes

My friend John, every time he boils potatoes, adds to the pot a huge fistful of fresh mint (practically the size of a geranium) from his garden. "Garden" is a misnomer, really, because it's actually a massive mint patch on his lawn, overgrown and underpaid and in constant use. The mint (which is discarded at the end of cooking, so keep the leaves on the stalk) imparts a very mild and intriguing flavor to the potatoes. On top of that, flinging sprigs of mint into the pot makes you look and feel like a real *artiste*. I do it all the time now, as if I'd come up with the notion myself.

One point, before you launch in, is that not all mint is created equal. John's variety is a type with fuzzy leaves that gets quite big and has a very strong taste. That's ideal for these potatoes because you really taste the herb, but it's not good for much else, being too coarse and overpowering for most palates. Other, more feminine mints, by contrast, are useless for boiling (too mild to impart any real taste), but much better for, say, shredding and tossing with cantaloupe or salad or making mint sauce. Even if you don't have the right mint, I like the mere gesture of throwing some into the potato pot. Serve the potatoes tossed with butter, freshly ground pepper, and fleur de sel.

Salade d'Everything

MAKES: 6 SERVINGS

My uncle Freeman lives off this salad from June through August, a bit like a cow put out to pasture. He makes an enormous batch and keeps it in the fridge for a week, nibbling away at it until the hillside is bare and he has to make another one. It has so many different ingredients in it, it practically constitutes a meal in itself, but it's also a good accompaniment to salmon. Indeed, the pairing constitutes Freeman's number one summer dinner-party menu. He puts the salmon on a platter and the salad in an antique wooden butter-whipping thing. Everything is laid out on the table so people can drift past with plates, load up, then float out onto the deck to eat overlooking Belleisle Bay. Food with a view is always spirit lifting.

By the way, I give the recipe its Frenchy name because Freeman, at the age of 72, admirably decided he should learn French, so he packed himself off for a month of immersion. At around the same age, he also decided to turn a bog on his property into a garden, all of which proves that whatever your age you can pretty much accomplish anything if you put your mind to it. Certainly you can whip up a Salade d'Everything.

2 generous handfuls of arugula

1 celery rib, sliced

10 ounces (280 g) cauliflower florets, sliced

10 ounces (280 g) small broccoli florets

1/3 English cucumber, peeled and chopped

1 red pepper, cut into short strips

2 avocados, cut into pieces

1/2 red onion, diced

8 ounces (225 g) mushrooms, sliced

8 ounces (225 g) cherry tomatoes

2 garlic cloves, minced

8 ounces (225 g) feta cheese

2 handfuls of chopped fresh walnuts

6 tablespoons (90 mL) olive oil

A few drops of balsamic vinegar

White wine vinegar or white wine, to taste

Salt and pepper, to taste

Put everything in a bowl and toss your little heart out. Cover and refrigerate until serving.

RASPBERRY TART

MAKES: 1 LARGE TART

This is the simplest raspberry tart there could be, so don't be put off by the long description that follows. You'll be able to make it faster than I, in my pontificating mood, describe it.

The *pâte sucrée* (sweet pastry) is one I was taught by my mentor in all things French, Anne Willan, when I was studying in France. She was strict about pastry (not to mention everything else) and liked it made the old-fashioned way: on a marble counter with a bench scraper and a lot of yolks. I had abandoned that method upon returning to *l'Amérique,* probably because it annoyed me to use four yolks and have no use for the whites—no longer a problem, what with Pavlova (p. 74), Coconut Cake (p. 164), Peachy Patti Cake (p. 162), and Almond Cookies (p. 149), to name a few recipes that will come to the rescue. But when I visited Anne a while ago in Los Angeles, where she now lives, I was reminded of its merits. One lunch she served a raspberry tart (this very same) that was one of the most perfect things I have ever eaten: simply fresh raspberries tossed in some melted apricot almond jam and tumbled into the baked shell. It wasn't the filling that made it (although you can't go wrong with fresh, ripe berries); it was the long-forgotten pastry from France. I couldn't get over the quality: firm and steady on the plate, yet crumbly and melting in the mouth. You could eat it without any filling at all and you'd still swoon. Read the recipe through before you start in. The charm is in the method, not the ingredients.

If you really can't stand the thought of weighing anything, go with the following cup measures, which are a very close approximation: 1 2/3 cups (400 mL) flour, 1/2 cup (125 mL) butter, and 1/2 cup (125 mL) sugar.

FOR THE PASTRY (notice, weighing-phobes, that the cup measures are in the paragraph above)

7 ounces (200 g) flour

3 1/2 ounces (100 g) cold unsalted butter

3 1/2 ounces (100 g) sugar

4 egg yolks

1/2 teaspoon (2 mL) salt

1/2 teaspoon (2 mL) vanilla

Clear off a space on the countertop. Sift the flour onto the surface and make a well in the center, which is to say move it around so it sits in a ring with an open space in the middle about the size of a salad plate.

Pound the butter with a rolling pin a few times to soften it, then cut into small pieces. Put the pieces in the well with all the remaining ingredients and, without touching the flour, mix them with your fingertips until they look a bit like scrambled eggs. When they are nearly combined, you can gradually start drawing in the flour. Continue working with the mixture, cutting with a bench scraper, until it forms coarse crumbs, looking rather like a pile of raw *Spätzle*. If it feels too sticky, add a spoonful or two more of flour.

Now, gather the pastry up into a mound and slide the heel of your hand along the side of it a few times, pushing the dough away from you to blend in the fat, without overworking. (The French term for this is *fraisage*.) When you're done, the dough should be, in Anne's words, "soft, and as smooth as putty," and it should peel away from the countertop in one piece, without crumbling at the edges. This is important if you don't want a battle with the rolling pin and pastry later—and you definitely don't because they will win. Shape the dough into a disk, wrap in plastic, and chill for 30 minutes or until firm. (You can freeze the dough at this juncture if you want it for another day.)

Heat the oven to 425°F (220°C). Roll out the dough on a lightly floured surface and fit it into a tart tin with a removable bottom. Trim the edges. Line the pastry with parchment paper and fill with dried beans right to the top. Bake 10 minutes, then remove the beans and parchment. Reduce the heat to 375°F (190°C) and continue baking until the pastry is golden and cooked through, about 10 minutes longer, but check because it may want a few more, depending on your oven. Cool on a rack, then remove the sides of the tin.

FOR THE RASPBERRY FILLING

You need enough raspberries to cover the base of the tart, so for a 9-inch (23 cm) tart, that's about a pound (450 g). Then you need jelly, red currant or apricot (apricot almond is very nice, too), which someone at your local farmer's market should sell if you're not a jelly maker yourself. Scoop about 1/2 cup (125 mL) jelly into a small pot and add 2 tablespoons (30 mL) water or orange juice. Heat, stirring from time to time, until melted. Paint the bottom of the tart shell with some of the melted jelly, then arrange the raspberries neatly on top. Carefully paint the berries with the remaining jelly until the berries glisten. Set the tart aside for about an hour to set. Serve with or without whipped cream.

Fresh Blueberry Pie

MAKES: 1 PIE

For a North American approach to berries in pastry, I'd put blueberry pie in this menu, and in that case use pastry (p. 215) instead of the tart shell used in the previous recipe. This particular pie is not a traditional baked one, but rather one where you make a thick, jammy sauce using a few berries and then fold in many more fresh ones, which will pop pleasantly in the mouth when you bite in. I have seen recipes that add a cream cheese layer beneath the blueberries, and I used to make that pie myself, but for some reason it tastes a bit churchy to me now. I prefer it with berries alone, albeit with lemon- or nutmeg-whipped cream on top, which is just a matter of a bit of sugar and lemon zest (or nutmeg) in the cream you whip, and a spoonful of sour cream whipped with the cream as well.

1 baked pie shell (p. 215)

About 5 cups (750 g) fresh blueberries

3 tablespoons (50 mL) cornstarch

1/2 cup (95 g) sugar

1 tablespoon (15 mL) butter

Zest of 1 lemon

A squeeze of lemon juice

Scoop out 2 cups (300 g) blueberries for the sauce and set the rest aside. In a medium saucepan, stir the cornstarch and sugar into 1/2 cup (125 mL) water to make a slurry with no lumps. Add the blueberries for the sauce and bring to a boil. Reduce the heat and simmer until the blueberries pop and the whole mixture becomes a thick sauce, about 10 minutes. Stir in the butter, lemon zest, and lemon juice.

Stir the reserved berries into the sauce, and tilt the whole lot into the baked pie shell. Cool completely, then refrigerate to set, about half an hour, before serving. Serve with lemon (or nutmeg) whipped cream.

Traditional Blueberry Pie

MAKES: 1 PIE

Much as I adore Fresh Blueberry Pie, not including a traditional version made me feel disloyal to my grandmother Ethel, who baked a pie from which the purple juices oozed out all over your plate and usually ended up somewhere on your shirt. Just to mention her pie makes me feel nostalgic for home, where, once the blueberries are all gone, the fields stretch into oblivion, turning the landscape into a flaming, woven red and purple magic carpet. An empty, autumnal blueberry field is one of my favorite visions to behold, right up there on my personal bliss list with the smell of wood smoke and the hushing sound of wind in treetops.

Sweey lard pastry (p. 318)

4 cups (600 g) fresh blueberries

3/4 cup (155 g) sugar, more for strewing

1/4 cup (30 g) flour

2 tablespoons (30 mL) butter, melted

Zest of 1 lemon

1 tablespoon (15 mL) lemon juice

1 egg

Heat the oven to 425°F (220°C). Roll out one disk of pastry to fit a 9-inch (23 cm) pie plate. Do not trim the overhang. Combine the blueberries, sugar, flour, butter, lemon zest, and lemon juice. Spoon into the shell. Roll out the top pastry and lay it over. Trim the edges and press together. Cut vents in the top.

Beat the egg with a spoonful of water. Paint the top of the pie and strew over some more sugar. Bake 15 minutes. Reduce the heat to 350°F (180°C) and continue baking until the filling is bubbling and the crust golden, about 40 minutes.

CHOCOLATE CREAM POTS (P. 102)

Eats in the Heat

PERHAPS PEOPLE DON'T ENTERTAIN AT HOME ALL THAT OFTEN ANYMORE BECAUSE they think they need a reason, such as an anniversary or a marginal "raise" at work. I used to be a bit like that. When I was living the wild life in Paris, my roommate Camille and I used to get a kick out of making up excuses for our parties. We must have thought we'd get more guests that way.

That was a footloose time of our lives when we were both freelancing (emphasis on the "free"), and quite simply because we didn't have much else to do we entertained about four nights a week. I could tell when a party plan was about to hatch. We'd be sitting at coffee in the morning, or taking a break from our Great American Novels, and I'd feel a restlessness breeze through the window. The next thing you know we'd be drawing up a guest list, plotting a menu, and scheming up some completely superfluous and often impractical theme as a hook to hang our party from. Such as the Fire and Ice party we threw during a heat wave, or that party where people could send anonymous messages to one another all night: you'd write your wee note, unsigned, and slide it into a ballot box. Occasionally we'd empty the box and tape the notes onto a wall of mirrors. Everyone could wheel through the hall of mirrors and check the messages they were getting and write back. That led to the odd scandal before the night was out.

These days, in my great maturity and wisdom, I don't do themes, although occasionally one feels like giving a toast to something or someone. Recently, at the eleventh hour, I decided to make dinner into "Bill appreciation night," so we all raised our glasses to that. It's not a bad idea sometimes to let the spur of the moment take the lead, as demonstrated by my friend Jean-Louis, who at a recent dinner raised his glass and said, "Well . . . here's to the first bottle."

Right in the middle of writing this, I had a phone call from a friend who announced, "It's the anniversary of the Battle of Agincourt, you know." I didn't know. "Oh yeah, about 1,500 Brits against 7,000 Frenchmen, and we Brits won, thanks to the murky battlefield and the longbow. I'm doing roast beef and Yorkshire pudding in celebration." After that amazing announcement, I wonder if themes aren't a good idea after all . . .

As it happens, this menu does have a bit of a theme, in that it was designed for a summer's night when you're hot and tired and don't feel like cooking but still have an appetite and a craving to see friends. The cream pots are quick, but you have to make them a few hours before you eat. You also have to soak white beans overnight so they're ready to cook. Otherwise, this menu is a wink to throw together, and its simplicity sets a good example if you're trying to make a statement about not needing to fuss just because you're having people in.

COOK'S BLOODY MARY
NIBBLES

✳

TUNA AND WHITE BEAN SALAD
ON TOASTED BAGUETTE

✳

COCONUT CREAM POTS

COOK'S BLOODY MARY

MAKES: I

I am not a magazine junkie by any stretch, but there are a select few I can devour cover to cover, especially when I have a long flight ahead. *Vanity Fair* is in my top three (second place after *The Spectator*). I like it for the long, juicy articles, but also for the quirky tidbits of information that pepper each issue, such as the few recipes for cocktails that were in the issue I wolfed down on an interminable flight from Seoul. Come to think of it, I could have used a decent Bloody Mary on that (bloody) flight . . . Now, about the recipe. I know no bartender would ever write a drinks recipe down in terms of cups, so this does look a bit strange. What can I say, I am but a home cook, not a "mixologist" (which word I despise almost as much as "blog"). So here's the recipe written for people like me who, without it in these terms, would be hard pressed to mix a cocktail if their life depended on it.

1/2 cup (125 mL) tomato juice

1/4 cup (60 mL) vodka

1 tablespoon (15 mL) lime juice

1 tablespoon (15 mL) lemon juice

2 teaspoons (10 mL) grated fresh horseradish

Dash Worcestershire sauce

Tabasco sauce and black pepper, to taste

1/2 slender celery rib, for garnish

Stir everything but the celery together in a glass. Add ice to taste, poke in the celery rib, and serve.

NIBBLES

The other day, having coffee in a posh grocery store (if indeed there is such a thing), my yoga buddy Nancy and I started devouring her just-bought sack of roasted almonds. I'd forgotten how dangerously good they are (along with their potential to destroy the whole effect of the yoga class you just did), but I thought, after about three palmfuls, they were probably the right thing to serve with a Bloody Mary when you're a little peckish but don't feel like cooking.

Alternatively, the Frenchy thing to do would be to buy salted pistachios in the shell and a dried sausage, making sure the latter is truly a dry one. Sometimes "dried" sausages are not dry enough and they have a soft, oily texture, which is creepy. Avoid those: you want the dried kind that are really hard to cut and require your sharpest knife. Lop the end off the sausage, then make a slit down the length of it and peel off the white casing. Slice it ultra-thin, which is ultra-important: a thickly sliced dried sausage is a leathery no-no.

TUNA AND WHITE BEAN SALAD
ON TOASTED BAGUETTE

MAKES: 6 SERVINGS

A cyclist friend made this for me when I visited him and his family in Singapore, where I just about melted into a boiling puddle the second I stepped off the airplane. *Mamma mia,* what hot nights and sweltering days! When you're a serious athlete like my amigo and temporarily living in the tropics, it's dishes like this tuna one that you cling to like a well-rooted tree trunk in a flood zone. It might just be the best dish for summer eating I've ever had. Made right, it's a super-refreshing, ultra-lemony, flavor-packed Mediterranean salad, light and hearty all in the same breath and gorgeously rustic. It is perfect for a lunch or light supper, and conveniently keeps a day or two in the fridge.

Remember this forever: the simpler the recipe, the more vital the quality of the ingredients. That's why Italian food tastes so great in Italy and so ho-hum almost everywhere else. Recipes have only so much power; the rest is in our hands. Do, for this recipe, use top-quality chunk tuna packed in olive oil in a jar, and cook your own white beans. You'll need 3/4 cup (150 g) dried beans to yield the amount needed for the recipe. Soak them covered in cold water overnight, simmer them in fresh water (no salt) until tender, about 40 minutes, drain, and carry on.

2 red peppers

2 yellow peppers

About 1/2 cup (125 mL) olive oil, more for the
   baguette

3 garlic cloves, minced

3 celery ribs, sliced

A scant cup (100 g) pitted Kalamata olives,
   roughly chopped

A few handfuls of fresh parsley leaves

2 cups (400 g) cooked lima or cannellini beans

Salt and pepper

Zest and juice of 2 lemons, more to taste

14 ounces (390 g) high-quality tuna chunks
   packed in olive oil, drained

1 to 1 1/2 baguettes

Heat the oven to 350°F (180°C). Seed and julienne the peppers, toss on a baking sheet with a few tablespoons of olive oil, spread into a single layer, and bake until soft, about half an hour. Remove from the oven and turn the heat up to 400°F (200°C).

Tip the peppers into a large bowl. Add the garlic, celery, olives, parsley, and beans. Season with salt and pepper, and toss with the lemon zest and juice and the remaining olive oil. Add the tuna last and carefully mix it in with your hands so the chunks don't break up too much. Taste and adjust the seasonings.

Slice the baguette(s) in half lengthwise and then into pieces the length of the palm of your hand. Arrange on the baking sheet and drizzle with olive oil. Toast until golden and crisp on top but still squishy within, about 5 minutes.

Put a piece of toast on each plate and top with a generous heap of the salad, including the juices. (Or make a whole platter of slightly smaller versions and let people help themselves.)

COCONUT CREAM POTS

MAKES: 8 SERVINGS

Texturally, these are right up my alley. I love the unimpeded silky smoothness of these pots, and they can be varied for all kinds of flavors by using milk in the place of coconut milk, then adding vanilla or a proportion of lemon juice or coffee in place of part of the milk/cream total.

If a *chocolate cream pot* is what you're craving, bring 1 1/2 cups (375 mL) whole milk or half-and-half to a simmer. While whisking, gradually pour the milk over 6 ounces (170 g) melted bittersweet chocolate, stirring until completely smooth. Add 1/4 cup (60 mL) espresso and 1/4 cup (60 mL) Kahlúa or Irish cream liqueur. The sugar, eggs. and vanilla are as below. Finally, if you're feeling sneaky, you might even hide some crushed ripe raspberries in the bottom of each pot for a surprise. Bake as below.

1 cup (250 mL) coconut milk
1 cup (250 mL) heavy cream
1/4 cup (55 g) sugar
1 egg + 2 egg yolks
1 teaspoon (5 mL) vanilla

Heat the oven to 250°F (120°C). Bring a full kettle to the boil.

Put the coconut milk and heavy cream in a saucepan with half the sugar. Heat just to the boiling point. Meanwhile, beat the remaining sugar with the egg and yolks until thick and pale. Stir in the vanilla. When the cream is very hot, slowly add to the egg mixture, stirring constantly. Remove from heat.

Pour into 8 ramekins and set in a baking dish. Slide into the oven, then pour water from the kettle around the pots to come halfway up the sides. Lay over a piece of foil. Bake until just set, 1 1/4 hours. Remove from the water, cool, then chill before serving.

Poppysicles

This is just a reminder, not a recipe, but it seems the right place for it. I got the idea for popsicles from a girl called Poppy, whom I met one midsummer when she was tearing with her friends through the woods and across the beach and around the village where I was staying. Once, when I was out walking on the gravel roads through the woods, she whizzed past me like a hornet on a miniature motorbike wearing a bright yellow jacket. I thought, not without a flash of envy, "I wish I'd been that cool at 11!"

One day Poppy invited me over to her house to teach me how to make popsicles, which she makes every day all summer. When I arrived for the demonstration, she was wearing a white apron scattered with red poppies, and she had the whole kitchen counter covered in organic juices, Greek yogurt, berries, chopped bananas . . . She set to work making all sorts of combinations of popsicles, some with banana and coconut yogurt, some with mango, lemonade, and raspberries, some orange and peach, some apple juice. . .

Later, I read up on popsicles and found that one approach is to start with fruit coulis, such as raspberry or peach. Just purée the fruit (peeled if it has skin) and add sugar (dissolved first in a little hot water) and lime or lemon juice to taste. If you do a variety of purées, you can make striped popsicles by freezing the bottom layer, then adding the next and freezing, then adding another. Maybe you want to make one layer by combining one of the purées with yogurt. Really, your imagination is the only limit.

Mango Frozen Yogurt

My friend Johanna (also with growing children) has this in the freezer at all times. You make it with 2 cups (500 mL) sweetened mango pulp (which you can buy in specialty shops), mixed with 3 1/2 cups (750 g) Greek yogurt, and 2 tablespoons (30 mL) sugar or to taste. Fold in 2 beaten egg whites and churn in the ice-cream maker.

Zucchini and Swiss Chard Gratin (p. 111)

An Honest Country Dinner

AT ONE OF OUR HABITUAL FRIDAY-NIGHT PUB *RENDEZVOUS*, MY FRIENDS AND I GOT onto the topic of snobbery. Perhaps I brought it up because it's a word I can't stand, especially when it's thrown around unjustifiably, as is so often the case. "What is a snob anyway?" I solicited. "Surely a person is allowed to have standards." That's nothing to do with it, according to my friend JB, who explained that the definition of a snob is someone who is simply not a "nob" (i.e., nobility); they just try very hard to pass for one, which is why a snob disdains anyone who is not of the class to which he himself fruitlessly aspires.

I don't know what all that does to the notion of food snobbery, which term also gets tossed carelessly about. Fast-food defenders in particular like to aim the accusation like a dart at anyone who dares to express an interest in getting their hands on an apple that actually tastes like an apple. That's not fair in my books, but I can fathom the label being accurately applied to chefs and cooks who, in an attempt to approximate what they imagine to be three-star dining, gussy up dishes until they're the gastronomic equivalent of Priscilla Queen of the Desert (with all due respect to the dame). The pretentiousness label can also be applied to restaurants that use great ingredients and make extremely simple food—but then won't shut up about it and way overcharge for it. I remember a restaurant like that in Paris: you could order a pot of very good quality steamed mussels, fine, but that involves zero imagination and no skill, so why were they priced like a racehorse and served with self-righteousness and pomposity?

Which brings me around to that dreadful word: *foodie*. It sounds to me like the name of a poodle cross, and I've never really understood what it meant. I used to think it referred to people who obsess about trendy restaurants and ingredients: types who dined at elBulli before it even opened, whose cupboards were spilling over with 30-year-old balsamic vinegar before the rest of us had even heard of pizza, who can't eat in a Michelin-starred restaurant without taking a photograph of every dish . . . On closer observation, though, it seems to mean anyone who enjoys food beyond its fuel function, which hopefully is most of us. Still, I'd rather come up with a better name, which might make a good dinner-party game one night . . .

This reminds me that I do like the notion of keeping a dictionary in the dining room. I seem to remember knowing someone once who kept one on a pedestal, like the Holy Bible, right by the head chair just in case an etymological debate flared up some night over stew and dumplings.

Anyway, those silly food terms came to mind as I contemplated what is essentially pork chops and zucchini gratin as a menu for guests. It's doubtful any "foodie" would ever dare to serve anything so pedestrian to the ear, but I like the honesty of this menu. It's comforting, satisfying home-cooked food that doesn't try to be anything other than what it is.

Make dessert first, then the gratin. The roast you put in the oven just over 3 hours before you plan to eat it (the gratin you can reheat while the meat is resting). Tomato salad you make more or less just before you eat it. Just make sure the tomatoes are not in the fridge because they're unpleasant, as you know, cold (and, as you also know, they should never be stored in the fridge in the first place).

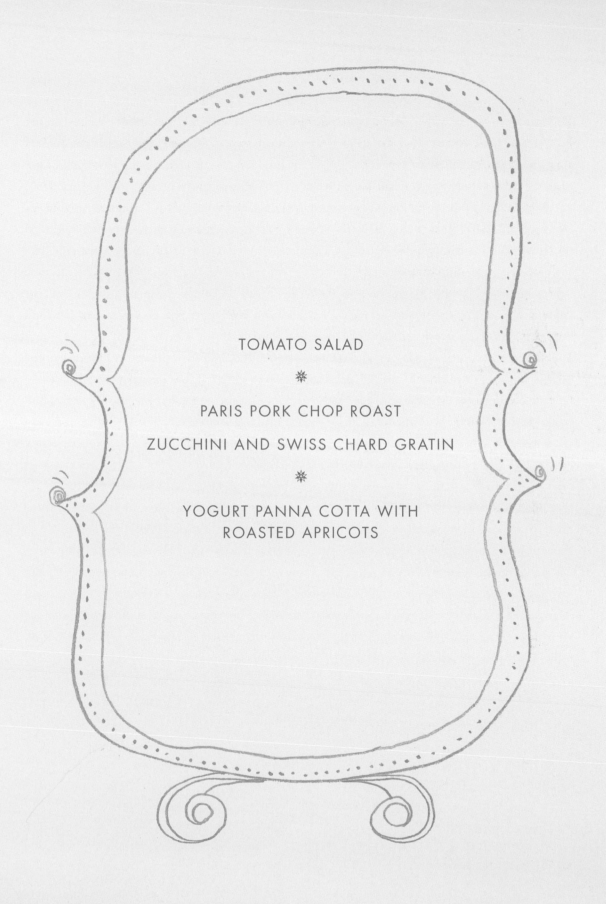

TOMATO SALAD

✳

PARIS PORK CHOP ROAST

ZUCCHINI AND SWISS CHARD GRATIN

✳

YOGURT PANNA COTTA WITH
ROASTED APRICOTS

TOMATO SALAD

One summer evening, despite threats of rain, a rather impressive theater was erected on my friend John's lawn. When the curtains were drawn, Poppy, Tibault, Zola, Sigovia, and Brady re-enacted the "Teddy Bears' Picnic," singing their little hearts out and dancing like a merry-go-round of leprechauns. This was followed by a heart-wrenching drama, written by themselves, about a stolen fish. The children had cardboard costumes to disguise themselves as various benevolent sea creatures, and their role was to come to the rescue of a poor fisherman called Tim when his prized Derby-winning catch was stolen by an evil villain called "The Dude." (We laughed, we cried, we videotaped . . . two thumbs up!)

None of this has anything to do with the recipe, which doesn't even contain fish. It's just that Poppy and Brady's mom told me that night about a tomato salad she makes, and so tomato salad and this event are linked in my mind. Besides, I thought you might like to hear the tale of the play in case sometime you have little people coming to dinner yourself who need an outlet for their creative urges. There's nothing like a children's play or concert to get everyone in jolly pre-dinner spirits.

Back to this easy first course. It goes without saying that you want only the juiciest, ripest summer tomatoes. Nothing else will do. Estimate about 1 medium tomato per person. Slice them thickly and arrange on a platter. Drizzle over exceptionally good extra virgin olive oil, and season with freshly ground high-quality pepper and fleur de sel. You can serve that salad plain, or scatter over shredded basil. It's as simple as that.

Another friend, Henry, is a fanatic of *tomatoes with burrata*—burrata being a creamy type of mozzarella that comes in the shape of a pouch. He races to the market at the crack of dawn on the day he knows it arrives, because if he doesn't, all of it gets snapped up before mid-morning by other gluttons in the know. The cheese costs a fortune, so only splash out on people you really love. If burrata is not easy to find, you can use good buffalo mozzarella instead. Slice either about the same thickness as the tomatoes (note that burrata slices will be on the messy side) and arrange in a ring on a platter, crowning the whole lot with shredded basil. Dress as above, noting that the olive oil must be absolutely top-notch. In fact, Henry's name for this dish is "Olive oil, with tomatoes and burrata," not the other way around.

Pan con Tomate

All this tomato talk reminds me of something I more or less lived on one summer I spent in Spain pretending I had it in me to write a novel. You need firm white bread from a rustic loaf, which you slice and toast lightly. Rub the rough, crunchy surface of the toast with the cut side of a split clove of garlic, then vigorously rub the bread with the cut side of a tomato half so that the juices soak into the bread and the surface becomes coated with a film of tomato mush. A drizzle of olive oil and a pinch of fleur de sel sprinkled over are all you need for a fantastic snack. I spent my whole summer eating it: *pan con tomate* in one hand, plume in the other.

PARIS PORK CHOP ROAST

MAKES: 8 GENEROUS SERVINGS

Friends of mine in Paris a long time ago had an apartment on the high floor of a building overlooking the loud rue de Rivoli. There was only one common room, which accommodated kitchen, living room, and dining room together, so it was a bit tight. For some reason, I also remember that the floors were linoleum, and instead of cupboard doors there were little curtains, flowery and prone to rustling if a breeze came through the window. You might expect, walking into a place like that, something like bought cheese straws and Beaujolais Nouveau on the menu, but instead full-blown feasts of grandmotherly generosity would be set before you, sometimes for crowds. This magnanimous pot roast, for example, came out of that kitchen. It couldn't be simpler to prepare, and the results are juicy and succulent. You probably wonder why I'm serving it in warm weather. You have a point, but we can't live on cantaloupe and lemonade for an entire season just because it's sunny out. Besides, despite the fact that I had it in Paris, I think the Provençal nature of the beast makes it legitimate here.

1 8-chop pork rib roast, about 5 pounds (2.2 kg), fat on	A head of unpeeled garlic, smashed
Salt and pepper	2 small leeks, washed and cut into lobs
3 tablespoons (50 mL) herbes de Provence	2 sprigs fresh rosemary
3 tablespoons (50 mL) olive oil	A generous fistful of fresh thyme sprigs
2 to 3 onions, roughly chopped	A generous fistful of fresh parsley sprigs
3 carrots, peeled and cut into big logs	1 cup (250 mL) white wine
	1 cup (250 mL) chicken stock

Heat the oven to 400°F (200°C). Season the roast generously with salt and pepper. Rub on the herbes de Provence. Heat the oil in a large Dutch oven over medium-high heat and brown the meat all over, about 5 minutes per side.

Add the vegetables and herbs, tucking them in around the meat, season them with salt and pepper, and pour in the wine and stock. Bring to a boil, cover the pot, and transfer to the oven. After 20 minutes, reduce the heat to 325°F (160°C) and continue braising, basting occasionally, for 3 hours. It should be well done, but still very juicy. Transfer the meat to a cutting board and tent it with foil to keep it warm. Strain the juices (discarding the solids) and boil them down a little. Carve the roast into chops and spoon the juices over.

ZUCCHINI AND SWISS CHARD GRATIN

MAKES: 6 TO 8 SERVINGS

When I was apprenticing in a restaurant long ago, in Lourmarin in the south of France, the staff lunched practically every day on zucchini gratin, and I couldn't stand the stuff. It consisted of thick slabs of zucchini that had been boiled to translucence, then tossed in béchamel sauce. If I ever see one again, I'll run screaming over hill and dale into Austria and live the rest of my days on miniature Sachertorten. Explain to me, will someone, how it is that cooks in restaurants go to such pains to prepare divine eats for the patrons, but then subsist themselves on slop?

This recipe is a completely different kettle of fish. I found the inspiration for it in the *Provence the Beautiful* cookbook (a wonderful cookbook series the complete set of which I am determined to own) and immediately adapted it for my repertoire, cutting down on the eggs and adding some tart cream to lighten it up. The result is a refined and unexpected gratin that raises the banal and ubiquitous zucchini several notches in everyone's estimation. A new summertime hit! It's great with the pork roast, and with many other things too. The mixture makes a wonderful stuffing for tomatoes, which you can serve as a side dish, or even as a first course, especially if you've thought to put a pinch of goat cheese in the bottom of the tomatoes first.

About 2 pounds (900 g) zucchini

Salt and pepper

2 to 3 tablespoons (30 to 50 mL) olive oil

4 ounces (110 g) bacon, cut into lardons (optional)

1 large onion, fairly finely chopped

3 garlic cloves, minced

Leaves from 1 pound (450 g) Swiss chard, parboiled, squeezed dry, and chopped

2 ounces (60 g) finely grated Parmesan cheese

1 large or 2 small eggs, lightly beaten

A generous 1/2 cup (125 mL) crème fraîche (or sour cream)

1/2 teaspoon (2 mL) paprika

1/2 cup (40 g) fresh bread crumbs

A small handful of chopped fresh parsley

1 to 2 tablespoons (15 to 30 mL) butter, melted

Shred the zucchini on the large holes of a box grater. Layer with salt on cake racks, set in the sink, and let stand for 30 minutes. Rinse in cold water and squeeze dry in a clean tea towel. Transfer to a large bowl. Heat the oven to 350°F (180°C). Smear an 8-cup (2 L) baking dish with olive oil.

Heat a tablespoon (15 mL) of the olive oil in a frying pan and fry the bacon pieces (if using) until cooked but not crisp. Remove. Add another spoonful of oil, and when it's hot add the onions and cook until soft, about 15 minutes. Finally, add the garlic and cook 1 minute. Add to the zucchini. Add the chard leaves and two-thirds of the Parmesan. Stir through the egg, crème fraîche, and paprika. Taste and adjust the seasonings. Spoon into the gratin dish.

Mix the remaining Parmesan with the bread crumbs and parsley, scatter over the gratin, and drizzle with the melted butter. Bake 40 minutes or until very hot and the top crisp and golden. Serve hot.

Parsleyed Kasha

MAKES: 8 SERVINGS

I had to put a plug in somewhere for buckwheat groats (or kasha) because it's one of my favorite foods. It's more wintery, I guess, so perhaps save it for a side dish when you serve the pork in a snowstorm. It's important that you buy kasha from a reputable source, because the kind you find in bulk stores will, in my experience anyway, yield nothing but mush. I buy my good stuff from a Ukrainian food shop, and the cooked grains stay separate and have the right al dente bite. To cook it, put 2 cups (400 g) kasha in a pot. Cover with 4 cups (1 L) water. Bring to a boil, cover, reduce the heat, and simmer gently until cooked al dente and the liquid is absorbed, about 15 minutes. Stir through a piece of butter and some chopped parsley, if you like, and season with salt and pepper. It will be wonderfully fragrant, nutty and honey-scented, with just the right amount of bite.

YOGURT PANNA COTTA WITH ROASTED APRICOTS

MAKES: 8 SERVINGS

If you're in a rush, you can always scrap the panna cotta and instead serve the apricots with a spoonful of ricotta or Greek yogurt drizzled with warm honey. If you do make panna cotta, know you don't have to make it in a terrine. You could also use ramekins or teacups or small glasses to vary the shape; just don't forget to line them with plastic wrap so you can turn them out. If rosemary in the honey is not for you, simply sprinkle the apricots with a scraping of nutmeg. Peaches, of course, can replace apricots. (And here, I might also alert you to the custard and peaches concept on p. 47.)

Finally, if apricots are unavailable, *blueberry sauce* is equally scrumptious. For 1 1/2 cups (375 mL) sauce, put 4 cups (600 g) blueberries, 1/4 to 1/2 cup (55 to 95 g) sugar or 1/2 cup (125 mL) maple syrup, a squeeze of lemon juice, and 2 tablespoons (30 mL) water in a sauccpan. Gently bring to a full boil, stirring, then cool.

FOR THE PANNA COTTA

2 cups (500 mL) Greek yogurt

1 envelope gelatin

1 cup (250 mL) heavy cream

1/3 cup (70 g) sugar

1 teaspoon (5 mL) vanilla

FOR THE APRICOTS

12 apricots, halved and pitted

1/4 cup (60 mL) honey

1 sprig rosemary

Put the yogurt in a medium bowl; set aside. Scatter the gelatin over 2 tablespoons (30 mL) water in a ramekin and set aside to soften a few minutes. Set the ramekin in a small saucepan of just boiled water, off the heat, for a few minutes and stir to melt it to liquid. Heat the cream with the sugar and vanilla, stirring so the sugar dissolves. When the gelatin has dissolved, add it to the cream, stirring to mix well. Then stir the whole mixture into the yogurt. Line a terrine mold with plastic wrap and pour in the yogurt mixture. Refrigerate until set, at least 4 hours. Turn the terrine out onto a platter and remove the plastic wrap.

For the apricots, heat the oven to 400°F (200°C). Spread the apricots cut side up in a baking dish. Heat the honey and rosemary and let steep 10 minutes. Discard the rosemary and drizzle the honey over the apricots. Roast until soft, about 15 minutes. Serve alongside slices of panna cotta.

New-Fashioned Berry Ice Cream (p. 127)

Eggs with Elegance

*I*NSPIRATION WOULD BE A GOOD SUBSTANCE TO BE ABLE TO BUY IN JARS. JUST THINK: you could wake in the night, sneak downstairs, open the fridge, swallow a few big spoonfuls, then go back up, lie down, and be struck instantly by a lightning bolt. "I know! I'll paint the house *chartreuse!*" Or, "Delphiniums! Just the plant to parade along the garden wall." We wouldn't have to toss and turn for hours beneath the sheets agonizing over what to do with the rest of our lives or how to spin straw into gold. We'd have the answer in one bite.

Of course inspiration is not much use if it isn't motorized by energy. I've always wondered where people get that, too, when I've popped by for a visit and discovered them absorbed in some obscure activity like starting a worm farm to fuel their compost heap or fermenting vats of sourdough starter just to make one loaf. All just for the hell of it, too! I remember one day my brother looking up from the newspaper and saying, "What do you know, there's some Brit doing a jig across the UK." How *do* people come up with these ideas? And what magic potion gets them off their butts bringing these ideas to life? Some days it's all I can do to take a walk.

Dinner parties, at one time or another, bring inspiration problems to the surface for all of us. If I get inspired to cook before I've invited people, there's no problem: the food's there. It's when I get inspired to invite people and then find no urge to cook that I'm in hot water. Cook's block is as real as writer's block.

What I've discovered is that just as the way over the writer's-block hurdle is simply to force myself to put pen to paper and write *something*, so too is cook's block curable simply by opening the fridge door and taking some things out. Believe me, it's not uncommon to think you have nothing in the house to eat, only to discover that, with a little ingenuity, in fact you have the fixings for a feast. Perhaps inspiration is always in the fridge after all!

I'm of the persuasion that if, for example, you have a box of eggs in the fridge, you can feed anybody and be pretty classy about it. Quiche is easy to make and glams eggs up. (James Bond impressed the pants off a chick in a movie doing that once.) Cocotte eggs are cute as a bug's ear and a little more surprising, if you just want something light. And Spanish tortilla is downright brilliant, because it's hearty and delectable and not something people see every day unless they live in Spain, which most of us don't. The other appealing characteristic of a dish like this: it is utterly unintimidating and makes guests feel that you might not be such a tough customer to invite back to dinner yourself sometime.

Actually, I served this menu as a lunch originally. It was a lazy day, a few people dropped by, we opened the fridge door and ended up throwing this together. Not only that, we had the sudden inspiration to set up a table in the greenhouse to eat. A change of environment almost gives familiar foods a whole new taste.

If you're serving the cookies, obviously bake them ahead. If any of the spreads are on offer, prepare those ahead as well. The tortilla, too, can be made ahead and served room temperature, but I find people like to watch the process, so maybe wait until they show up to launch in.

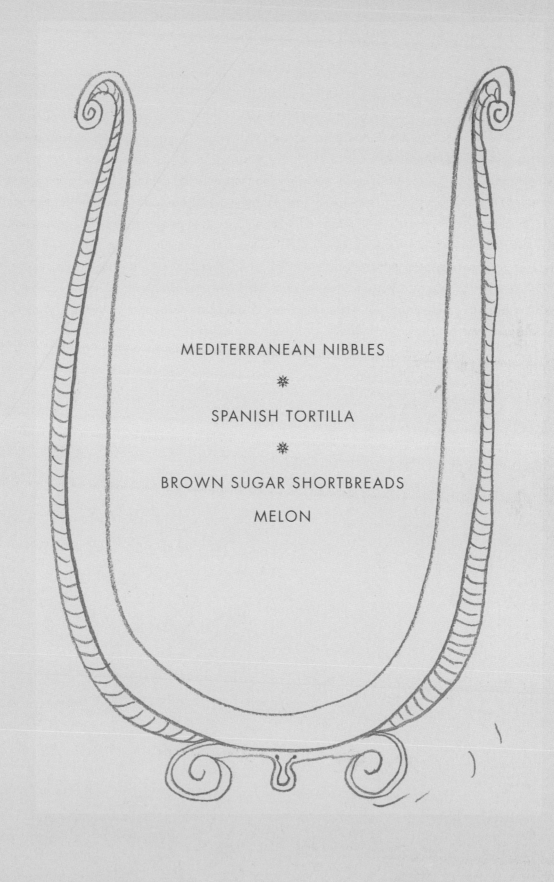

MEDITERRANEAN NIBBLES

✳

SPANISH TORTILLA

✳

BROWN SUGAR SHORTBREADS

MELON

MEDITERRANEAN NIBBLES

Set out some nuts, sliced chorizo sausage, radishes, and yummy fat green olives in separate bowls. *Basta.* Or, you could also offer a mound of *herbed goat cheese* for spreading on crackers or croûtes. To make that, put 8 ounces (225 g) goat cheese in a food processor along with 2 or 3 tablespoons (30 or 50 mL) heavy cream. Pulse to blend, then transfer to a bowl. Mix in 2 small handfuls of chopped fresh herbs and plenty of lemon zest, and season with salt and a generous grinding of black pepper. (If you put it all in the processor at once, be warned: you'll end up with something not prettily flecked, but frog green.) Wrap in plastic and shape into a disk. Chill 1 hour. To serve, unwrap the disk and set it on a small board. Make a depression in the top and drizzle olive oil over. (Actually, what I usually do is just put a room-temperature log of goat cheese on a board, drizzle some olive oil over, and shave on lemon zest. If you have lemon-infused olive oil on hand, so much the better. All you have to do is pour.)

Beet Hummus

MAKES: 2 CUPS (500 ML)

One fine morning, I received an email from my friend Bridget with the heading "A beautiful thing." The letter began in a leisurely, chatty tone talking about the new lawnmower, the children's piano lessons, her budding organic food business . . . On and on it meandered while I writhed with curiosity, until finally in the last paragraph she let me in on what the "beautiful thing" was: hot pink hummus! Blow me down. I raced from computer to kitchen to test it out, and B was right, it's a stunner. She wrote that she loves it with jalapeño oil dribbled on top, as I'm sure I would too if I knew where to get any. In the meantime, I'm blissed out with it mopped up just as it is onto the ragged edge of a pita, or tackily piped into the groove of a celery rib. (If fussy, remove threads from back of celery first.) You can also toast thin rounds of baguette in the oven to use as crackers. Just brush the slices with olive oil and toast on a baking sheet at 400°F (200°C) for about 5 minutes.

1 medium beet, roasted, peeled, and chopped
About 1 1/4 cups (250 g) cooked chickpeas (1/2 cup/100 g dried)
1/3 cup (75 mL) tahini
1/4 cup (40 g) toasted pine nuts
2 garlic cloves, crushed
1/2 cup (125 mL) olive oil
Juice of 1 lemon, to taste
Salt and pepper

Purée all the ingredients in a food processor. Check the seasonings, and serve.

Prawns with Cocktail Sauce

MAKES: 4 SERVINGS

This reminds me of hotel dining in the fifties, not that I was there, of course, but I wish I had been, just for the clothes, and for the fact that my body type back then would have been ideal. Oh well. Eventually we have to come to terms with the times (and the body) we live in, or so *they* say.

Anyone who knows me will pass out cold seeing ketchup in the ingredients list. It's not something I keep in my kitchen, but it is something that's kicking around most summer cottages, and the cottage is not the place to stick one's nose up at such things. There's also Tabasco sauce, which I have, but rarely use, although I might warm up to it since a friend recently told me a little joke—Q: What's the definition of a long marriage? A: Any couple on their second bottle of Tabasco. Put all these condiments together for a quick cocktail sauce for fresh seafood and you've got an easygoing starter for an outdoor lunch by the seashore, gulls in the distance, buoys bobbing on the breaking waves . . .

1 cup (250 mL) ketchup or chili sauce
2 tablespoons (30 mL) lemon juice
1 tablespoon (15 mL) prepared horseradish
1/2 teaspoon (2 mL) salt
1/4 teaspoon (1 mL) Tabasco sauce
24 medium shrimp or prawns

Combine everything except the shrimp in a bowl, cover, and chill until serving. Boil the shrimp in salted water until just cooked, about 5 minutes. Drain and peel. Serve warm with the cold sauce, or cover and chill the shrimp to serve with the sauce later.

Spicy Baked Shrimp

MAKES: 4 SERVINGS

I went for years without owning a bathing suit. For some reason I just didn't like the idea of getting wet. What that has to do with spicy shrimp is beyond me, apart from the fact that the originator of this recipe told me about it one hot day on the beach as I sat covered head to toe in cotton swaddling, loath to stick so much as a toe in the water. Thank God that phase is over, although, come to think of it, I still haven't gone out and bought a swimsuit. It could probably come in handy for this dish, though, because it's just the attire to don for eating slightly messy, spicy seafood at a picnic table.

1/2 cup (125 mL) olive oil
2 tablespoons (30 mL) Cajun spice mix
2 tablespoons (30 mL) chopped fresh parsley
2 tablespoons (30 mL) lemon juice
1 tablespoon (15 mL) honey
1 tablespoon (15 mL) soy sauce
Pinch cayenne pepper
1 pound (450 g) deveined shrimp

Toss all the ingredients together, cover, and refrigerate 1 hour. Heat the oven to 450°F (230°C). Spread the shrimp with their coating on a baking sheet and bake until pink, 5 to 7 minutes.

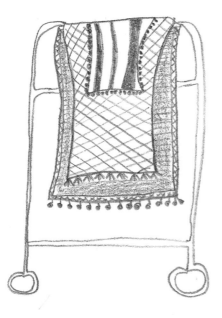

SPANISH TORTILLA

MAKES: 4 TO 6 SERVINGS

One summer I spent in Spain I had a neighbor, Mercedes, who made an excellent tortilla, which she topped with wide slices of oven-roasted green pepper (400°F/200°C for 30 minutes if you want to do that). She was a great card player, I remember, gathering with the neighbors many nights a week to smoke, drink rosé—and win. I am not a great fan of green peppers as a rule, so I recommend red, yellow, or orange instead, but you don't need them at all, really—that's just if you want to be festive.

It's a wonder this recipe isn't a classic the world over, really, because the ingredients are available to all of us, and yet, mysteriously, it seems to remain in Spain "where the rain stays mainly in the plain." A green salad with halved cherry tomatoes tossed through is nice on the side, or simply a juicy salad of heirloom tomato wedges tossed with salt, pepper, and coriander leaves.

I watched Mercedes make tortillas many times and was always desperately impressed with the flipping activity, which as it turns out isn't hard. You do need a well-seasoned cast-iron pan, and here's how you achieve that: put lard or peanut oil in the pan, heat for several minutes until sizzling hot, pour the oil out, and let the pan sit 10 minutes. Wipe the pan out with paper towel and swear on the honor of your grandfather's grave that you'll never, ever after, wash it with soap.

1 1/4 cups (300 mL) olive oil

1 onion, minced

1 1/2 pounds (675 g) Yukon Gold potatoes, peeled and cut into 3/4-inch (2 cm) cubes

6 eggs, lightly beaten

Salt and pepper

In a well-seasoned cast-iron (or nonstick) pan, heat 2 tablespoons (30 mL) of the oil over medium heat and gently cook the onions until soft. Remove to a plate. Add the remaining oil, and when it's sizzling hot, add the potatoes. Fry until crisp and golden outside and soft in the center, up to 30 minutes. Pour off the oil and save for other uses (it's delicious). Scatter the onions evenly over the potatoes. Season the eggs and pour over. Cook over medium heat until set, about 10 minutes. Flip the tortilla onto a large plate or saucepan lid, then slide it back into the pan to cook the underside, 5 to 10 minutes longer. Remove to a cutting board or platter and serve warm or at room temperature.

Fried Eggs on Asparagus

MAKES: 2 SERVINGS

This dish comes to mind while I'm thinking of tortilla because we often forget, when faced with feeding people spontaneously, how knight-in-shining-armor a carton of eggs can be. Eggs are the perfect food, coming in their own packaging and all, and nothing cooks faster. Of course, you want to serve only very good farm eggs with high whites and bright, happy yolks, not supermarket eggs with pale and peaked yolks that look up at you from the plate like the faces of consumptives in a 16th-century hospice. A good egg, like a good tomato, speaks for itself, and oh how eloquently!

My Italian teacher used to prepare this lunch for us after my morning lessons in Emilia-Romagna. I make it now as a light supper for one or two, and if I were into brunch, which I'm not, that would be a good place for it. Serve with a loaf of crusty bread.

1 bunch asparagus
1 tablespoon (15 mL) olive oil
Salt and pepper
4 eggs

Trim the asparagus. Heat the oil in a sauté pan until sizzling. Fry the asparagus, seasoning while it's in the pan, until tender and golden, about 7 minutes. Remove to 2 plates. In the same pan, adding a little butter if you like, fry the eggs, seasoning with salt and pepper. Arrange the eggs on top of the asparagus, and serve.

Fiala's Dill Fried Egg

Once, when I showed up starving at my friend Peter Fiala's place, he made me a fried egg that restored not just my energy, but also my faith in the universe. He fried a beautiful farm-fresh egg in butter, sunny-side up, seasoned it well and strew over a generous handful of chopped fresh dill before slipping it onto my plate. Accompanied by good bread and a cold glass of wine, it was "welcome" done right.

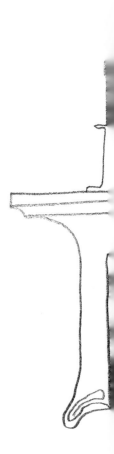

Carrot and Cheddar Soufflé with Dill

MAKES: 6 FIRST-COURSE SERVINGS OR 4 MAIN-COURSE SERVINGS

If you've never made a soufflé before, I urge you to make this one. It is one of the most delicious and savory soufflés I know of—easy as a pancake, too—and it's a perfect supper with a light green salad on the side. You can use other vegetables in place of carrots another time, and if you do then consider a different cheese, too, and changing the herb. This is an excellent, elegant basic to have in your repertoire for last-minute entertaining. It's worth knowing you can make it ahead, too (nobody ever tells us this about soufflé, but it's true!), right up to the point of beating the egg whites and folding them in, so it's far less stressful than people would have you believe.

1 1/4 cups (300 mL) milk

1 bay leaf

1 slice onion

7 ounces (200 g) carrots (about 3 medium),
  thinly sliced

2 tablespoons (30 mL) butter

2 tablespoons (30 mL) flour

3 eggs, separated + 2 egg whites

4 ounces (110 g) Cheddar cheese, grated
  (about 3/4 cup/175 mL)

1/2 teaspoon (2 mL) paprika

A generous pinch of cayenne pepper

A generous handful of chopped fresh dill

Salt and black pepper

Butter a 6-cup (1.5 L) casserole or 4-cup (1 L) soufflé dish. Heat the oven to 400°F (200°C).

Heat the milk in a saucepan with the bay leaf and onion just to the simmering point, then remove from the heat, cover, and let infuse 5 to 10 minutes. Meanwhile, cook the carrots in a pot of boiling salted water until very tender. Drain, and mash to a coarse purée with a fork. You'll have about 1 cup (250 mL) of mashed vegetable.

Remove the bay leaf and onion from the milk. Melt the butter in a saucepan over medium heat. Whisk in the flour and cook 1 minute. Whisk in the infused milk and cook gently, stirring, until smooth and slightly thickened, about 2 minutes. Remove from the heat and whisk in the egg yolks, 1 at a time, working quickly so they don't clump. Stir through the cheese, paprika, cayenne, and dill. Season very well with salt and pepper. (At this stage, you can cover with plastic wrap and put in the fridge to use later.)

Boil a kettle of water for the water bath. Beat the egg whites to firm but not dry peaks with a pinch of salt. Stir a spoonful into the cheese mixture to loosen, then fold in the remaining whites gently but thoroughly. Spoon into the soufflé dish. Set in a deep baking dish and slide it into the oven, then pour boiling water around the dish to come halfway up the sides. Bake until the soufflé has risen and browned on top, 25 to 30 minutes. Serve immediately, although soufflés taste fine slightly fallen too, so don't worry.

BROWN SUGAR SHORTBREADS

MAKES: ABOUT 40 SHORTBREADS

This is my family's Christmas cookie recipe, which is a bit of an odd suggestion for lunch on a hot summer's day, unless you're in Australia where everybody's used to that. Simply serve them on a plate along with a platter of melon slices. I'm not saying you need cookies, because melon alone is fine, but in case you or your guests have a serious sweet tooth, these aren't hard to throw together. Brown sugar makes them a bit rustic and gives them more taste, but white works too, obviously.

2 cups (450 g) salted butter, softened
1 cup (225 g) light brown sugar
4 cups (500 g) flour
1/2 teaspoon (2 mL) baking powder

Heat the oven to 350°F (180°C). Lightly grease a baking sheet (or use nonstick). Cream the butter and sugar together until light and fluffy. Sift over the flour and baking powder and stir in to make a smooth dough. Roll out on a lightly floured surface to 1/2-inch (1 cm) thickness and cut into roughly toonie-sized rounds. Transfer rounds to the baking sheet and bake until cooked through but not brown, about 20 minutes. Cool on racks and store in an airtight tin. The shortbreads will keep for a few weeks.

MELON

I can't have a warm-weather section and not suggest melon for a menu. It's one of those fruits that is really only worthwhile very ripe and in season, so you must get them "while they're hot." Melon is so versatile that it can be served as a first course, too—give everyone a half with the seeds scraped out first, or serve in slices, with or without the classic accompaniment of prosciutto. For dessert, you can fill halves with sweetened sliced strawberries or raspberries, adding a splash of liqueur, such as kirsch, if you like. Or just put out a platter of juicy melon slices to grab with the hands and sink your teeth straight into.

Old-Fashioned Berry Ice Cream

Wild strawberry ice cream was a Christmas Eve tradition in our house in my youth. My father made it with berries we'd picked in the summer and frozen. I'm not saying you have to crawl through ditches on your hands and knees in search of the wild things to make a decent ice cream, but do use very ripe, sweet summer berries, not tasteless, jumbo, white-centered imported impostors. Follow the Vanilla Ice Cream recipe on p. 280 (or, for a lighter, egg-free version, use the Vanilla Milk Ice recipe on p. 281). For *strawberry ice cream,* before freezing fold through 1 1/2 pounds (675 g) strawberries that you've chopped and mashed with a fork. For *blueberry ice cream,* sprinkle 2 cups (300 g) berries with 2 tablespoons (30 mL) sugar, bring to a boil, cool, and mash slightly with a fork. Chill thoroughly, and add to the ice cream halfway through churning.

New-Fashioned Berry Ice Cream (or Berry Fool)

MAKES: ABOUT 3 CUPS (750 ML)

You can churn this into ice cream if you like, or simply spoon it into parfait glasses for fool.

2 cups (300 g) blueberries

2/3 cup (150 mL) sweetened condensed milk

2 cups (500 mL) heavy cream, whipped

1 teaspoon (5 mL) vanilla

Put the berries in a saucepan and boil, stirring frequently, until the juices run, about 5 minutes. Remove from the heat and let cool completely. Chill until very cold, at least 30 minutes.

Put the condensed milk, cream, and vanilla in a large bowl and whisk to stiff drifts. Fold the chilled berries into the cream. For fool, spoon into glasses and chill until serving. For ice cream, churn in an ice-cream maker and freeze.

Scotch Eggs (p. 132)

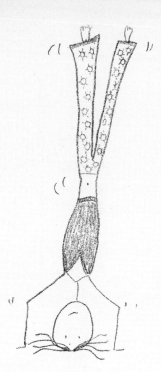

An Impressive Pub Lunch

I READ A BOOK A FEW YEARS AGO CALLED *THE ART OF SIMPLICITY*, WHICH WAS WRITTEN BY a Frenchwoman who had spent most of her life in Japan. There were some odd bits of advice in there, such as the recommendation that you wash your eyes out every morning. Actually, I was going to adopt that practice, remembering the eyecups (a bit like egg cups, only oblong) that used to be in the medicine cabinet of the house I grew up in, but I haven't yet got around to it. (I do, however, give my face a good, cold splash.) What did impress me as being sound thinking I could put to immediate use was the author's idea that we should get rid of the things in our life that don't work and replace them with things that do work.

This may sound obvious, but when you think about it, there are all sorts of pains in the neck we put up with for years on end, such as a chair that's too big for the space it's in and half blocks a doorway, a fissure in a windowpane, a key that constantly sticks in its lock . . . As the author stressed, although these things may seem like molehills, over time they have a mountainous effect, making us frustrated and gloomy and often turning an otherwise fine start to a day into a complete stop. I used to be sent into rages fighting with cheap coat hangers in my closet every morning, for example. After reading this woman's book, I went out and bought armfuls of matching wooden coat hangers and the world was suddenly a whole new place. I mean, you could call me before 7 a.m. and actually get someone pleasant on the line. So you see, it is important to nip these things in the bud.

Kitchens, centers of gadgetry that they are, tend to have more than their fair share of such woes. I think of several peppering my existence right now: the wooden spoon with so deep a bowl that it's no good for stirring, the whisk so thick-limbed and heavy it's like trying to whip cream with a lamp, the ugly pan with the half-melted plastic handle that is not just hell to cook in but also miserable to look at . . . Why are these in my kitchen?! And why have I done nothing about the hot tap, which, every time I open it anything less than full blast, rattles and roars as if I had a werewolf chained in the basement?

My friend Cathy went through a phase in which she wanted to pare everything down. Every time she passed a piece of furniture, she'd threaten to have it hauled to the dump. Her family was about to start bolting their favorite chairs and chests to the floor.

Perhaps we all reach a point in our lives when we've accumulated too much and want to feel lighter. Certainly we go through phases in which we want to simplify our diets and our cooking. I'm in one of those phases right now. I don't want fussy ingredients or fancy recipes; I just want to know what to do with carrots, potatoes, and eggs. If I were invited to someone's house for lunch today, I'd be thrilled to be served exactly that sort of thing, something calm and simple that I don't have to think too much about, something just right. In case you plan to ask me over for lunch later today and don't know what to make, here's a menu I'd consider ideal.

Make the jelly cakes in the morning. Prepare the coleslaw and refrigerate until serving. Finally, make the eggs before your guests' very eyes because they're such a joyful process to behold. You can continue working on your yard sale project later.

SCOTCH EGGS

COLESLAW

✳

VIDA'S JELLY CAKES

SCOTCH EGGS

MAKES: 4 TO 6 SERVINGS

One of the most impressive things I was served, ever, was a Scotch egg, and I know you won't want to believe me because it's hardly an appetizing name. It sounds like a hard-boiled egg wrapped up in Scotch tape or served with single malt—or both—which is not exactly picturesque or otherwise tempting. But wait until you see the real thing!

There's not much of a connection, but this recipe reminds me of my university days in London. I lived in a brick quadrangle with a rather grand name situated at the top of Lamb's Conduit Street. A fellow resident (Scottish) would parade around the courtyard practicing bagpipes every day, sometimes rather early in the morning, much to the chagrin of the other residents. I forget his name. Alisdair? Dugald? Anyway, all I remember is that he wasn't actually all that good at playing bagpipes and that he would drink a pint of ale and eat a pickled egg every afternoon at 4 o'clock at the pub on the corner. Andrew, maybe his name was . . .

Anyway, this is not the bagpiper's recipe; it's another from my Welshman with the kitchen up in the wilds on the edge of the Pacific. All his food comes in by one boat or another, and one day while I was visiting, eggs arrived from the "egg lady." Magnificent eggs they were, too: the yolks ruddy rather than yellow from the hens' exposure to so much fresh air and sunshine, enough almost to make me want to move into the same coop!

"I have to make you a Scotch egg," John said urgently, scurrying into the kitchen with his box of eggs, as if it were important that I not live one breath longer without this experience. Quite right. A Scotch egg in progress is an amazing thing to behold: the egg-boiling, the wrapping in spicy sausage meat, the dipping in this and that . . . but mostly the deep-frying, which to me always sounds like a monumental ordeal, but which in fact proved only to involve an inch of peanut oil in the smallest copper pot and about 30 seconds. I ate two of these magical eggs, and I'd have eaten another except there was only one left and I insisted we save it to serve to my cooking friend Mooney the next day. It was worth it, because the Scotch egg, even cold, so impressed M that he brought his entire family over to eat a batch of them the next day. To complete a feast with these eggs, serve with crusty bread, inexpensive wine, and a lightly dressed, herb-heavy salad—or the coleslaw that follows. For the eggs, there is a recipe for Spiced Sausage Meat (p. 134), but you can also just buy spiced sausages and squeeze the meat out of the casings.

1 egg

Flour, for dredging

About 1 cup (60 g) dry bread crumbs

A handful of chopped fresh parsley

A handful of finely grated Parmesan cheese

4 to 6 freshly hard-boiled eggs, preferably still warm (method follows)

About 2 cups (450 g) spiced sausage meat (recipe follows)

Peanut oil, for frying

In a shallow dish, lightly beat the raw egg. Place the flour in a second shallow dish. In a third dish, toss the bread crumbs with the parsley and Parmesan. Peel the boiled eggs and lightly dredge in the flour to help the sausage stick. Pack a layer of sausage around the eggs, making sure there are no gaps. Dip in the beaten egg, then roll in the bread crumbs.

Heat 2 inches (5 cm) of oil in a small pot until a cube of bread dropped in it sizzles. Fry the eggs until very golden brown and the sausage cooked through, about 4 minutes each, turning occasionally. Remove to paper towels to drain. Serve warm or cold.

Hard-Boiled Eggs

If you don't have your own method, mine is to put eggs in a pot, cover with cold water, and bring them to a boil uncovered. As soon as the water bubbles, shut off the heat and cover them. Wait 8 to 10 minutes, depending on the size of the egg, lift them out, shock under the cold tap, then peel.

Spiced Sausage Meat

MAKES: 2 CUPS (450 G)

This is Jane Grigson's recipe (more or less). You can adjust the herbs and spices according to your tastes. For example, I am sure my mother wouldn't dream of making such a thing without including summer savory, probably in place of the sage and thyme.

1 pound (450 g) ground pork
1 1/2 teaspoons (7 mL) brown sugar
3/4 teaspoon (4 mL) salt
1/2 teaspoon (2 mL) ground sage
1/2 teaspoon (2 mL) ground thyme
1/4 teaspoon (1 mL) ground allspice
1/4 teaspoon (1 mL) nutmeg
1/8 teaspoon (0.5 mL) cayenne pepper
Plenty of freshly ground black pepper

Mix everything well with your hands. Fry a small piece of it, taste, and adjust the seasonings if necessary.

Deviled Eggs

In my Paris days, I used to make deviled eggs all the time for cocktail parties and they'd disappear like peanuts! If you aren't equipped for Scotch eggs, then a plate of these with a salad will make a very respectable lunch instead. I know they're ho-hum in print, but they are delicious in real life. The French call them mimosa eggs, which is a lovely name, but I'm keeping the devil attached to mine since I like them with the mild heat of curry and a dusting of paprika.

To make, let's say, 24 deviled eggs, hard-boil 12 eggs (see p. 134). Peel them, halve them, and remove the yolks, setting the whites on a platter. Grate the yolks on the small holes of a box grater or mash with a fork. Mix in 1/2 cup (125 mL) mayonnaise, salt and pepper, and 1 teaspoon (5 mL) curry powder. Spoon or pipe into the whites. Sprinkle the tops with a dusting of paprika. Cover and refrigerate until serving, perhaps with a leaf of fresh coriander or chervil on top for color.

For deviled eggs, I use *traditional French mayonnaise,* which is 1 egg yolk whisked with a teaspoon (5 mL) each of white wine vinegar and Dijon mustard, and finally 3/4 cup (175 mL) grapeseed oil (not olive oil, which is too strong), added drop by drop. I heighten the acidity at the end with lemon juice rather than more vinegar, but either would do; then season with salt and pepper.

If you've never made classic mayonnaise, the one thing to remember is not to add the oil too fast, or the emulsion will split and take on an indigestible curdled appearance. If you get thinking nostalgically about your youth to the point of distraction and wreck the mayonnaise, there is, mercifully, a way to repair it: put a teaspoon (5 mL) of water in a clean bowl and, paying attention this time, madly whisk in the ruined mayonnaise drop by drop. Perfect mayonnaise with no sign of a false start in life will result.

Mom's "Mayonnaise"

MAKES: ABOUT 1 1/4 CUPS (300 ML)

My mother made something *called* mayonnaise, but it was really a sort of cooked dressing. It's an odd thing, but tasty, and you can use it in place of traditional mayonnaise for the deviled eggs (p. 135), or for *potato salad*, which would be a nice second dish if you wanted. My mother makes her potato salad with crushed boiled potatoes into which she stirs plenty of this "mayonnaise," along with a little grated garlic and plenty of finely chopped fresh parsley and minced onion. It must be served cold.

1 egg, lightly beaten

3/4 cup (175 mL) milk

1/4 cup (60 mL) cider vinegar

3 tablespoons (50 mL) oil

4 teaspoons (20 mL) sugar

1 tablespoon (15 mL) flour

1/2 teaspoon (2 mL) dry mustard

1/2 teaspoon (2 mL) salt

Put everything in a saucepan and stir over medium heat until the mixture thickens to the texture of paint and coats a spoon, 5 to 7 minutes. Cool, then chill.

COLESLAW

This creamy salad is as simple as equal amounts shredded cabbage (large ribs removed) and grated carrot, tossed with mayonnaise and perhaps a little sour cream, possibly a spoonful of Dijon mustard, a splash of cider vinegar, and a pinch of sugar. If you want to jazz it up, you could add some thinly sliced fennel or a fine julienne of celeriac, and perhaps a shredded Granny Smith apple. Celery seed is fairly *de rigueur,* and you can even add fennel seed if you're feeling particularly adventurous. Don't forget the salt and pepper. And come to your own conclusions as to whether a handful of currants shouldn't be tossed in. Make the salad about 30 minutes before you eat it, then keep it in the fridge, tossing it once more just before serving. For 4 people, you'd need about a pound (450 g) of cabbage and 2 carrots, 1/4 cup (60 mL) mayonnaise, and a spoonful of sour cream as the basic building blocks.

VIDA'S JELLY CAKES

MAKES: 30 TO 36 CAKES

I've been collecting recipes since I was a little girl, which is lucky because this one comes via someone who was already very old when I was very young, so if I hadn't started early we wouldn't have it now. Vida was a neighbor who lived at the end of a long driveway, in a white farmhouse with linoleum kitchen floors and a wooden icebox in the vestibule. She always had fresh cream and butter on hand, and eggs still warm from the hens' feathery bellies. No wonder everything she made tasted so good.

She used to walk, even in her nineties. If you said you'd pick her up for some community event or other, she'd be waiting for you at the end of that interminable driveway, on which, incidentally, I learned to drive, the only thing to ram into if you lost control being the odd fence post. At the end of the lane, there would wait Vida holding a tin of home baking for whatever event we were heading to: a play at the elementary school, a tea for the Historical Society . . . Her lemony jelly cakes were a specialty, and I used to keep an eye out for them. They're unusual because they're not actually cakey; they're almost a cross between a cake and a cookie, baked in mini muffin tins with a jewel of jelly at their hearts. Unusual, and truly excellent.

3/4 cup (170 g) butter, softened
3/4 cup (155 g) sugar
1 egg, beaten well
1 tablespoon (15 mL) milk
Zest of 1 lemon
Pinch salt
1 1/2 cups (185 g) flour
About 1/2 cup (125 mL) red currant or crabapple jelly

Heat the oven 350°F (180°C). Grease and flour a mini muffin tin (or use nonstick). Cream the butter and sugar until pale. Beat in the egg, milk, lemon zest, and salt. Stir in the flour. Spoon 2 teaspoons (10 mL) of the batter into each muffin cup. Make an indentation in the center of each with your finger and spoon in about 1/2 tsp (2 mL) of the jam. Bake until just very lightly golden, about 15 minutes. Cool on racks.

Jam Yo-yos
MAKES: 8 YO-YOS

These delightful powder-puff-sized sponges filled with cream and raspberry jam are right out of a Victorian garden party, evoking ladies in hats and lace wielding croquet clubs. The cakes could easily go macho, too, however: consider them the size of hockey pucks, use blackberry or blueberry jam, and serve them off a platter so everyone can grab them and wolf them down like hamburgers.

1/2 cup (60 g) flour
1/2 cup (60 g) cornstarch
3/4 teaspoon (4 mL) cream of tartar
1/2 teaspoon (2 mL) baking soda
3 eggs, separated
3/4 cup (155 g) sugar
Raspberry or blackberry jam
About 2/3 cup (150 mL) heavy cream, whipped with vanilla and sugar
Icing sugar, for garnish (optional)

Heat the oven to 425°F (220°C), and line a baking sheet with parchment paper. Combine the flour, cornstarch, cream of tartar, and baking soda; set aside. Beat the egg whites to soft peaks and beat in the sugar a spoonful at a time to make a stiff meringue. Whisk in the yolks one at a time. Sift the dry ingredients over the meringue and gently fold them in with a spatula (do not stir). Drop the batter in sixteen 2-tablespoon (30 mL) mounds (not larger), spaced well apart, on the baking sheet. Bake until well risen, lightly golden, and cooked through, about 7 minutes. Cool on racks.

Spread the flat side of one cake with jam, top with some whipped cream, and then sandwich with another cake. Continue with the rest. Let sit a couple of hours before serving so they soften and meld. Dust with icing sugar, if you like, then eat them right away.

SEA BASS ON FENNEL (P. 147)

An End-of-Summer Supper

MONG THE MANY TIMES I'VE PREPARED THIS MENU, OR SOME VARIATION THEREOF, was one occasion following a full moon when my friends and I realized, not without regret, that summer was over for good. That was the same night we discovered that our host owned a musical carafe, a sort of hurdy-gurdy and wine vessel in one, so all the Burgundy got poured to the tune of a Russian lullaby. That cheered us up!

This particular group of friends happens to be extremely fussy about the *placement*. "Who did the placement?!" I remember Mollie protesting one party when she got stuck next to Bill. "What's wrong with me?" Bill protested back. "I see you all the time!" said Mollie.

When it's just a small group—up to six—seating doesn't matter too terribly much because you'll all be sharing the same conversation anyway. When numbers get higher, however, you really have to think about who's going to be placed next to whom. You may be restricted a bit by the boy/girl/boy/girl rule, and of course you'd never seat a couple together; after all, they woke up in the same bed together and they're going to crawl back into it again together later, so for heaven's sake give them something fresh to talk about when they get there. As the cook, I always take the seat closest to the kitchen, so I can bop in and out without disturbing the peace. Beyond those guidelines, though, the idea is simply to seat people in such a configuration as to elicit the best conversation and have the most fun.

This will never happen if you've invited a bunch of duds, although sometimes that's difficult to forecast; you need to invite a good group to begin with. To paraphrase Agnes Jekyll (she of *Kitchen Essays*): before worrying about what to put on the table, worry what to put on the chairs.

Generally speaking, if you have nice and interesting friends, they'll get along and be amusing, or at the very least have the decency to pretend. Sometimes you have to invite the same people a few times, mixing them up in different ways, before you can really be an expert on their type. It's like cooking: once you've made a few dishes with, say, capers, you start to know what other ingredients capers will bring out the best in, and vice versa; same principle with people.

Here's a simple menu of highly congenial dishes that will get along even if your guests do not. The cookies you should make well in advance, but the rest is a bit last minute, so it's the kind of meal you need to be relaxed enough to enjoy at leisure, and also share with friends who don't mind hanging around the kitchen while you stir risotto. If you're worried about that, make the chickpea salad as a first course instead; you can even make that the day before if you like.

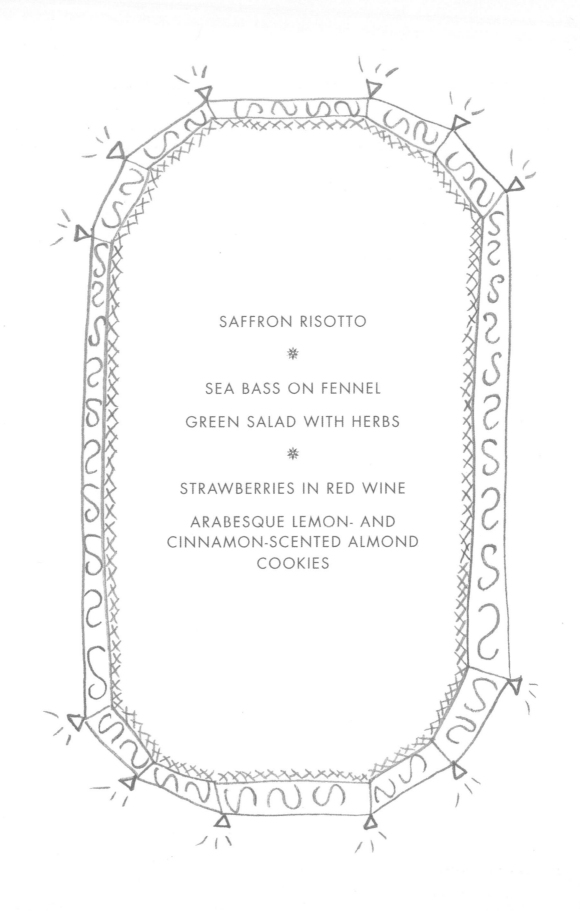

SAFFRON RISOTTO

✳

SEA BASS ON FENNEL

GREEN SALAD WITH HERBS

✳

STRAWBERRIES IN RED WINE

ARABESQUE LEMON- AND
CINNAMON-SCENTED ALMOND
COOKIES

SAFFRON RISOTTO

MAKES: 6 SERVINGS

I prefer simple risotto with not too many bits and bobs in it, such as classic risotto Milanese, which this is, but which in fact I learned to make in Reggio Emilia. It was my Italian teacher, Luisa, who taught me, and I remember we had debates about the validity of wine and butter as ingredients. Artusi, who wrote the famous *La Scienza in Cucina e L'Arte di Mangiar Bene* in the 19th century, didn't use wine, but I find risotto flat without its gentle acidity. The butter question was whether it shouldn't be replaced by olive oil. I think, with this particular risotto, butter is nicer, but depending on what flavors you might be adding another time, olive oil is reputed to give a cleaner taste, for example in seafood risotto. Cream, on the other hand, is a big no-no, even though I knew an Italian in Paris who always finished his risotto with a scandalous spoonful of crème fraîche. A friend of Luisa's, also called Luisa and who happened to be an amateur expert in religious art, gave me a lecture once about cream (this on a tour of Venice analyzing variations on *The Last Supper*). "It shouldn't be used in Italian cooking," she insisted. "It does nothing but dilute flavor." I've thought about that quite a lot and I have to confess that for the most part, perhaps she's right.

Saffron is expensive, so it's a treat to save for friends you really love. You may actually need a pinch more than what I call for below, but it depends on the quality of your saffron. Whenever I use it in cooking, I think of a job I once applied for in England when I was a naive young thing: crocus warden. Don't ask me where I came across the ad for that one, but I called up about it. The job was this: stand in a field of crocuses all night with a flashlight and make sure nobody comes along and steals them. That sounded rather amusing . . . for about 10 minutes. I sent in my CV, but then promptly fled to Scotland to avoid the possibility of an interview.

About 6 cups (1.5 L) chicken stock

1/2 teaspoon (2 mL) saffron threads

1/4 cup (60 mL) olive oil

2 onions, minced

2 cups (400 g) arborio rice

1 cup (250 mL) dry white wine

Salt and pepper

2 tablespoons (30 mL) butter

1 cup (40 g) finely grated Parmesan cheese

In a saucepan, bring the stock to a simmer; keep hot. Pour 1/2 cup (125 mL) hot stock over the saffron; let steep 5 minutes.

Heat the oil in a large pot over medium heat and gently cook the onions until soft and translucent. Add the rice and cook, stirring to coat the rice with the oil, about 3 minutes. Add the wine and cook, stirring constantly, until it's absorbed. Add the saffron with its liquid. Season with salt (unless you're using bought stock that's salted already).

Now start adding the stock in increments. Start with about 1/2 cup (125 mL) and cook the rice, stirring, until the liquid is completely absorbed before adding the next ladle. Continue until the rice is al dente and the mixture creamy, about 20 minutes. Remove from the heat and stir in the butter and cheese. Taste and add salt if needed. Spoon into warm serving bowls and grind over black pepper. Serve immediately.

Chickpea Salad

I tend to associate chickpeas with rustic dishes, as indeed this one is, but as long as you chop all the vegetables small it looks quite chic, and it's certainly flavorful and refreshing. I've served this before the sea bass dish on occasion and it works well. Another time, you can make a big bowl of it to take to a picnic.

2 cups (400 g) cooked chickpeas (about 3/4 cup / 150 g dried)

2 tomatoes, seeded and finely diced

1 small zucchini, finely diced

1/2 red onion, minced

A handful of shredded fresh basil

A handful of chopped fresh parsley

2 teaspoons (10 mL) red wine vinegar

3 tablespoons (50 mL) olive oil

Salt and pepper

Lemon juice, to taste

Combine all the ingredients in a bowl. Taste and adjust the seasonings. Serve on its own or on a bed of lightly dressed juvenile spinach leaves.

SEA BASS ON FENNEL

MAKES: 4 SERVINGS

My friend Sarah worked for years in far-flung countries with not much on offer in the way of groceries, then suddenly she was transferred to Rome and found herself in food heaven. She gave me this recipe over the phone one day, and when I finally made it for a small dinner party I was flabbergasted. It is seriously one of the best things I've ever eaten. Pure and perfect. That's all I have to say.

2 large fennel bulbs
1/4 cup (60 mL) olive oil
Salt and pepper
A generous splash of Pernod
4 skinless sea bass fillets, 6 ounces (170 g) each

Trim the fennel, reserving the fronds, and slice the bulbs crosswise about half a finger's width thick. Heat the oil in a large frying pan over medium heat. Turn the heat down to medium-low and add the fennel; season with salt and pepper. Cook, stirring occasionally, until fennel only just starts to turn lightly golden, 3 to 4 minutes. Add the Pernod. Season the fish fillets and lay them on top, then cover the pan and steam until the fish is just cooked through, just over 5 minutes. Chop the fennel fronds, scatter them over, and serve.

GREEN SALAD WITH HERBS

This is more of a suggestion than a recipe. If I sound repetitive, it's because I believe in green salad after most main courses, especially when the latter isn't heavy on vegetables. Toss together a mixture of light leaves, chopped dill, ripped coriander leaves, and the like to make an exciting mix. Dress lightly with oil and the slightest amount of vinegar, then salt and pepper. My house vinaigrette includes a bit of Dijon mustard at the outset, a drop of soy sauce, and a pinch of powdered beef stock—but I've printed that before so I mustn't repeat myself . . .

STRAWBERRIES IN RED WINE

MAKES: 6 SERVINGS

My longtime cooking teacher in France, Anne Willan, used to make strawberries in port wine in a slightly different way, and I remember it was absolute ambrosia. She crushed a pint (330 g) of strawberries with 3 tablespoons (50 mL) of sugar, poured over a cup (250 mL) of tawny port, and stuck that, covered, in the fridge all day. Before serving (at room temperature), she stirred in 2 more pints (660 g) of berries, halved. There is no need for cream with that recipe, and neither is there with this slightly quicker but equally refreshing variation, which concluded a very lovely dinner on the eve of a friend's wedding. If you like, sprinkle a tablespoon (15 mL) of brown sugar over the berries before serving. And if you're not in the mood for the almond cookies on the side, try the lemon loaf on p. 35.

1 pound (450 g) strawberries
1/3 cup (70 g) sugar
2 cups (500 mL) red wine

Trim the strawberries, slicing them in half if very large, and put them in a beautiful glass bowl. Sprinkle over the sugar, toss gently, and set aside for an hour to macerate. Pour over the wine and chill for 30 minutes before serving.

ARABESQUE LEMON- AND CINNAMON-SCENTED ALMOND COOKIES

MAKES: 16 COOKIES

The texture of these cookies is just "ever," as my grandmother used to say: chewy, but with the right amount of softness. "Cookies" is a bit of a misnomer, as they contain no butter or flour. I suppose they're macaroons, but I wasn't sure that painted the right picture since these taste so sophisticated. I like the mystery of the cinnamon, because you can barely tell it's there, and even the lemon is subtle. For decoration, a few toasted slivered almonds or pine nuts on top of each cookie is elegant.

1 cup (110 g) finely ground almonds

1/2 cup (95 g) sugar

1 egg white

1/2 teaspoon (2 mL) lemon or orange zest

1/4 teaspoon (1 mL) cinnamon

About 50 lightly toasted sliced almonds or pine nuts

Heat the oven to 325°F (160°C). Grease a baking sheet if it isn't nonstick.

Mix all but the toasted nuts together in a bowl until it forms a dough. Wet your hands and roll the dough into roughly 1-inch (2.5 cm) balls. Place on the baking sheet, spaced well apart. Press down to flatten them just slightly, then press 3 toasted nuts on top of each. Bake the cookies until cooked through, 12 to 15 minutes. Cool on a rack.

Butter and Watercress Tea Sandwiches (p. 152)

Afternoon Tea on the Lawn

$\mathscr{I}$T'S TIME WE GOT OUT OF OUR HEADS THE IDEA THAT TEA IS SOMEHOW PRISSY. IT'S actually an excellent way to entertain, especially if children are participating. Teas are inclusive and can be scaled down for an intimate party in the shade of a gazebo or scaled up for larger numbers by spreading tables across the lawn. I love that you're free to stroll around, nibbling, which you can't get away with indoors under normal circumstances, and the best part is that you can host tea in the middle of the day so you're free later to enjoy the sunset in peace.

I suppose you could make a tea party where you just serve sweets, but if the event is more or less going to replace lunch then some savory bites should be on offer. This is way easier for tea than it is for a drinks party (unless you take my lead on cocktail parties, from p. 173) because you just need to make a few dainty tea sandwiches (ignore that they're sometimes called "funeral sandwiches"), which is child's play. Indeed, the last tea party I hosted was largely prepared by children. I set up a station for them with three different sandwich fillings and stacks of bread and they put them all together while I turned my attention to a few cakes. The only thing to monitor with your sandwich-making elves is that they spread the fillings right to the edges of the bread and that they don't put in too little or too much.

Incidentally, there's no point buying fancy breads for this type of sandwich. What you want are plain, bought, soft white and whole wheat loaves. A 2-pound (900 g) loaf will make 10 regular sandwiches. Make your sandwiches, then chill them (this will make cutting easier), remove the crusts (very important), and cut the sandwiches into squares, triangles, or fingers (one sandwich should yield three fingers). You'll get 30 to 40 little sandwiches out of each loaf. Arrange them artfully on platters or boards and you're all set.

Highly inventive types will want to experiment with groovy sandwich fillings. I'm not, alas, one of them, so I veer toward the traditional. The variety needn't be vast; anywhere from three to five kinds of sandwiches is fine. Here are some classic options (don't forget to season with salt and pepper):

Butter and watercress
Herb butter and thinly sliced radish
Cucumber with cream cheese and mint
Egg salad with mayonnaise, minced onion, and paprika
Tinned tuna/salmon/crab/lobster with mayonnaise, lemon, and chives
Smoked salmon with cream cheese and dill
Butter, ham, and minced dill pickle with mustard
Turkey with cranberry sauce and butter
Avocado, bacon, thinly sliced tomato
Sharp Cheddar and Branston pickle

For sweets, it's nice to have a bit of a selection. Here are some to choose from elsewhere in the book:

The Midwife's Molasses Cake, p. 188
Tiffany's Saucepan Brownies, p. 190
Coconut Macaroons, p. 251
Honey Hearts, p. 293
Victoria Sponge, p. 308
Cherry Pound Cake for Christmas, p. 21
Glazed Lemon Loaf, p. 35
Walnut Squares with White Chocolate Cream Cheese Icing, p. 201
Brown Sugar Shortbreads, p. 126
Vida's Jelly Cakes, p. 138
Jam Yo-yos, p. 139
Arabesque Lemon- and Cinnamon-Scented Almond Cookies, p. 149
Crazy Cake, p. 160

SUMMERY TEAS

Unless you're a small party, then racing back and forth from the garden to brewing teapots in the kitchen is not a relaxing way to spend an afternoon. One romantic way around it is to offer large quantities of *sun tea* instead. This is nicest made from herbal teas. Simply throw a few bags into large jars along with a few slices of lemon and orange and a fistful of mint. Pour over water, cover, and set in the sun for a day. Strain to serve.

Many tea shops now sell *fruit- or herb-based teas,* which are delicious cold. Simply brew them and have them chilled and at the ready to serve out of glass jugs. The other obvious option is iced tea, which uses black tea (see p. 154) and requires *simple syrup.* For the latter, put 1 1/2 cups (375 mL) water in a saucepan with 1 1/4 cups (250 g) sugar and bring to a boil 5 minutes to dissolve the sugar. Cool. For the iced tea itself, make black tea, cool it, and chill it. Stir in simple syrup to taste, and serve with ice cubes and lemon slices.

HOW TO MAKE A PROPER CUP OF BLACK TEA

If you're a small party and entertaining late afternoon, you'll probably want black tea; and if you're a die-hard tea drinker like me, you'll want it made right, which is to say with cheap English-style tea that has a rather powerful taste.

I once spent part of a year working in California's wine country, and my parents traveled down to visit me from the Maritimes. One late afternoon, worn weary from a day of sightseeing, I repeated what I'd often heard my mother and grandmother say in nerve-frazzled moments: "Oh! I need a cup of tea in the worst possible way!" My father snapped back, "Well, you're in luck, because that's exactly how they make it down here."

He was referring, of course, to the most unfortunate of fast-food-inspired habits, now apparently standard throughout North America and even Europe, of serving mugs of lukewarm wash, stained gray with no-fat milk, and set before you with a paper tea bag floating lifelessly on top like a drowned toad. In more upscale establishments, sometimes you're served a small pot of microwaved water and then, with ridiculously incongruous pageantry, presented with a small wooden box of assorted teas individually wrapped in preposterous little envelopes. Either way you know you're in for what my family calls "swill."

These days, people love to position themselves at the righteous, democratic extreme, proclaiming, "There is no such thing as one right way to do something." With tea it's different. As I learned it, there is only one way to make decent tea, and this is how:

First, you need water that is freshly drawn, not stale from sitting in a kettle all night. Our house had its own well of spring water that trickled down out of the woods from the back hill. I remember when I moved into my first apartment in the city, my mother and father would come to visit carrying with them a large Thermos of "country water." "Your tap water," they said, "is not fit for tea." Alas, my tap water is now all I've got.

Then there's the tea itself. You can use leaves and a strainer, or a tea ball full of leaves, which is more convenient because it is easily removed, giving you the luxury of a second cup. Some people are against tea bags, but when it comes to basic black tea I'm all for them, as long as they have some flavor. I've got my favorite brand, King Cole, which is cheap, strong, and comes in a cardboard box. It's the only tea we ever drank at home, but there are other good ones and I'm sure you'll find a brand you like (including loose leaf, obviously, if that's your preference).

To make tea, first bring water to an unambiguous boil. When it is plumping, pour a bit into a teapot and swirl the water around to warm it. Then empty the pot and put in the tea leaves (or bags). Don't skimp. Put in enough to be proportionate with the amount of water you're adding: there is nothing worse than wishy-washy tea. Pour the boiling water in on top and give a quick stir to release the flavors. Put the lid on and let the tea steep for 3 to 4 minutes.

Now you must watch, because in that time there will be one precise moment when the tea is ready to pour: too soon and the tea will be weak, too late and it will be bitter and undrinkable. Tea should have definite color and strength, but no alarming tannic taste. With practice, you'll know when it has steeped long enough to suit you. Pour the tea, serving those who prefer it on the pale side first and ending with those who take it stronger.

When the milk goes into the cup (cold; never the no-fat kind and never, ever cream) is a matter of debate. Most people over the age of 75 (and some younger) are of the "milk in first" school and not only argue it's good manners but also insist tea tastes better that way. Most of my generation (at least those who care one way or the other, which most don't) would say that milk in second is correct and that it doesn't make one bit of difference to taste. Personally, milk in second seems the only *sensible* thing to do because how would you know how much milk to put in your tea if the tea wasn't there first so you could see how strong it was? (Don't talk to anyone Chinese about it, because they'll just tell you it's blasphemy to put milk in tea in the first place. With the best teas, they certainly have a point.) Anyway, whatever you do, use china teacups or porcelain mugs with thin rims. Clay and thick rims are death to a good cup of tea.

Some people, such as Russians, add a lemon slice to black tea, others like it plain, a few take sugar. No need to scorn this sort of variety as long as the quality of taste and experience isn't compromised— because tea is, after all, an experience. At best, it's a civilized ritual that has nothing whatever to do with the morning kick-starts associated with coffee, too often downed from a paper cup large enough to use as a vase for sunflowers.

In defiance of the modern world, tea takes a bit of time. That's what I was taught. So I'll no doubt grow old making it this way, and be just as batty and uncompromising as the late, great aunt of mine who used to say: "When I make tea, I make tea . . . When I make water, I make water."

A FEW
BIRTHDAY
CAKES

Generally speaking, I find layer cakes heavy after a meal, but when there's a birthday to celebrate it would seem unsporting not to serve one. Besides, it's vital to have a focus for making wishes, blowing out candles, and singing in voices all out of tune. Without such revelry, what's life?

I shall now, in honor of your impending festivities, tell you my balloon story: One summer's evening in Halifax, when the sun was low in the sky but the sky still light, I found myself walking home down South Street. I was feeling a bit lifeless after a long week, and as I walked my mind wandered off in its own directions. Suddenly, at the intersection of South and Morris, I encountered a curious sight: a lone white balloon was floating up Morris Street toward me. Just when it reached the intersection, it turned and bobbed down South Street in the same direction I was heading.

I followed behind. The white balloon breezed along, miraculously dodging traffic; occasionally it would get caught behind a discarded pop bottle or a small branch, but after a few seconds it would wiggle out again and carry on, until finally, a few blocks into the game, it got wedged behind the tire of a parked car. "Well, that's that," I figured, a little disappointed, and walked on, allowing my thoughts to return again elsewhere.

The next thing I knew, the white balloon was right beside me, floating along at my heel like a loyal puppy. We proceeded together companionably like this all the way down to where South Street meets the harbor, long enough, pretty well, to become friends. The breeze off the water picked up here, and any minute, I realized with a slight tremor, it would sweep the white balloon away and out to sea. I held my breath, waiting for the moment of doom, but the wind never got a chance. You know why? Because that bold balloon, now a pace or two ahead of me again, turned left down my street instead! I hadn't touched it, I swear: it just did a little twirl in the air and changed course of its own accord.

By now, people were pointing and giggling because it truly was a ridiculous sight. (Who was this mad woman out of an evening walking a white balloon?!) The balloon took no notice and kept bouncing in pace with my step, until right in front of my building where it came, no joke, to a complete stop on the sidewalk. I stepped up beside it and stared down. It all felt like a strange visitation from the spirit world come to deliver an urgent message. What could it be?

"Well, balloon," I accepted, "obviously you want me to take you home. You followed me all the way here, you've stopped at my front door—clearly you want to be mine." I bent over and picked up the balloon, preciously holding it by the tip of its knotted end, and there, finally safe in my hand, it burst into smithereens.

CRAZY CAKE

✲

CHOCOLATE DUCK

✲

PEACHY PATTI CAKE

✲

COCONUT CAKE
WITH MARSHMALLOW ICING

✲

CARAMEL CAKE WITH VANILLA BUTTERCREAM

✲

BANANA CAKE WITH COFFEE ICING

CRAZY CAKE

MAKES: 1 CAKE

Now that you're convinced I need my head examined, I might as well put this cake first. This recipe (not unlike the above balloon) came to me out of the blue. For no reason in particular, an acquaintance from down the road delivered it one fine morning, neatly written on a greeting card that bore a painting she'd done of the house where I was staying. It's a Depression-era cake, which sounds a bit grim, and you'll notice it contains neither butter nor eggs and not even real chocolate. This is not to its detriment, but rather to its glory. I, who do not love chocolate, love this cake, because for once it's not like being batted over the head with a giant tablet of Callebaut; instead it's mild and moist and dangerously more-ish.

I make it as a snack cake generally, and therefore don't bother to ice it, but if it's destined for a birthday celebration you might want to nick one of the icing recipes for Chocolate Duck (p. 161) and swath it over. The painter who gave me the recipe told me she often uses coconut milk in place of water in the cake (not a very wartime move . . .). Since that's thicker than water, you may have to add a bit extra, say 1/4 cup (60 mL) or so, to thin out the batter enough. And in that case, perhaps you want to nick the marshmallow frosting off the coconut cake (p. 164), but make half as much.

1 1/2 cups (185 g) flour	1 teaspoon (5 mL) salt
1 cup (200 g) sugar	1/3 cup (75 mL) vegetable oil
1/4 cup (30 g) cocoa powder	2 tablespoons (30 mL) vinegar
1 teaspoon (5 mL) baking powder	1 teaspoon (5 mL) vanilla
1 teaspoon (5 mL) baking soda	1 cup (250 mL) water

Heat the oven to 350°F (180°C). Line the bottom of a 9-inch (23 cm) springform pan with parchment paper.

Sift the dry ingredients into a large bowl and make a well in the center with a spoon. Pour the liquid ingredients into the well. Mix thoroughly and pour into the cake pan. Bake until a toothpick inserted in the center comes out clean, 35 to 45 minutes.

CHOCOLATE DUCK

MAKES: 1 CAKE OR 16 CUPCAKES

In my youth we had an ancient cake tin shaped like a duck in which we used to bake this cake for birthdays. There must have been something wrong with the tin, thinking back, because our duck cakes always looked as though they had flown up from Florida through a hurricane. Notwithstanding that, I did win first prize with this cake in a baking contest when I was six. It had peanut butter icing smeared all over it, which is surely what tipped the balance with the judges, and I went home with a prize in the form of a radio modeled after a can of Coca-Cola.

If you happen to be under the age of 10, *peanut butter icing* will please you to pieces. Cream together 3/4 cup (175 mL) peanut butter, 1/2 cup (110 g) softened butter, and 2/3 cup (80 g) icing sugar. If think you might prefer *chocolate buttercream,* you'll want 1/2 cup (110 g) softened butter beaten with 3/4 cup (90 g) icing sugar. To this add 3 tablespoons (50 mL) milk, then beat in 4 ounces (110 g) dark chocolate, first melted until completely smooth. Finally, beat in a further 3/4 cup (90 g) icing sugar to thicken the icing to spreading consistency.

1/2 cup (110 g) butter, at room temperature	1/2 cup (125 mL) boiling water
1 cup (200 g) sugar	1 teaspoon (5 mL) baking soda
1 egg	1/2 cup (125 mL) sour milk (or 1/2 cup/
1 1/2 cups (185 g) flour	125 mL milk with 1 teaspoon/5 mL cider
1/2 cup (60 g) cocoa powder	vinegar, left to sit 5 minutes)
1 teaspoon (5 mL) baking powder	1 teaspoon (5 mL) vanilla

Heat the oven to 350°F (180°C). Grease and flour an 8-inch (20 cm) springform pan or line a muffin tin with paper liners.

In a large bowl, cream the butter and sugar, then beat in the egg. Sift together the flour, cocoa, and baking powder. Stir together the boiling water and baking soda, then stir in the sour milk and vanilla. Alternately add the flour mixture and the milk mixture to the creamed mixture, making 3 additions of each. Pour into the prepared pan (or liners) and bake until a toothpick inserted in the center comes out clean, about 30 minutes (20 to 25 minutes for cupcakes).

PEACHY PATTI CAKE

MAKES: ONE 2-LAYER CAKE

This cake was never going to work, I thought, because the method is unlike anything I've ever seen. I mean, who on earth makes cake with unwhipped egg whites bereft of their yolks? But it's a great cake: it has a nice dense texture that's ideal for holding up pastry cream and fruit, and the flavor is right out of this world. My friend Patti, who is a food stylist, is the one who added all the bells and whistles, turning a weird white cake into a summery peachy wonder. It's perfect for a birthday in peach season, but you can always use tinned peaches in syrup if you can't find nice flavorful ripe ones in the supermarket. The cake is best assembled not too long before eating. If you want it to keep longer than one occasion, don't put the peaches in and on the cake, just serve them alongside.

FOR THE CAKE

1 cup (250 mL) milk

6 egg whites

1 teaspoon (5 mL) almond extract

1 teaspoon (5 mL) vanilla

2 1/4 cups (280 g) cake-and-pastry flour

1 3/4 cups (355 g) sugar

4 teaspoons (20 mL) baking powder

3/4 cups (170 g) butter, softened

FOR THE PEACHES

4 to 5 medium-sized ripe, firm peaches

1/2 cup (95 g) sugar

1 tablespoon (15 mL) lemon juice

FOR THE PASTRY CREAM

1/4 cup (55 g) sugar

2 tablespoons (30 mL) cornstarch

2 egg yolks

1 cup (250 mL) milk

1/4 vanilla bean, split (or 1/2 teaspoon/
   2 mL vanilla)

1 tablespoon (15 mL) butter

FOR THE BUTTERCREAM

3/4 cup (170 g) butter, softened

4 1/4 cups (510 g) icing sugar

1/4 cup (60 mL) milk

2 tablespoons (30 mL) lemon juice

Heat the oven to 350°F (180°C). Grease and flour two 9-inch (23 cm) cake pans.

For the cake, whisk together the milk, egg whites, almond extract, and vanilla. Put the flour, sugar, baking powder, and butter in a stand mixer with the paddle attachment and beat to combine evenly. Add half the milk mixture and beat 1 1/2 minutes. Add the remaining milk and beat 30 seconds.

Divide the batter between the pans and bake until a toothpick inserted in the center comes out clean, about 30 minutes. Cool on racks.

While the cake bakes, peel, pit, and slice the peaches. In a bowl, sprinkle the slices with the sugar and lemon juice, toss gently, and set aside for at least 20 minutes until a syrup pools around the fruit.

For the pastry cream, in a medium bowl whisk together half the sugar and all of the cornstarch, then beat in the yolks and half the milk to make a paste. In a saucepan, heat the remaining milk with the remaining sugar and the split vanilla bean just to the boiling point. Remove from the heat, cover, and infuse 10 minutes. Remove the bean and slowly whisk the scented milk into the yolk mixture. Return the whole thing to the pan and bring to a boil, stirring constantly. Cook, stirring, until the pastry cream is very thick, dropping from the spoon in heavy mounds, a matter of minutes. Remove from the heat and beat in the butter. Lay a piece of plastic wrap directly on the surface to prevent a skin from forming, and cool completely.

For the buttercream icing, cream the butter and half the icing sugar. Beat in the milk and lemon juice, then gradually beat in the remaining icing sugar until you have a thick, smooth, spreadable frosting.

Set a cake layer on a serving plate. Spoon over a little of the peach juice. Spread over the pastry cream, then arrange a layer of peaches over top. Spread buttercream on the top layer of cake before setting it on top of the peaches, then carefully ice the sides of the cake. Arrange the remaining peach slices on top.

COCONUT CAKE WITH MARSHMALLOW ICING

MAKES: ONE 2-LAYER CAKE

This may be the most exquisite white cake I've ever tasted. The crumb is extremely fine, soft, and tight, and the coconut flavor so delicate that I frankly like it without icing at all. However, birthday boys and girls want their cakes fully decked out, so don't skip the shiny, luscious, marshmallow boiled icing, and if you're really nice, remember to scatter toasted coconut over the icing both between the layers and on top. To toast coconut (you'll just need a couple of handfuls), spread it on a baking sheet and put it in the oven at 400°F (200°C) for a few minutes, stirring occasionally. Do *not* walk away from the oven, because the coconut will burn in a flash.

As for the icing, I felt very much ego-boosted for having made this (without a candy thermometer to boot). But if you are afraid of hot syrup, just put the ingredients, vanilla exempted, into the top of a double boiler—only use 1/3 cup (75 mL) water in this case. Beat over simmering water until peaks form, classically 7 minutes. Beat in the vanilla at the end and there you go.

FOR THE CAKE

3 cups (375 g) cake-and-pastry flour

2 teaspoons (10 mL) baking powder

1/2 teaspoon (2 mL) salt

1 cup (225 g) butter, softened

2 cups (390 g) sugar

4 eggs

1 teaspoon (5 mL) vanilla

1 cup (250 mL) coconut milk

FOR THE ICING

2 egg whites

1 teaspoon (5 mL) cream of tartar

1 1/2 cups (300 g) sugar

1/2 cup (125 mL) water

1 teaspoon (5 mL) vanilla

FOR THE TOPPING

Toasted coconut (optional)

Heat the oven to 350°F (180°C). Line the bottoms of two 10-inch (25 cm) cake pans with parchment paper.

For the cake, sift the flour, baking powder, and salt into a bowl. In a separate bowl, and preferably using electric beaters, beat the butter and sugar together until light and fluffy. Beat in the eggs, 1 at a time, then beat in the vanilla. Alternately beat in the dry ingredients and the coconut milk, adding about a third of each at a time. Divide the batter between the pans and bake until a knife inserted in the center comes out clean, about 30 minutes. Cool on racks.

For the icing, put the egg whites and cream of tartar in a bowl. Put the sugar and water in a saucepan and boil until a drop in a cold glass of water forms a soft ball (238°F/115°C if you use a candy thermometer). Remove from the heat. Beat the whites and cream of tartar to peaks, then continue beating while pouring in the syrup in a thin stream. Add the vanilla at the end. You'll have thick, spreadable fluff that tastes like childhood.

Place a cake layer on a serving plate. Spread some icing on top and sprinkle over a handful of toasted coconut if desired. Spread icing on the other layer before setting it on top, then ice the sides of the cake. Strew some toasted coconut on the top to decorate.

CARAMEL CAKE WITH VANILLA BUTTERCREAM

MAKES: ONE 2-LAYER CAKE

I love when I see an unusual idea that I can run right into the kitchen and try without having to go out in search of exotic ingredients. Sugar is the hero here: just boil it until it turns golden, then rain it into cake batter and *voilà,* caramel cake. Vanilla buttercream is the perfect foil, and the nutty praline ties it all together and adds a celebratory touch.

FOR THE CAKE

2 cups (390 g) sugar

2 1/2 cups (310 g) cake-and-pastry flour

4 teaspoons (20 mL) baking powder

1/2 teaspoon (2 mL) salt

3/4 cup (170 g) butter, at room temperature

1 teaspoon (5 mL) vanilla

2 eggs, separated

FOR THE HAZELNUT PRALINE

1/2 cup (95 g) sugar

1/3 cup (40 g) chopped, lightly toasted hazelnuts

1 tablespoon (15 mL) butter

FOR THE BUTTERCREAM

3/4 cup (170 g) butter, softened

4 1/2 cups (540 g) icing sugar

1/4 cup (60 mL) milk

2 teaspoons (10 mL) vanilla

Heat the oven to 350°F (180°C). Grease and flour two 9-inch (23 cm) cake pans.

For the cake, melt 1/2 cup (95 g) of the sugar in a heavy pan, swirling but not stirring, until the caramel is golden brown. Remove from the heat and very gradually add 1 cup (250 mL) boiling water—it will splatter like mad so stand back. Put the pot back on the stove and simmer to dissolve the caramel.

Sift together the flour, baking powder, and salt. In a large bowl, cream the butter until smooth, then gradually add the remaining sugar until fluffy. Beat in the vanilla and egg yolks. Alternately beat in the dry ingredients and the caramel, making 3 additions of each. In another bowl, beat the whites to soft peaks. Gently but thoroughly fold into the batter and divide between the pans. Bake until a toothpick inserted in the center comes out clean, about 25 minutes. Cool on racks.

For the praline, butter a baking sheet. Put the sugar in a heavy saucepan with 2 tablespoons (30 mL) water. Melt, swirling but not stirring, until the caramel is richly golden. Lift off the heat and stir in the hazelnuts and butter. Pour onto the baking sheet and set aside to harden. Remove from the baking sheet to a chopping board and reduce to crumbs, first by chopping it, then by running back and forth over it with a rolling pin.

For the buttercream icing, cream the butter with half the sugar. Beat in the milk and vanilla, then gradually beat in the remaining sugar until you have a thick, smooth, spreadable icing.

Place a cake layer on a serving plate. Spread over about a third of the icing, then scatter over a generous handful of praline. Top with the second layer and ice the cake completely. Sprinkle more praline decoratively on top.

BANANA CAKE WITH COFFEE ICING

MAKES: ONE 3-LAYER CAKE

This very delicious firm-textured cake, slightly salty/sweet, comes from my friend Nancy, who once had a black bear walk right into her kitchen and remained unfazed. She simply backed out of the house and did some petunia planting in the garden until he left. I can imagine, then, that she doesn't get too worked up if a pot boils over or a meringue weeps.

Nancy's icing tastes outstanding and I definitely recommend you make it, but if you have an uncooked-egg issue, then here's an alternative coffee icing, also excellent: 1 cup (225 g) butter, 3 cups (360 g) icing sugar, and 1 to 2 tablespoons (15 to 30 mL) espresso, beaten smooth.

FOR THE CAKE

1/2 cup (110 g) butter, softened

1 1/2 cups (300 g) sugar

2 eggs

2 ripe bananas, mashed

1 teaspoon (5 mL) vanilla

2 cups (250 g) flour

1 teaspoon (5 mL) baking soda

1/4 teaspoon (1 mL) salt

1/2 cup (125 mL) buttermilk

FOR THE ICING

1 cup (225 g) butter, softened

3 egg yolks

2 cups (240 g) icing sugar

1/4 cup (60 mL) espresso or very strong coffee

Heat the oven to 350°F (180°C). Grease and flour three 9-inch (23 cm) round cake pans.

For the cake, in a large bowl, cream the butter and sugar until light and fluffy. Beat in the eggs, 1 at a time. Add the bananas and vanilla, beating again until light. Sift the dry ingredients together and add them alternately with the buttermilk to the banana mixture, making 3 additions in all, beating well after each addition. Pour the batter into the lined pans and bake until the cake is firm to the touch and a toothpick inserted in the center comes out clean, about 40 minutes. Cool cakes before removing from the pans and cooling completely.

For the icing, beat the butter, yolks, sugar, and coffee together until smooth. Spread between the layers and over the cake. (Leftover cake with egg yolk icing will keep, covered and refrigerated, a day or two at the most. With the non-yolk icing, the cake, covered, will last out of the fridge, easily, for the same amount of time.)

MOSTLY
COLD-WEATHER
MENUS

OPEN-FACED SANDWICHES (P. 175)

snap snap

The Cocktail Party–phobe's Cocktail Party

"THE EVER POPULAR COCKTAIL PARTY IS AN INFERIOR FORM OF ENTERTAINING AT BEST." James Beard, the great American gastronome, said it first, but it could just as easily have come out of my mouth. Pecking at morsels of puff pastry as they fly past like bread tossed to pigeons whilst standing in high heels making small talk to strangers is my idea of a very bad time. More nightmarish, however, is the prospect of having to fiddle around producing those morsels myself. Toothpick cookery has never been my forte. On top of it, I am virtually incapable of mixing drinks. These flaws combined, I reckon, make me a world authority on how to give a respectable drinks party if you're hopeless at them.

Sometimes, for better or for worse, it's the only form of entertaining that will do. Say, for instance, it's your turn to host the office party over the holidays. You don't want your colleagues in the house for more than a few hours (after all, isn't getting away from those people what holidays are partly about?), so a full-blown meal is out. The only solution is to ask people in for a *cinq à sept*. So that's the first step: nailing down a precise two-hour (or so) period for the affair.

Next, buy drinks and make sure you have enough glasses, which won't take a moment if you follow my lead: serve only sparkling water and Champagne. *Basta.* Let's not waste any more time racking our brains over that business. I say leave the mixology to the masochists. (Well, I suppose a choice of white or red wine in place of Champagne would be fairly gentle on the mind too, so I wouldn't rule that option out, especially if you're on a budget.)

Now, about the food. A few years ago, I was on a sort of classical music aficionados' tour of Germany, Austria, the Czech Republic, and Hungary, and it was in a minor opera house that I was struck with inspiration for ideal cocktail-party eats. The opera ruled out dinner because it would have been too early to eat beforehand and too late to dine afterward in any serious way unless we'd been in Barcelona, which we weren't. The opera house itself served the solution to this problem: during intermission, you could wander into a lovely room with tall, elegant windows framed by thick, elaborate moldings that looked as though they'd been applied with a piping bag fitted with a star tip. There were elbow-height tables placed about the room, and at these you could get yourself a flute of Champagne and nibble on a tasty and artfully arranged open-faced sandwich. Eureka! I who have feared cocktail-party nibbles all my life (a bit the way elephants fear mice: they're tiny, but terrifying) would never have to quake in the face of the task again. No more mini quiches. Hurrah! No more "dips" and toothpicks and Chinese spoons. Oh, sing me a swan song for cold soup in shot glasses! The open-faced sandwich revelation was better than the opera.

Rye or sourdough breads are best for cocktail sandwiches, thinly sliced, if they don't already come that way from the deli section of your grocery. The advantage of this bread is that it's sturdy and won't collapse when you pile things on top of it. It's also substantial in a way that white bread is not, so people really get something decent in their stomachs to prevent the Champagne bubbles from geysering straight into their noggins.

The open-faced sandwiches I'm talking about are of the eastern European and Scandinavian variety. They're about four bites each, and the topping at one end of the bread can be slightly different from that at the other end. In other words, each bite can be different, because artistic you may have thought to put a slice of dill pickle at one end and a slice of egg and a ring of red onion at the other. (Why, this isn't cooking, it's crafts!) So be creative and stress not. With Champagne and sandwiches, you too (even moi!) can pull together a smashing cocktail party in no more time than a cocktail party itself lasts. God forbid, we may even have fun doing it.

Here's a list of topping ideas, by no means exhaustive, but enough, I hope, to get your creative juices flowing. The smartest thing is to sit down and make a list of sandwich ideas (for example, smoked trout with apple, dill, and sour cream; or roast beef with horseradish mayonnaise and arugula) and then go shopping. Sometimes, though, I can't be bothered to plan, so I just race around the grocery store buying random bits of this and that, then I figure out how to put it all together once I'm home. You might want to take a personality test before you decide which option is best for you.

SANDWICHES PICTURED ON P.172
(CLOCKWISE FROM TOP LEFT):
Mayonnaise, bacon, lettuce, tomato
Hummus, dill, carrot strips, capers
Dijon mayonnaise, smoked mackerel,
    capers, boiled egg
Cream cheese, dill, watercress, and
    smoked salmon, red onion
Hummus, fig, chervil, butter, grapes
Goat cheese, asparagus, cucumber, red pepper
Hummus, apple, ham, cornichons
Pear, blue cheese, pomegranate, mint
Mayonnaise, boiled egg, mustard, sprouts
Horseradish, Dijon, beef, red onion

SPREADS
Butter
Mayonnaise
Horseradish
Hummus
Mustard
Relish
White bean purée
Tapenade
Cream cheese
Sour cream
Crème fraîche

TOPPINGS AND GARNISHES
Roast beef
Cured meats, such as salami and ham
Smoked fish
Pickled fish
Lobster or crab
Sardines
Tuna or salmon
Egg salad or sliced boiled eggs
Arugula
Watercress
Dill, basil, parsley, mint, coriander, etc.
Endive
Cucumber
Apple
Beets
Grapes
Radishes
Sprouts
Red onion
Cooked asparagus
Cooked red pepper
Pickled artichokes
Sun-dried tomatoes
Pickles
Capers
Walnuts
Pistachios
Pine nuts
Hazelnuts
Goat cheese
Brie
Blue cheese
Cheddar
Shaved Parmesan

APPLE CHICKEN (P. 182)
AND PAPYRUS LEEKS (P. 184)

Love in a Cold Climate

THIS MENU STARTED OFF A ROMANTIC DINNER FOR TWO, BUT THEN IT SEEMED LIKE IT might be more fun to have four, or more. I'm not sure what I ever thought was romantic about these dishes anyway, because there's not an aphrodisiac in sight, and yet the whole thing somehow feels like a plot to sweep someone off their feet. Not that I wouldn't make the same dinner for my parents.

No matter whom you invite, the main point is to cook honestly. True colors will show eventually, so you might as well wave them in front of people right from the start. This means, for example, that you should leave your kitchen as is and not start minor renovations for fear of what people might think. Who cares if you have only one operational burner, that you store your winter boots in the oven, and, as a rule, make stir-fry six nights a week? That's what makes you *interesting*.

Apropos, let me tell you about a kitchen I ate in once that really shut me up as far as having any prejudice goes. It was in Brooklyn. I'd arrived from France and was going to stay at a friend's place, but she was out of town, so I was to get the keys from her neighbor across the hall. At some wildly early hour of the morning, straight from JFK, I rang the bell, and a woman probably in her late sixties, a sort of cross between Big Bird and Ronald McDonald, opened the door. "Come in!" she said. "You must be *starved*." I have an idea her name was Evelyn.

The Formica-topped table in the kitchen was already decked to the nines, with those translucent plates that promise not to break even if you drop them from the top of the Empire State Building, wineglasses with moss-green paper napkins poking out their tops in a stylish twirl, and a toast stand with the Wonder bread already golden and upright within it.

"Broccoli?" she asked as I set down my bags and picked my jaw up off the floor. *Whoosh*, she swooped down and whipped up a cardboard box, snipped the top off, then lowered a plastic bag into a simmering pot of water. "Fish," she declared, spinning around and sliding a Corning Ware dish of breaded fingers into the microwave. "Thirty seconds," she promised. And whoop and hoop—in no time I was sitting on a brown-eyed Susan plastic upholstered chair, ketchup bottle to my left, feasting forth. Remember, this was roughly five in the morning.

I am, of course, feverishly against packaged food. On the other hand, this must have been one of the most touching displays of hospitality I'd ever encountered. Evelyn, if indeed that was her name, had got up *before* the crack of dawn and done everything she knew how to do, using the ingredients familiar to her world, to make me welcome. God bless her! So what if the food wasn't what I'd normally want to eat? The fact that my hostess was so confidently frank about who she was ("what you see is what you get") endeared her to me no end, and it was a lesson I've never forgotten: that I should be brave enough myself to be as honest when it comes to feeding people, no matter who they are.

Which is how you get molasses cake in this menu, for example. Here I am suggesting how to seduce someone with food and I give you gingerbread; am I out of my mind? Also, how is it we go from Italian gnocchi to a French sauté, to a vaguely eastern European salad, to an American dessert? Not sure, but we do . . . Oh well, it will only make you look more mysterious. It reminds me of advice my friend Nancy once gave me: "Never give one explanation for anything. Tell 10 completely different stories and keep everybody guessing."

Make the molasses cake a few days beforehand because it's better after it sits. Prepare the gnocchi so they're ready to cook—you can even freeze them on a baking sheet and, once frozen, store them in a bag. The chicken and leeks are made in the hour before eating, started late enough so that you have time to eat the gnocchi before the main course is done.

SQUASH GNOCCHI
WITH BROWN BUTTER AND SAGE

✳

APPLE CHICKEN

PAPYRUS LEEKS

GREEN SALAD WITH WALNUTS
AND PAPRIKA DRESSING

✳

THE MIDWIFE'S MOLASSES CAKE

SQUASH GNOCCHI
WITH BROWN BUTTER AND SAGE

MAKES: 4 SERVINGS

Gnocchi are very easy to make, much faster and less fussy than most homemade pasta. You may have to try a few times, as I did, to get the hang of shaping them, but it's worth it. A perfect bowl of these divine little dumplings anointed with nutty brown butter and sage is a treat!

I got this recipe from Chef Keith Froggett at Scaramouche restaurant in Toronto after I was served the softest, lightest, most pillowy little gnochetti I ever did taste alongside braised beef cheeks. His were potato gnocchi, for which he recommends Yukon Gold potatoes, but I was desperate for an orange first course in this menu, so I made a modification. Sweet potato would work in place of squash, but whatever way you go, keep in mind that gnocchi success depends almost entirely on the dryness of the vegetable you're using. I've not had success with butternut squash, for example—it's always too wet to work with, and if you add too much flour to compensate, the resulting dumplings will have the texture of a bowl of erasers. I've used buttercup squash grown in my father's garden, however, and the gnocchi were perfect. If you're worried about wet squash, try using half squash and half sweet potato. If you don't care about color, do like Chef Froggett and go for the Yukon Golds. For the record, with the weight given below, once through the ricer you'll have about 3 cups (750 mL) of purée.

FOR THE GNOCCHI

1 1/2 pounds (675 g) very dry squash, sweet
   potatoes, or Yukon Gold potatoes

1 cup (125 g) flour

1 egg or yolk (optional, depending on the
   wetness of the dough; with squash, I leave it
   out altogether)

Generous pinch nutmeg

Salt and pepper

FOR THE SAUCE

1/4 cup (55 g) butter

A large handful of shredded fresh sage

A handful of finely grated Parmesan cheese

Toasted chopped pecans, for garnish
   (optional)

Heat the oven to 350°F (180°C). If you're using squash, peel it, remove the seeds, and cut it into chunks. If you're using potatoes, leave them whole and prick them with a fork in several places. Put the vegetable on a baking sheet and bake until very tender, about 45 minutes (whole potatoes will take a little longer). When the flesh is soft, remove the peelings and put the pulp through a ricer and into a bowl while still hot.

With a fork, mix in the flour, egg (if using), nutmeg, salt, and pepper. Do not over-mix. Pat into a ball and cut into 4 pieces. Roll each piece into a rope 3/4 inch (2 cm) thick and dust with flour. Cut into 1-inch (2.5 cm) pieces. Freeze the gnocchi on a lined baking sheet for 30 minutes before cooking; they'll be much easier to handle that way. (Transfer to plastic bags if you want to freeze them longer.)

When you're ready to eat, bring a large pot of water to a boil. While the water heats, melt the butter in a small saucepan over medium heat and leave it on the heat, swirling it a couple of times, until it turns nutty brown, which it will do after the second foaming. Remove from the heat.

When the water boils, salt it and add the gnocchi. After a minute or two they will float to the surface. Let them poach 1 1/2 minutes longer, then drain. Toss with the brown butter, sage, and Parmesan, and serve immediately with the toasted pecans (if using) scattered over.

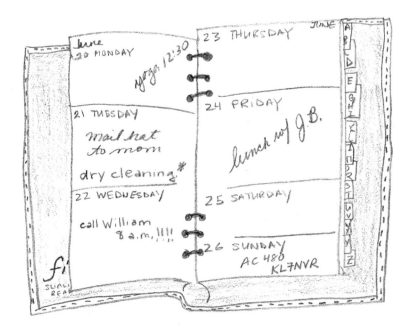

APPLE CHICKEN

MAKES: 4 SERVINGS

This beautiful Norman dish is incredibly simple to make, but luxurious tasting and elegant, the kind of thing that reminds you why French food really never goes out of style. It's chicken cooked in cider and finished with cream, then garnished with golden rings of sautéed apple. Aphrodisiac or not, apples have an age-old reputation for getting people into trouble, so in a way this dish could be considered provocative.

If you can't find Calvados, simply use regular brandy in its place. If you can't find crème fraîche, use half cream and half sour cream, knowing it won't have quite the same tangy perfection, but it will be very good. And a word of warning: chicken breasts in North America these days tend to be too big for one serving. Unless you can find cuts from a tender, small organic bird, then you'll have to cut them in half and plan for one breast to serve two.

FOR THE CHICKEN

4 slices bacon, cut into lardons

1 tablespoon (15 mL) butter

4 small organic bone-in chicken breasts,
   with skin

Salt and pepper

1/4 cup (60 mL) Calvados or other
   apple brandy

1 cup (250 mL) hard cider

1/2 cup (125 g) crème fraîche

A small handful of finely chopped fresh parsley

FOR THE APPLES

2 Granny Smith apples

1 tablespoon (15 mL) butter

1 teaspoon (5 mL) sugar

Fry the bacon in a sauté pan until cooked but not crisp; remove and set aside. Add the butter to the pan. Season the chicken with salt and pepper and brown the skin side, about 4 minutes. Pour off all but 1 to 2 tablespoons (15 to 30 mL) of fat. Deglaze the pan with the Calvados and boil to reduce. Put the bacon back in, pour over the cider, cover the pan, and cook over medium-low heat until the chicken is done, about 20 minutes, uncovering the pan for the last 5 minutes to reduce the liquid to about 1/2 cup (125 mL).

While the chicken cooks, prepare the apples. Peel, core, and slice them into 1/4-inch (5 mm) rings. Melt the butter in a frying pan over medium-high heat and fry the apples on both sides until golden and tender, a matter of minutes. Sprinkle over the sugar and continue cooking, turning the apples once, for a minute or two until the sugar has melted and slightly caramelized.

Stir the crème fraîche into the chicken sauce and heat through. Place the chicken breasts in a warm serving dish. Taste the sauce and adjust the seasoning. Pour it over the chicken and arrange the apple pieces on top. Sprinkle with the parsley, and serve.

PAPYRUS LEEKS

MAKES: 4 SERVINGS

It's the papery quality of the roasted scrolls of leek that inspired this name. The outside edges around the soft interior get brittle and slightly browned like old love letters, and they crinkle and crumble in the mouth, perfectly foiling the creamy apple chicken.

6 leeks, trimmed, halved lengthwise, and rinsed
2 tablespoons (30 mL) olive oil
Salt and pepper

Heat the oven to 425°F (220°C). Arrange the leeks, cut side up, on a baking sheet. Drizzle over the oil, season with salt and pepper, and roast until they're tender and have fanned out, and the edges are slightly brown and quite crisp, about 30 minutes.

GREEN SALAD WITH WALNUTS
AND PAPRIKA DRESSING

MAKES: ABOUT 1/3 CUP (75 mL) DRESSING

Salad greens will refresh the palate while paprika adds excitement. Before you cook the Papyrus Leeks, put a couple of handfuls of walnuts on a baking sheet and toast them for about 5 minutes, then chop them up and set them aside. Have mixed greens washed and wrapped in a tea towel in a plastic bag in the fridge. When the time comes for salad, put a good handful of greens per person in a bowl, add the walnuts, and toss with just enough dressing to coat them lightly. A little chopped fresh dill in here wouldn't hurt, and you can always substitute hazelnuts and hazelnut oil for walnut.

FOR THE DRESSING

1 teaspoon (5 mL) Dijon mustard
1 teaspoon (5 mL) sherry vinegar
Salt and pepper
1/4 cup (60 mL) walnut oil, more to taste
1/2 teaspoon (2 mL) paprika

Whisk together the mustard, vinegar, and salt and pepper. Gradually add the oil, mixing until the dressing is emulsified, then whisk in the paprika. Taste and adjust the seasonings.

THE MIDWIFE'S MOLASSES CAKE

MAKES: 1 CAKE

This is a slightly fluffier than usual, sticky-topped cake that demands a pile of whipped cream on the side. It's best made a few days ahead for the flavors to mellow and the stickiness to be at its prime.

Now that I've got those essential points off my chest, I can tell you that getting the recipe was like something right out of Indiana Jones. One of my oldest friends, Erin, who summered not far from my family home, had got a taste of this cake because her mother had saved her a slice after some sort of community-hall function. Erin then had to save some of her saved piece and call me to come taste it so I could get her the recipe. "Me?" I protested. "What makes you think I can get it?" I was given one clue: the cake was made by Beth Fullerton's mother.

At the time, I only vaguely knew who Beth Fullerton was because she was older than me in school, and you know how continentally distant a few years can seem when you're in your early teens. I quizzed members of the community as to her character, and when I felt I had gathered enough data and was dealing with friendly fire, I called her to gather the same sort of data on her mother. At long last, after that connection, I had the phone number of the cake maker and the OK to make a cold call.

I wonder if I shot back a whisky before I dialed Beth Fullerton's mother's number . . . it probably wouldn't have been a bad idea. Anyway, I telephoned, and the funniest thing happened. I confessed I'd been worried she'd tell me the recipe was top secret and slam down the phone. Instead she laughed and said, "You think *you* had a hard time getting it!"

Well, she'd got the recipe from a midwife she'd once known (and now we're really shuffling back through the generations). The midwife, whoever she was, used to deliver babies for a certain family in the back of beyond, and her consistent post-birth report was that every time she went to the house to deliver a baby there was "the most delicious gingerbread!" sitting in a warm spot on the back of the woodstove. "It took me five babies to get that recipe!" the midwife told Mrs. Fullerton. Comparatively speaking, my treasure hunt was easy.

2 cups (250 g) flour	1 cup (250 mL) hot black tea
2 teaspoons (10 mL) ground ginger	1 egg
1 teaspoon (5 mL) cinnamon	1/2 cup (95 g) sugar
Pinch salt	1 cup (250 mL) fancy molasses
1 teaspoon (5 mL) baking soda	1/2 cup (110 g) butter, melted

Heat the oven to 350°F (180°C). Grease a 9-inch (23 cm) cake pan and line the bottom with parchment paper.

Sift together the flour, ginger, cinnamon, and salt and set aside. Dissolve the baking soda in the tea. In a large bowl, beat the egg and sugar together until very light, pale, and fluffy. Beat in the molasses. Alternately add the dry ingredients and the tea, making 3 additions of each and beating well after each addition. Finally beat in the butter. Pour the batter into the pan and bake until a toothpick inserted in the center comes out clean, about 50 minutes. Cool on a rack. Wrap in plastic and let sit for a day or two, if you can, before serving.

Applesauce

Someone I know can't fathom eating molasses cake without applesauce on the side, so I thought I'd better let you know how to make some in case you know someone from the same tribe. Chop 6 apples—skins, cores, seeds, and all—and put them in a saucepan with 2 tablespoons (30 mL) sugar, a pinch of nutmeg, and 1/4 cup (60 mL) water. Cook, stirring occasionally, until very soft. Run through a food mill to remove the skins and seeds. You should have about 1 1/2 cups (375 mL) applesauce that's slightly pink and gels a bit as it cools. Not to meddle, but you might want to make some just in case your dinner guest also ends up at the breakfast table. . .

Tiffany's Saucepan Brownies

MAKES: ABOUT 12 BROWNIES

It was pointed out to me by a chocolate fanatic who took a look at the first draft of this book that there were almost no recipes for chocolate in it. (Gasp!) Well, I'm not a huge fan of chocolate, so I hadn't really noticed, but I do know all about how along with sea cucumbers and hot peppers it's supposed to be an aphrodisiac. I thought I'd better slide a chocolate option in here in case you don't think molasses cake will do the trick with the object of your desires.

Just as an aside, the infamously romantic French make the worst brownies known to man. They pronounce them "broo-nays," and that just about sums up my reaction to those incarnations, only I'd remove the "r." If you're looking for a rich, deeply dark, chewy, chocolaty brownie, this recipe is it, and it's the easiest one on earth, all mixed together in a saucepan. Amazing how so little chocolate can deliver so much on taste! I bake them in a round cake tin and then slice the whole cake into diamonds. (Diamonds, get it, another hint?)

My real mental association with brownies, I should confess, is not romance, but rather a feeling of nearly yogic peace and ease. I was at a friend's place long ago—a little house with pale pink walls on the edge of a river, pale pink walls the color of Rome at sunset—and she got a phone call informing her that about 10 people would be landing within the hour for tea. I'd have hung up from a call like that and started ripping my hair out, but not she (luckily, because she has the most stunning mane of auburn locks you've ever seen). No, she instead said, "Lovely!" then hung up the telephone and drifted into the kitchen where, in about 10 minutes, she was sliding a giant pan of brownies into the oven. The party landed, spilled themselves all over the living room, drank tea, ate the brownies all up, and went away again. It turned out to be a rather jolly afternoon, actually, and the redhead handled her spontaneous crowd without a flap. I've never forgotten that afternoon because I remember thinking at the time, "That's the kind of hostess I want to be: serene at all times." I haven't quite (*cough*) got there yet, but I think perhaps if I were surrounded by heavenly pale pink walls all the livelong day it might help. Anyway, you can contemplate this little tale over dinner, because there is a link: if the person you're feeding doesn't make you feel as calm and collected in the kitchen as the redhead, then I'd suggest this be your last date.

1/2 cup (110 g) butter

1 cup (225 g) brown sugar

1 egg, beaten

3/4 cup (95 g) flour

3 tablespoons (50 mL) cocoa powder

1/2 teaspoon (2 mL) baking powder

1 teaspoon (5 mL) vanilla

Heat the oven to 350°F (180°C). Line the bottom of an 8-inch (20 cm) round cake pan with parchment paper.

Melt the butter in a large saucepan. Remove from the heat and beat in the sugar, followed by the egg. Mix the flour, cocoa, and baking powder, then beat them in. Finally, stir in the vanilla. Pour into the pan and bake until just set, about 20 minutes. Cool on a rack before cutting.

Walnut Squares with White Chocolate
Cream Cheese Icing (p. 201)

Boy Bait

I GREW UP WITH TWO BROTHERS AND IT'S PERHAPS FOR THAT REASON THAT I LIKE TO feed men. There's something about the way boys go at food sometimes, a combination of unbridled voracity and complete indifference, that I find endearing. All cooks crave positive feedback, but I don't necessarily need to hear "Yum, this is delicious!" I'm more of the show-don't-tell school; I want to see people dig in, lick their lips, reach for another helping. This is how it was when at around age 10 I used to concoct for my brothers an early invention called "fruit cocktail whip" (don't ask). It was very rewarding to watch them eat that. Cook's logic: you ate more, *ergo* you must love me!

The main point, in adult life, is that when dining in company that I've been looking forward to seeing all week, I don't want to waste precious time verbally dissecting the food on our plates. I want to find out how they are and what they're up to—unless I'm testing a new recipe, in which case I may ask about a particular aspect of a dish and do a little hemming and hawing over how to improve it next time—but otherwise I want my guests to revel in lunch, while allowing brains to be off debating sex, politics, and religion.

This menu actually *was* created for "boys," by the way. I used to have a small loft right beside a big market, and occasionally I'd host lunches for a handful of food journalist types, all coincidentally men. (They used to joke that "Laura sleeps on a shelf in her kitchen" because my "bedroom" hung above the kitchen on a mezzanine—just to make the point that small digs should never be a deterrent to entertaining.) We talked about food, of course, at those lunches—indeed that was half the point—but not about the food in front of us. Instead, we gossiped about chefs and authors, about trends and follies in the restaurant world, and we left more "full" because of that exchange. Nourishment, after all, encompasses so much more than omega-3s and vitamin D.

Right. So, now that we've agreed we're not going to mention food at the table today—not a murmur—let's talk about the food! This is lunch. The boys are racing out of the office, screeching into my place, and then whizzing out afterward straight back to the office. They are food connoisseurs, so they do not want pasta salad or sandwiches; they want something new, and they want a proper hot lunch. This menu delivers on all fronts.

Make the walnut squares well ahead. Next make the broth part of the cabbage dish, and keep it separate. Roll up the sausage in leaves and keep them separate too until just before cooking them with the broth. The potato skins (as long as potatoes are baked) are last minute, as of course is salad if you want to toss one in there. If you think of it, have a loaf of crusty bread to go with the main dish, too.

FRIED POTATO SKINS

✷

CABBAGE-WRAPPED SAUSAGES
IN VEGETABLE BROTH

✷

WALNUT SQUARES WITH WHITE
CHOCOLATE CREAM CHEESE ICING

FRIED POTATO SKINS

If pressed at age five to name my favorite food, I'd have bellowed, "Fried potato skins!" We ate baked potatoes a lot, and we always saved our scraped-out skins. We'd cut them into strips, sprinkle with salt and pepper, and fry them in butter in a cast-iron pan until golden and crisp. They were and are the most delicious things on earth (organic potatoes a must), delectable to nibble on while staring out the window upon a field of new fallen snow and contemplating your next snowman. Or so I recall. (If this all sounds like too much, then you could put out some good-quality potato chips to go with the aperitif instead. I'm not above it.)

You wonder, now, what to do with all that scraped-out potato flesh, and I can tell you. Make the gnocchi on p. 180, mashed potato torte on p. 66, potato soup on p. 211, or the potato hash on p. 317.

CABBAGE-WRAPPED SAUSAGES IN VEGETABLE BROTH

MAKES: 6 SERVINGS

I bought a book once for this recipe alone (*How to Feed Your Friends with Relish* by Joanna Weinberg). Dark, wintergreen, sausage-stuffed leafy bundles sit in a golden pool of broth that's cheerfully flecked with a delicate dice of vegetables and flat, smooth, seashell-like white beans. Although very quick to make, this dish does constitute proper cooking, wherein flavors blend to make something far more than the sum of its parts. I particularly love how the white beans act somewhat as a starchy bridge between the light broth and the hearty bundles of sausage.

You can use some drained beans from a tin if you're in a rush, but they'll be way better if you prepare them from their dried state. I recommend doing a bigger batch than required for the recipe and freezing them in measured quantities for next time. For this recipe, you need only about 1/2 cup (100 g) dried beans, so why not increase that to 2 cups (400 g) for a reasonable quantity of freezable leftovers? Put the beans in a very large bowl and cover generously in cold water. Leave them on the counter to soak overnight. The beans will go through a quite remarkable transformation: the insides push rebelliously against their smooth skins until the edges become crinkled with tight lines, ready to burst. Then, after a while, the beans settle into themselves again, smoothing back out into a softer, more polished version of their former selves. It's only when they take on this comfortable new look that they're ready to cook. Don't be tempted to cook them any sooner or the beans will be tough and inedible. Keep back about a cup (200 g) for the sausage dish, and freeze any beans you're not using. To cook, put them in fresh water in a pot, without salt (which would make them tough), and simmer until tender, about an hour.

Sometimes a good savoy cabbage with plenty of big green outside leaves is hard to find. If so, use another green, such as chard, which is not as sturdy as cabbage, but holds up nonetheless. Separate the leaves from the stems and blanch them very briefly, just so the leaves are pliable. This will go faster than cabbage and the leaves will be a bit messy, but overlap them as best you can to make a bit of a lily pad for each bit of sausage, and wrap as described on p. 198.

6 large green savoy cabbage leaves (the outer-
   most leaves)

6 spicy pork sausages, about 3 pounds (1.3 kg)

2 tablespoons (30 mL) duck fat or olive oil

2 ounces (60 g) pancetta, finely chopped

1 large carrot, finely diced

1 onion, finely diced

1 celery rib, finely diced

Salt and pepper

1 garlic clove, minced

1 bay leaf

A small handful of chopped fresh thyme
   leaves

1/2 cup (125 mL) dry white wine

1 1/2 cups (375 mL) chicken stock

1/2 cup (125 mL) crushed tinned tomatoes
   (or 2 tomatoes chopped to pulp)

About 1 cup (200 g) cooked lima beans

Bring a pot of water to a boil, salt it, and blanch the cabbage leaves for a few minutes, until pliable. Drain and rinse under ice-cold water. Pat dry, then cut out and discard the largest part of the rib. Squeeze the sausages out of their casings.

Now, you can make globe-shaped cabbage bundles or log-shaped. For globes, shape the sausages into rounds, lay them on a cabbage leaf, and fold up the leaf to enclose the sausage. Wrap in plastic, twisting the ends tight, like a puppet head. Release and remove the plastic. It should now stay together without the need for string or toothpicks. For logs, roll the sausages into shape, and wrap each in a cabbage leaf, folding the sides in. Wrap these in plastic too, tightly twisting in the ends of the plastic like the handles of a rolling pin. Release and remove the plastic. Set the bundles aside.

Heat the duck fat in a sauté pan or casserole over medium-high heat. Add the pancetta, carrots, onions, and celery, and fry until the pancetta is cooked and the vegetables are slightly softened, about 10 minutes. Season with salt and pepper. Add the garlic, bay leaf, and thyme. Pour the wine over the vegetables and boil the liquid down for a couple of minutes. Stir in the stock and tomatoes. Set the cabbage bundles down into the mixture. Cover and simmer 20 minutes. Add the beans and cook 5 minutes longer to heat through. Discard the bay leaf.

Remove the cabbage bundles. Check the vegetable-and-bean broth for seasoning. Ladle it into 6 soup plates and set a cabbage parcel on each.

Three-Hour Meatballs

MAKES: ABOUT 70 MEATBALLS

One bite of these meatballs at my friends Anne and Ian's one night and I could not believe my tongue. I'd gone through life thinking meatballs were crass: dense, rubbery, nubbly boulders clumsily strewn across spaghetti fields. What I was eating bore no resemblance. Here were slowly simmered, mollified meaty morsels, as light and soft as feather pillows. I felt positively dainty lifting them to my lips, an experience not remotely like that I'd had in the past with the on-top-of-spaghetti variety.

This recipe comes from Ian's father, who was kind enough to share it even though he'd promised the original source he never would. (That was 40 years ago, mind you, and I did beg.) The story goes that the dad, Bruce, and his friends long ago used to have regular bowling nights after which the loser would have to pay for the whole team's food and drinks. Or sometimes, I suspect rather more often than not, feeding the team would fall on the loser's unsuspecting wife. Everyone rejoiced when a guy called Edo lost because that meant they'd be going to his place and getting these meatballs. Sort of ironic to think that the recipe for the lightest and most feminine meatballs I've ever tasted has a past-life association with a men's bowling team.

Feel free to experiment with flavorings in both the meatballs and the sauce. The meatballs can take extra herbs, possibly herbes de Provence or oregano, and perhaps a dash of Worcestershire sauce if you like. The sauce is quite plain tasting and on the thin side, which you may find desirable. If you prefer a chunkier version, sauté equal quantities of finely diced carrot, onion, and celery and add to the sauce. For punchier taste, add garlic and chili flakes. For more depth of taste, you could add some finely diced smoky bacon to the sauce. Play around. Finally, I instinctively reject the idea of meatballs on spaghetti. I'd choose wider, flat noodles myself, such as pappardelle, or generic egg noodles.

1/4 cup (60 mL) olive oil

1/4 pound (110 g) lean ground beef

3 tins (each 28 ounces / 796 mL) crushed
    tomatoes or tomato juice

3 tins (each 5 1/2 ounces / 156 mL) tomato paste

1 tablespoon (15 mL) honey

2 bay leaves

Salt and pepper

FOR THE MEATBALLS

1 pound (450 g) ground beef

1 pound (450 g) ground veal

1 pound (450 g) ground pork

1 loaf of fresh French bread (oval type),
    crust removed

3 eggs

2 tablespoons (30 mL) finely grated
    Parmesan cheese

2 tablespoons (30 mL) herbes de Provence

Salt and pepper

Heat the oil in a large pot and fry the lean ground beef until cooked through, 5 minutes. Pour over the crushed tomatoes and tomato paste. Stir in the honey and bay leaves, then add 2 1/2 cups (625 mL) water. Season with salt and pepper. Bring to a simmer.

Meanwhile, combine the ground beef, veal, and pork in a large bowl. Put the crustless French bread in a strainer and run hot water over it. Squeeze the water out of the bread, break it into crumbs, and add to the meat along with the eggs, cheese, and herbs. Season with salt and pepper. Combine thoroughly.

Rub your hands with a bit of oil, then roll pieces of the meat mixture into 1 1/2-inch (4 cm) meatballs. Put them on a baking sheet and freeze for 30 minutes to firm slightly. Add the meatballs to the simmering tomato sauce and cook gently, partly covered, until soft and light, about 3 hours. Serve with pasta.

WALNUT SQUARES WITH WHITE CHOCOLATE CREAM CHEESE ICING

MAKES: ABOUT 16 SQUARES

When I was at university in Montreal moons ago, I used to buy vegetable pâté sandwiches at some outfit called the Biotrain, which was down in a Metro station en route to my French Lit class. If I could eat one now, who knows what I'd think of it, but back then I thought it was heaven on a bun. A few times I tried to replicate the pâté, but my attempts tasted more like pressed compost, so I gave up and accepted that the magnificent veggie pâté was lost forever. Sniff.

That tragedy has made me extremely sympathetic to other people's stories of lost recipes. So when my friend John was waxing on one day about the walnut squares he used to spend fortunes on at a pastry shop in Vancouver (until it thoughtlessly closed), I felt the least I could do was try to track down a recipe for him. I assumed this would be easy because "walnut squares" doesn't exactly sound exotic. I mean, he wasn't after the secret code to deep-fried guava juice and sea urchin fritters. (Well, who would be, I suppose?)

Anyway, it took ages to find a recipe for anything that sounded remotely like what John had described. I even resorted to Googling, which is not habitual since I never trust recipes on the Internet. (A thousand times bitten, two thousand times shy.) Case in point: the closest to his description I found was a recipe with completely impossible quantities such as "a bag of brown sugar" (a whole bag!?). Using this outrageous blueprint as my guide, I attempted to rebuild the recipe. It took several tries (and my friend Patti's intervention on the icing front), but finally we arrived at walnut squares to match those in John's memory: crumbling shortbread base, chewy sweet walnut center, and vaguely lemony white chocolate and cream cheese top. If I do say so myself, they're almost as good as vegetable pâté, although I can't say I feel quite as virtuous eating them.

I can hear you asking, "Why on earth would you serve boys *squares*? Aren't those for the Ladies Aid annual bake sale?" I serve squares because it's lunch and therefore dessert doesn't have to be serious. Besides, I've never met a boy who didn't like seriously sweet squares—at least the kind that come in a pan.

FOR THE BASE

1 cup (125 g) flour

2 tablespoons (30 mL) brown sugar

1/2 cup (110 g) butter, softened

FOR THE FILLING

1 cup (100 g) walnuts, chopped

1 cup (225 g) brown sugar

1/2 cup (50 g) unsweetened coconut

2 tablespoons (30 mL) flour

2 eggs, lightly beaten

1 teaspoon (5 mL) vanilla

FOR THE ICING

1/2 cup (110 g) cream cheese, softened

1/4 cup (55 g) butter, at room temperature

6 ounces (170 g) white chocolate, melted until completely smooth

1/4 cup (30 g) icing sugar

1 tablespoon (15 mL) lemon juice

Heat the oven to 325°F (160°C). Lightly grease a 9-inch (23 cm) square cake pan. Work together the ingredients for the base, either in a food processor or using your fingers, to make fine crumbs. Press into the cake pan and bake until cooked through, about 15 minutes.

Meanwhile, stir together the filling ingredients. When the base comes out of the oven, spread this over top, return to the oven, and bake until set, about 25 minutes. Cool completely on a rack.

For the icing, beat the cream cheese, butter, and melted chocolate until smooth. Gradually beat in the icing sugar, and lastly the lemon juice. Chill until spreadable, about 10 minutes. Spread the icing over the cooled walnut filling and cut into diamonds.

Sweet Chickpea Tart

MAKES: 10 SERVINGS

If the walnut squares haven't convinced you and you really want to show off, here's a recipe that will get you a few points (although if you make it in this menu, perhaps leave the white beans out of the main dish).

A word of caution: you *must not* use tinned chickpeas for this or you'll be disappointed, if not turned off for good. Buy dried and prepare them yourself, following the instructions for soaking on p. 197. You'll need to start with at least 1 cup (200 g) dried chickpeas, and, once soaked, simmer them until very tender, about 45 minutes. Drain and rinse, then rub with a towel to remove the skins. (You may have to rub and pick off skins several times to do a thorough job, which I recommend.) Purée in a food processor. Measure out 1 1/4 cups (225 g) and use any leftover purée for hummus (p. 119).

FOR THE PASTRY

1 cup + 2 tablespoons (140 g) flour

2 tablespoons (30 mL) sugar

Pinch salt

1/2 cup (110 g) cold butter, cut into pieces

1/2 teaspoon (2 mL) vanilla

3 tablespoons (50 mL) cold water

FOR THE FILLING

1 1/2 cups (300 g) sugar

1/4 cup (55 g) butter, softened

1 1/4 cups (225 g) chickpea purée (see above)

2 eggs + 4 egg yolks

Zest of 1 lemon

Icing sugar, for dusting

Heat the oven to 350°F (180°C). For the pastry, put the flour, sugar, salt, and butter in a food processor. Pulse to crumbs. Add the vanilla and water and pulse a few seconds, just until the pastry comes together in clumps. Pat into a disk and roll out on a lightly floured surface. Line a 12-inch (30 cm) tart pan and trim the edges.

For the filling, cream the sugar and butter, then work in the chickpea purée until smooth. Beat the eggs with the yolks, then beat them into the chickpea mixture along with the lemon zest. Pour into the tart shell and bake until cooked through and lightly golden on top, 30 to 40 minutes. Cool to room temperature.

Dust with icing sugar through a fine sieve and serve with whipped cream.

Beet and Orange Salad
with Arugula and Pistachios (p. 208)

A Soothing
Post-Holiday Supper

*I*T TOOK SOME COURAGE TO ALLOW MYSELF TO SERVE SOUP AND CALL IT A DINNER PARTY, but it was just after the Christmas holiday and I was sick of eating, so I called my friends and said, "Would you be terribly offended if it was just chowder tonight?" You should have heard the sighs of relief on the other end of the telephone. They were thrilled at the prospect of such a calm and comforting night out. Sometimes homey food and a quiet, cozy atmosphere is just what the doctor ordered.

Speaking of *atmospheah,* I was thinking lately about how that's created, because I'm becoming increasingly dismayed over the botched job so many restaurants make of it (one of the key reasons I prefer to eat at home). Chairs, for instance, play a large part. The current rage is for cheap, spindly, modern chairs, which besides being torture on the backside give any dining room all the ambiance of a high school cafeteria. How I crave some clubby plush in my life! (Am I alone?) The other chronic obsession that sends me twirling straight back out of a restaurant and into the street again is loud pop music—loud *any* music, really. I want to talk during dinner, not shriek at the top of my lungs as if I were in the farthest bleachers at a football game.

I should confess that I didn't always appreciate how golden silence can be; in fact, I remember exactly the occasion when it dawned on me. It was during my student days in London, when a South African friend and I were quite into testing restaurants. One night we went to a place called Chiaroscuro, not far from the British Museum and now, I believe, closed. I think Grant and I were the first people there that night, which meant you could hear a pin drop in the place. Forgive us, we were young and fidgety and probably half the menu in front of us was a mystery, but there was a particularly excruciating moment when, unable to choose between the lamb chops and a quail, Grant, squirming like a fish on dry land, called the waiter to beg, "Where's the music? Don't you people have any music?" A throat cleared. "No," said the waiter, "we don't play music here." Gasp!

Anything to drown our inhibitions in that moment would have been a godsend (a fire alarm, a sudden explosion), but instead we found ourselves stuck with each other and the surrounding emptiness. It was a great lesson, because by and by more customers came in; chairs shuffled, cutlery clinked, laughter rose above the clang of pots and plates on the move . . . and we could talk without our vocal cords going full throttle. I realized that night that restaurants can be much more interesting if they pipe down long enough to let life itself become the music. (Certainly restaurants like that are more interesting for anyone who's hard of hearing. I was in a noisy pub once with my friend John, who could use new ears. I leaned over and bellowed, "John, can you hear okay?" "Oh yes," he said, "the beer's fine!")

All this is not to suggest you have to leap right up this minute and turn your jazz off, but if you are one who has always played music through dinner, you might try out a party without it some time and see what happens. Music while cooking is another matter. I am a huge fan of "nostalgia radio." Those perky wartime tunes from the '30s and '40s instantly put a smile on my face and cheer me along. And it's good company when you're alone in the kitchen for a few hours, as you're about to be because bread takes a while. Make it first (or even a day before). Next make the chowder, which you can cool and refrigerate until you're ready to reheat it. Then on to the tart, and finally roast the beets for the salad, which you toss at the last minute.

BEET AND ORANGE SALAD
WITH ARUGULA AND PISTACHIOS

✳

CLAM CHOWDER

OATMEAL BROWN BREAD

✳

CARAMEL TART

BEET AND ORANGE SALAD WITH ARUGULA AND PISTACHIOS

MAKES: 6 SERVINGS

The beets for this pretty salad can be ruby, yellow, striped, whatever suits your fancy; all are gorgeous and would make worthy characters in a fabulous fairy tale called *Beauty and the Beet*, which I'm dying to write. There's no point measuring ingredients—just go by the guidelines below. And feel free to try hazelnut oil instead of olive sometime.

6 small beets

3 oranges

Balsamic vinegar

Red wine vinegar or a few squirts of
    lemon juice

A few spoonfuls of olive oil

Salt and pepper

A couple of handfuls of arugula

A couple of handfuls of chopped, lightly
    toasted pistachios

Curls of Parmesan cheese (optional)

Heat the oven to 400°F (200°C). Scrub the beets clean, trim the snouts, and cut them in half lengthwise. Then, either (a) wrap them in foil and bake, or (b) toss with olive oil, salt, and pepper in a baking dish, pour in about 1/2 inch (1 cm) water, and bake. They'll take about 45 minutes either way, depending on their size. What you're looking for is a fork sliding into them easily: no al dente business. When they're ready, cut the beets into 6 or 8 wedges each and keep them warm.

While the beets bake, prepare the rest. Grate the zest of 1 orange into a large bowl. Cut off and discard all peel and pith, then, holding the naked orange over the bowl to catch the juices, remove the sections from between their membranes with a sharp knife, and let them fall into the bowl. Squeeze the membranes over the bowl to extract any remaining juice. Repeat with the other oranges, only never mind zesting them. You want about 1/3 cup (75 mL) juice. If you have too much, pour the excess into a glass and drink it.

To the orange sections, add a drop or two of balsamic vinegar and red wine vinegar. Stir in a few spoonfuls of oil to make a light dressing. Season with salt and pepper to taste. Add the arugula and warm beet sections (you want the quantity of beet and orange to be balanced, and the arugula more or less in the background) and give it all a quick toss. Tip onto a serving platter, letting everything tumble this way and that. Scatter over the pistachios and some thin curls of Parmesan cheese.

CLAM CHOWDER

MAKES: 6 SERVINGS

Someone I know signs off her every email with "chowder" instead of *ciao* (as in, "I'll call you next week. Chowder, P). In French, a big cooking pot is a *chaudière*, which is the origin of the word "chowder," something I've always liked knowing, being a bit of an etymology junkie. (The origin of *ciao* is "slave," but that's another story, and Venetian, so it doesn't fit here because my mind right now is on the Atlantic ocean.)

In our house, growing up, we ate fish chowder, corn chowder, and clam chowder often, the latter being my least favorite back then. I remember being left alone at the table after everyone else was long gone and told I couldn't get up until I finished my bowl of clam chowder. Torture! Eventually someone came along and choo-chooed three bites into my mouth and I was released. It wasn't that I didn't like the taste, I just didn't trust the look of those meaty little squiggles floating around in my soup. Fortunately, I've overcome that phobia (along with my early fear that "feet eaters" lived under my bed) and I love clam chowder today like a favorite old sweater.

Clam chowder came back into my life recently with this soothing variation that has added depth from smoky bacon. The recipe comes from a friend who puts bacon in everything he makes; actually, he uses half pancetta and half bacon in his chowder, so do that if you like. (He also puts maple syrup in everything—*everything*—but I have to steer you away from that impulse here.) You can leave the bacon out; you'll still have delicious chowder. And obviously if you have fresh clams in a bucket delivered to your kitchen door within the hour, use those instead of tinned. The thing about tinned is that they're cheap and ever at the ready, so I don't apologize for using them.

Speaking of tinned, you're probably raising an eyebrow at the evaporated milk component. I don't normally use tinned things, but there is a quality in evaporated milk that I like in soups and chowders, a light richness often better than either regular milk or heavy cream. It's also a very East Coast thing to do, and old habits do die hard.

Chowder can be made a day or two ahead (minus the chopped-parsley garnish), so all you have to do is gently reheat it at the requisite hour. To serve, heat soup plates and distribute them around the table, then carry the soup pot right over and plunk it down with a ladle poking out of it. This way, people can serve themselves and have seconds without anyone having to leap up. Serve with the bread or, if that seems too heavy, crackers (although I'm a bit anti-crackers these days, especially the gourmet kind that have taken grocery stores by storm and are priced like private jets).

1 tablespoon (15 mL) butter

4 to 6 slices smoked bacon, cut into lardons (optional)

1 large red or yellow onion, finely chopped

1 celery rib, finely chopped

2 bay leaves

A small handful of chopped fresh thyme

1 pound (450 g) potatoes, chopped into small cubes

1/2 cup (125 mL) white wine

2 tins (each 5 ounces/142 g) baby clams in their own juice

12 fresh clams, scrubbed (optional)

1 tin (12 1/2 ounces/370 mL) evaporated milk

A few handfuls of chopped fresh parsley

Melt the butter in a soup pot and add the bacon (if using), onions, and celery. Sauté until the celery is soft and the bacon is cooked but not crisp, about 7 minutes. Stir in the bay leaves, thyme, and potatoes, then pour over the white wine, the juice from the tins of clams, and 2 cups (500 mL) water. Bring to a boil, reduce the heat, and simmer, partly covered, until the potatoes are very tender, about 20 minutes. Add the clams (if using) and simmer 5 minutes. Stir in the evaporated milk and heat through. Discard the bay leaves. Taste, correct the seasonings, then scatter over the parsley.

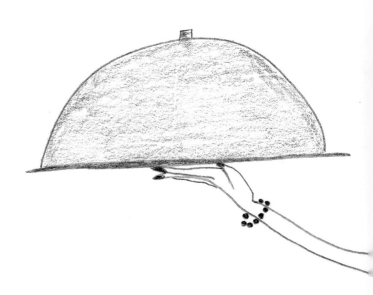

Potato Soup with Dill Seed and Cheddar

MAKES: 6 SERVINGS

This quick and inexpensive main dish, a creation of my soup-expert mother, is surprisingly flavorful and warmly satisfying. It's useful to know about for those impromptu moments when you have drop-in guests and not much of anything in the cupboard to feed them. It's also good to know about if you're feeling slightly destitute, because it's cheap to make, but at the same time richly comforting.

3 pounds (1.3 kg) Yukon Gold potatoes, peeled, diced

2 large onions, chopped

1 tablespoon (15 mL) dill seed, crushed

1 tin (12 1/2 ounces/370 mL) evaporated milk

Salt and pepper

Paprika

Chopped fresh parsley

Grated Cheddar cheese

Put the potatoes and onions in a pot and add enough water to just cover. Add the dill, bring to a boil, reduce the heat, and simmer until the vegetables are tender, about 10 minutes. Using a potato masher, crush smoothish (a bit of texture is nice, you don't want a perfect purée). Stir in the evaporated milk, and season with salt and pepper. Serve sprinkled with paprika, parsley, and Cheddar cheese.

OATMEAL BROWN BREAD

MAKES: 2 LOAVES

You can, of course, *buy* bread, but if you have the time and inclination to make your own, it's a treat for guests to witness hot, fresh loaves pulled from the oven before their eyes. The soft crumb and slight molasses sweetness of this bread contrasts beautifully with the milky clam soup. It happens to be the bread I grew up on (this is my father's recipe), so for me there's the added bonus of being able to give friends an intimate taste of my origins whenever I serve this.

This loaf makes excellent *open-faced grilled cheese sandwiches,* another staple of my childhood. I'm quite sure I ate a grilled cheese for breakfast every day all through high school, albeit of the fried variety. For the open-face, crowd-feeding kind, toast the bread, butter it if you wish, lay on a baking sheet, top with slices of old Cheddar cheese, and broil until the cheese has melted and is slightly bubbly. Eat with a knife and fork with a bit of salad on the side.

If you're in a more old-fashioned mood, then another way to enjoy this bread, which was typical of the Maritime provinces in my youth and long before, is for breakfast or dessert in the form of *bread and molasses:* spread molasses over a bare slice of this bread, then smear butter on top. The reason for this sequence is that if you put the butter on first, you create a seal that prevents the molasses from soaking into the bread, the very thought of which would have my grandmother spinning in her grave. Black tea with milk (see p. 154) is *de rigueur* with bread and molasses.

1 cup (100 g) large-flake rolled oats

3 tablespoons (50 mL) butter

2 teaspoons (10 mL) salt

1 teaspoon (5 mL) sugar

1 envelope (2 1/4 teaspoons/8 g) active dry yeast

1/2 cup (125 mL) fancy molasses

1/2 cup (80 g) cornmeal or oat bran

3 cups (375 g) whole wheat flour

3 cups (375 g) white flour, more if needed

Put the oats, butter, and salt in a large bowl and pour over 2 cups (500 mL) boiling water. Let sit until lukewarm. Stir the sugar into 1/2 cup (125 mL) lukewarm water and sprinkle over the yeast. Stir and set aside until it starts to foam, about 5 minutes. Stir into the oat mixture along with the molasses.

Stir the cornmeal into the mix, followed by the whole wheat flour. Now work in the white flour, which will eventually require you to spill the whole mixture onto the countertop and start kneading. More flour may be needed to make a smooth dough that no longer sticks to your hands but is still slightly tacky to the touch. Knead for a good 10 minutes, even once the flour is in, to give the bread a light, even texture. Pat the dough into a ball and put it in a greased bowl. Cover with a tea towel and let double in volume, about 1 1/2 hours.

Punch the dough down and divide it in half. Shape into loaves and put into lightly greased loaf pans. Cover again and let rise until doubled again, about 45 minutes. Meanwhile, heat the oven to 375°F (190°C). Bake the bread until it sounds hollow when you tap on the bottom of it, about 1 hour and 10 minutes. Turn out of the pans and cool on a rack at least half an hour before slicing.

CARAMEL TART

MAKES: 8 SERVINGS

A baker in Paris called Kayser made this tart famous a few years back. He was known mostly for breads, but then branched out in a tart-making frenzy, which is lucky for us because you can never have too many good ideas for fillings. This particular tart is extremely sweet—as sweet as Hallowe'en, Easter, and Christmas Day all put together—so be modest with your servings. Having said that, I'm now going to tell you that you can put the tart even farther over the edge if you like with a chocolate top. Make a *ganache* by putting 1/2 cup (125 mL) heavy cream and 4 ounces (110 g) chopped dark chocolate in a saucepan and melting it. Pour over the set caramel, turning the pan to swirl it smooth. If you like, garnish with a slight sprinkling of fleur de sel, and chill to set. Then go jog around the park a few times to ease your conscience.

FOR THE PASTRY

1 cup (125 g) flour

2 tablespoons (30 mL) sugar

1/2 cup (110 g) cold butter, cut into pieces

1 egg yolk

1 tablespoon (15 mL) ice-cold water

1/2 teaspoon (2 mL) vanilla

FOR THE FILLING

1 cup (200 g) sugar

1/2 cup (110 g) butter

3/4 cup (175 mL) heavy cream

Fleur de sel, for garnish (optional)

For the pastry, put the flour, sugar, and butter in a food processor and pulse to fine crumbs. Add the yolk, water, and vanilla, then pulse just long enough for the ingredients to come together in clumps. Pat into a disk, wrap in plastic, and chill 1 hour. On a lightly floured surface, roll out the dough and line a 9-inch (23 cm) tart pan. Chill a further half hour.

Heat the oven to 375°F (190°C). Line the shell with parchment paper and fill to the brim with dried beans. Bake 15 minutes. Remove the paper and beans, and continue baking until cooked through and starting to become golden in the base, about 10 minutes longer. Cool.

For the filling, put the sugar and butter in a roomy saucepan and melt to a richly colored caramel, 10 to 15 minutes. (Be careful not to let it burn.) Remove from the heat and slowly whisk in the cream until smooth. Cool slightly before pouring into the tart shell. Sprinkle judiciously with fleur de sel and chill a few hours to set.

Maple Pecan Tart

MAKES: 6 TO 8 SERVINGS

This is a very sweet tart, too, the kind of thing I usually claim to have no interest in. The first time I made it, however, I devoured a quarter of it on the spot, so then I had to wrap up the rest and give it away for fear of what I might do next. A cloud of whipped cream scented with bourbon or whisky is nice on the side.

1 baked 9-inch (23 cm) tart shell (p. 215)

6 ounces (170 g) pecan halves

3 eggs

3/4 cup (170 g) brown sugar

3/4 cup (175 mL) maple syrup

1/2 teaspoon (2 mL) vanilla

1/4 cup (55 g) butter, melted

Heat the oven to 375°F (190°C). Scatter the pecan halves over the tart base. Beat the eggs. Stir in the brown sugar and maple syrup, followed by the vanilla. Finally stir in the melted butter. Pour the mixture over the nuts. Bake until set, about 45 minutes. Cool before slicing.

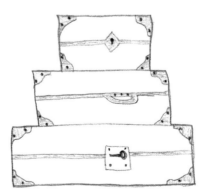

Toffee

MAKES: ABOUT 30 PIECES

Since this is such a family menu, and on weeknights most don't succumb to dessert, I thought I'd supply a recipe for toffee in case after soup you get a hankering to suck on a piece of hard caramel candy. I was put on to the idea when I was called by a friend in another time zone very early one morning. I think it was 3 a.m. in his part of the world and he couldn't sleep. "I've been lying here thinking about toffee," he said. "I think I'll get up and make some." "Mm-hmm," I humored him, thinking he'd roll over and dream of doing it and that would be the end of it. Hours later I got another call. "I'm eating my toffee . . ." Show-off.

We weren't toffee makers in our house growing up, but I do remember having some on a road trip to a ski resort once and liking it. This was in high school, and I was heading off to the slopes in Maine with a friend's family. She brought a plastic container full of toffee she'd made the night before, and we crunched away at it all the way down the I-95. I have a suspicion some of it may have been chocolate topped, although perhaps not because chocolate doesn't travel overly well, especially not when you forget about it in the sun-scorched back window of a Volvo. If you're staying home, though, and that notion strikes your fancy, melt 9 ounces (250 g) medium-dark chocolate, finely chopped, over a water bath and spread it over the set toffee. It won't take long to harden, and then you can cut the whole thing into pieces (not necessarily into perfect squares with any great ease, but who cares about that?).

1 1/2 cups (330 g) butter
2 cups (390 g) sugar

Lightly grease a 13 x 9-inch (33 x 23 cm) baking sheet. Put the butter and sugar in a heavy saucepan and melt together over medium heat. Don't stir once the butter has melted—just let it all go golden. When it's deep golden amber, pour it onto the baking sheet. Set aside to harden, about 45 minutes.

FOAMY LEMON PUDDING (P. 226)

An East Coast Feast for Doubters

IT WAS ON THE EXTREME WEST COAST THAT I MADE THIS EXTREMELY EAST COAST menu, one I now consider a speedy, last-minute, foolproof meal. I'd invited eight people to dinner, one of whom had promised to show up with armloads of fish and seafood luxuriously caught on the very day, with which he would demonstrate his sushi-making skills. Why, a seafood extravaganza, and we all couldn't wait!

At about three in the afternoon I called the "chef" to see what side dishes I might provide to flesh out his feast. "Oh, yeah," he said, "actually we can't come. I've gotta work." Some people have been raised by wolves and there's nothing you can do about it . . . except let out a blood-curdling scream and move on. (The culprit later redeemed himself by teaching me an excellent recipe for oysters—see p. 298—so he's forgiven.)

Once I had collected myself, I wandered over to the refrigerator to assess my options. Finding I had an impressive slab of corned beef in there, I decided to fall back on an old-fashioned peasant-style menu. This is, of course, about as far away from a sushi night as you can get, but that actually made the dinner quite amusing, especially as everyone showed up with white wine and Champagne for the fish fest.

We all adjusted our expectations, and some of us our presumptions, too. You see, food like corned beef and cabbage doesn't sound exactly high-end, which is why so many overlook it, even disdain it. You literally have to put this kind of food in front people (no better way than unexpectedly)

CHEDDAR OAT CRACKERS

MAKES: ABOUT 35 CRACKERS

My love of oatcakes goes back to a very long walk (seven hours long, to be precise) I once took with a friend over the roadless hills of rural Swaziland. She and I were both in crummy stages of our lives, angst-ridden, regretful, and faithless, and I had gone to visit her so we could vent our woes and analyze the daylights out of our respective predicaments. We set out on foot from her house in Mbabane for the countryside to "rinse our eyes" (as I once heard a Frenchwoman put it) and, thinking we wouldn't be gone long, we each took a small bottle of water and a packet of oatcakes. Well, as we walked we talked, and as we talked we craved more walk, and before we knew it the whole day had gone by and the sun was setting. At one point, mid-afternoon, we stopped to picnic on our oatcakes: three each. No wonder the Scots could live off the stuff, because we never felt a single pang of hunger the rest of the day.

What we took with us were the minimalist water-and-oats oatcakes, flat and fairly tasteless, which is just what you want in an oatcake. (Buy a box of Nairn's if you want to know what I mean.) The recipe I offer here is a distant, very debauched cousin of those: rich, crumbling, buttery crackers with the perky flavor of strong cheese fattening up the rustic, puritanical texture of the oatmeal. I give the "by hand" method, but the food processor does the job in about 20 seconds. Just mix everything except the egg, then add the egg and water and pulse for a few seconds until the dough comes together in clumps.

These biscuits are meant to be eaten on their own as a snack with aperitifs (I like a bowl of green olives on the table at the same time). If, another time, you're looking for a similar biscuit to serve with actual pieces of cheese on top, then omit the cheese from the recipe, or add perhaps only a handful of grated Parmesan.

2/3 cup (65 g) large-flake rolled oats

A slightly rounded cup (150 g) flour

1/3 cup (70 g) butter

4 ounces (110 g) Cheddar cheese, grated

1/2 teaspoon (2 mL) salt

A few grinds from the pepper mill

Pinch cayenne pepper or 1/4 teaspoon (1 mL) paprika or both

1 egg

Heat the oven to 400°F (200°C). Lightly grease a baking sheet (or use nonstick). Mix the oats and flour in a bowl. Pinch in the butter with your fingers until the mixture is evenly crumbly. Mix through the cheese. Season with salt, black pepper, and cayenne. Make a well in the center. Mix the egg with 2 tablespoons (30 mL) cold water and pour into the well. Quickly mix with your fingers until the dough comes together. Roll out on a floured surface to the thickness of 2 or 3 pennies. Using a 2-inch (5 cm) cookie cutter, cut into circles and, working in batches, bake on the baking sheet until golden and crisp, about 10 minutes. Cool on racks and store in an airtight container.

Cheddar Shortbreads

MAKES: ABOUT 60 BISCUITS

Without the oats, you get a savory sablé that is more refined (I wouldn't say better tasting, just different). These remind me, texturally, of a cross between shortbread and honeycomb candy. They are beautifully crumbly and rich, with full cheese flavor and just a hint of heat.

I have an almost identical recipe for *Roquefort and Walnut Shortbreads* (thanks to the *Le Gavroche Cookbook* by Michel Roux Jr.). They are gorgeous, and you must try them some other time. They call for 4 ounces (110 g) crumbled blue cheese, 1 cup (125 g) flour, a pinch of cayenne pepper, and 1/2 cup (110 g) butter, cubed and at room temperature. You mix them up and cut them as below, but then you brush the tops with egg wash (an egg or yolk lightly beaten with 1 teaspoon/5 mL of water) and place a walnut half on top of each. They take 12 minutes at 350°F (180°C) and yield about 40 biscuits.

8 ounces (225 g) finely grated Parmesan cheese
8 ounces (225 g) sharp Cheddar cheese, grated
1 cup (225 g) cold butter, cut into small pieces
1 1/2 cups (185 g) flour, more if needed
1 teaspoon (5 mL) cayenne pepper

Mix all the ingredients in a food processor until they just clump together. Turn out onto a board and pat into a smooth dough, without overworking. Shape into a 1-inch (2.5 cm) log, wrap in plastic, and refrigerate 2 hours or until firm enough to slice neatly. Slice into 1/4-inch (5 mm) rounds. Bake on a lightly greased (or nonstick) baking sheet at 375°F (190°C) until fully cooked through, 8 to 10 minutes. Cool on racks and store in an airtight container.

CORNED BEEF WITH MUSTARD SAUCE

MAKES: 6 SERVINGS

Cured meat has a slightly pickled taste, which I like, and an appealing confit-like texture that's a pleasant change from the usual roast. I take author Stephanie Alexander's approach to mustard sauce because it employs the cooking liquid from the meat, which keeps things light and economical.

FOR THE CORNED BEEF

About 3 pounds (1.3 kg) corned beef

1 large onion, studded with 3 cloves

1 large carrot, halved

1 celery rib

1 bay leaf

6 peppercorns

FOR THE MUSTARD SAUCE

2 tablespoons (30 mL) butter

2 tablespoons (30 mL) flour

1 tablespoon (15 mL) dry mustard, to taste

A palmful of chopped fresh parsley

1 to 2 tablespoons (15 to 30 mL) heavy cream

Salt, pepper, and lemon juice

Put the corned beef in a pot, cover with water, bring to a boil, and drain. Return the meat to the pot. Add enough fresh water to cover the meat. Add the clove-studded onion, carrot, celery, bay leaf, and peppercorns. Bring to a boil, reduce heat to low, and simmer, half-covered, until the meat is fork-tender, about 2 1/2 hours.

When it's done, remove the meat and wrap in foil to keep warm. Strain the broth and put it back in the pot. Scoop out 1 cup (250 mL) of the broth to make the sauce. (Use the rest to cook the carrots in.)

For the sauce, melt the butter in a small saucepan. When the foaming subsides, whisk in the flour and cook, whisking, 1 minute. Whisk in the dry mustard. Whisk in the broth to make a thick sauce, then stir in the parsley and cream and heat through. Season with salt, pepper, and lemon juice. Transfer to a warm sauceboat.

Slice the corned beef and arrange on a serving platter with the carrots, potatoes, and cabbage. Pass the sauce separately.

POTATOES WITH BUTTER AND PARSLEY

I love the grandmotherly sight of a bowl of boiled potatoes tossed in parsley, and it must be one of the most comforting things there is to eat. For eight attendees, you'll want about 12 medium-sized waxy potatoes (about 4 ounces/110 g each), peeled. Boil them in salted water until tender all the way through. Drain, and toss with butter and chopped fresh parsley.

CARROT RIBBONS

You'll need about 2 pounds (900 g) slender carrots, halved or quartered lengthwise with a little bit of green left on. I trim and slice them lengthwise ahead of time and put them in a big bowl of cold water, which makes them curl slightly. Once you've removed the meat from its broth, bring the broth back to a boil, adding more water if needed, and drop in the carrots. Boil until tender, about 10 minutes, depending on how thickly you've cut them. Drain and toss with butter.

SAVOY CABBAGE

Find a healthy savoy cabbage with its dark green outer leaves still attached—1 1/2 pounds (675 g) is probably all you need. Slice it into feminine ribbons, removing the fat ribs from the outer leaves as you slice, and discarding the core. Melt 3 tablespoons (50 mL) butter in a pot and add the cabbage ribbons. Cover and steam until tender, about 5 minutes. Season with salt and pepper, and toss.

FOAMY LEMON PUDDING

MAKES: 4 TO 6 SERVINGS

This light, easy, souffléed pudding is a specialty of my mother's, a quick family dessert that tastes a hundred times more impressive than it looks (better than the other way around), which is the fault of too many sweet dishes, especially the fancy ones in pastry-shop windows. The magic of this pudding is that the top two-thirds cooks like a foamy soufflé while underneath you find a nearly curd-like lemony sauce. Undercooking will yield more sauce; overcooking can make the sauce disappear altogether. It's fine to serve the dish on its own, but it's especially good with pouring cream or whipped cream on top. If you have a crowd, double the recipe and bake it in an extra-large dish (which may take slightly longer) or in two dishes of the size given below.

2 tablespoons (30 mL) butter

2/3 cup (140 g) sugar

Pinch salt

3 eggs, separated + 1 egg white

3 tablespoons (50 mL) flour

Zest and juice of 1 1/2 lemons

1 cup (250 mL) whole milk

Heat the oven to 325°F (160°C). Butter a 9-inch (23 cm) glass baking dish. Bring a full kettle of water to a boil.

Cream the butter, sugar, and salt in a bowl. Beat in the egg yolks and flour, followed by the lemon zest, lemon juice, and milk. In another bowl, whisk the egg whites to stiff peaks. Stir a spoonful into the yolk mixture, then gently fold the two mixtures together. Pour into the baking dish, then set this dish into a larger dish or roasting pan.

Slide the pans into the oven before pouring boiling water into the outer pan to come about halfway up the sides of the pudding dish. Bake until the top is lightly golden, the top two-thirds of the pudding set, and the bottom third still runny, 30 to 40 minutes. Serve warm or at room temperature with heavy cream or whipped cream.

Creamy Baked Rice Pudding

MAKES: 6 SERVINGS

Once, describing a weakling from his school days, a friend made the accusing remark that So-and-so "couldn't knock the skin off a rice pudding." It must be hard almost not to *like* getting insulted when the imagery is that good. I was never a great fan of the rice pudding we made at our house when I was growing up because it was too heavy with rice, and I didn't like the raisins (of which, notice, none here). When my friend Donnalu gave me her old recipe and had to shut her eyes as she raved about how good it was, I thought I'd better give baked rice pudding a second chance. This is a terrific recipe. It looks plain, but the brown sugar gives it depth, and because there is so little rice it is ultra-ultra-creamy and not heavy at all.

4 cups (1 L) whole milk
1/3 cup (65 g) short-grain rice
1/4 cup (55 g) packed brown sugar
1 tablespoon (15 mL) butter
1 teaspoon (5 mL) vanilla
1/4 teaspoon (1 mL) nutmeg
Pinch salt

Heat the oven to 300°F (150°C). Heat the milk in a saucepan until bubbles appear around the edge. Remove from the heat and stir in the remaining ingredients. Pour into an 8-cup (2 L) glass baking dish. Bake 1 hour, stirring twice during this time. Continue baking until the top is set with a golden skin and most of the milk is absorbed, about 1 hour longer. Serve warm or at room temperature.

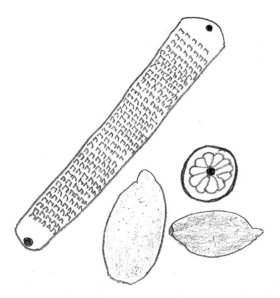

PRUNES AND FIGS IN ARMAGNAC SYRUP (P. 240)

France via Fork

THE FRENCH AND ITALIANS ARE STRONG ON REGIONAL COOKING, ON CONTINUALLY declaring their cultural identity by what they eat. When a Marseillais makes bouillabaisse, he's not just boiling up fish soup, he's reinforcing: *Bouillabaisse, c'est moi!* Likewise, this menu reflects southwest France: Roquefort, walnuts, duck, prunes, Armagnac . . . The ingredients paint a clear picture of place, enough to make you want to dash to the cupboard and dig out your long-lost beret. Some menus are pure table travel.

I suppose if food can paint a picture of place (for example: oats, molasses, dulse, shad = where I grew up), it can convey time, too. I don't just mean that chicken à la king says 1950s, say, or cheesecake screams 1980s, although in my mind they do, but that we can mark periods in our own lives with certain recipes. If I think of Nanaimo bars, for example, I'm suddenly 10, because that's when I used to make them and store them in the freezer because I thought they were better ice cold. If I think of spaghetti with tuna sauce and dill, I'm in second-year university in an apartment on Claremont Street, Montreal, the era when I used to run every night up and over Mont Royal in the dark (what was I thinking?!). Pretzels are my year in Munich. Back then I used to be interested in baking and horses, and I was constantly reading biographies of British writers and wanting to be one. I wrote a few poems at that time too, which is slightly embarrassing . . . one of them was about a jar of chutney.

Anyway, this menu takes me back to the southwest of France. Last time I visited the place I was with Australian friends. It was autumn, and in the frosty early-morning air you'd hear the clean crack of hunters' rifles shatter the peace, then the crunch of their hesitant footsteps on frozen leaves. They'd shoot unnervingly close to the house, I remember. We were staying in a small château where the lady of the house prepared dinner slowly in the evening, while we lazily sipped Pineau des Charentes by the fire . . .

The duck (or the pork belly) is great with the lentils (which in their own right are also fabulosity for lunch). If you need something super fast, serve the duck on buttered savoy cabbage (p. 225) and be done. You could also serve green beans with it or fried or roasted eggplant cubes tossed with parsley. Potatoes are classic, but serve those only if you are not serving the tart beforehand, otherwise it's all too much. Make the fruit dessert first, then the duck, but just up to the point before you broil it. That should be last minute. While the duck cooks, make the side dish. The salad is the last thing before dinner. Broil the duck between courses.

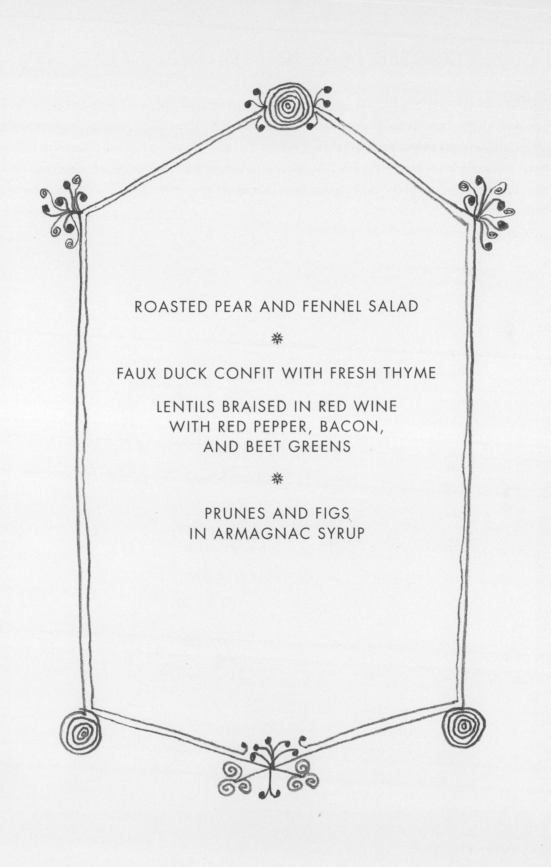

ROASTED PEAR AND FENNEL SALAD

✳

FAUX DUCK CONFIT WITH FRESH THYME

LENTILS BRAISED IN RED WINE
WITH RED PEPPER, BACON,
AND BEET GREENS

✳

PRUNES AND FIGS
IN ARMAGNAC SYRUP

ROASTED PEAR AND FENNEL SALAD

This is an easy way to begin. For four people you need 2 firm but ripe pears, peeled and quartered, and 1 large fennel bulb, trimmed and cut into thick slices lengthwise. Heat the oven to 400°F (200°C). Toast some walnut halves for about 7 minutes; set aside. Put the pears and fennel on a baking sheet, season with salt and pepper, dot with butter, and drizzle with olive oil. Roast, turning at least once, until very tender and starting to caramelize nicely, about 45 minutes. Serve with the walnuts and some blue cheese.

Onion, Blue Cheese, and Walnut Tart

MAKES: 6 SERVINGS

Whereas the beauty of quiche Lorraine is all in its perfect custard against crumbling crust, the charms of this one are in the contrasts between sweet strands of onion, sharp hits of creamy blue cheese, and the toasty crunch of walnuts. To toast the walnuts, wait until you have the oven on anyway for the tart. Pop the walnuts in on a baking sheet until they're just lightly colored and fragrant, 5 to 10 minutes, then chop. If you just want a pre-dinner nibble instead of a first course, Roquefort and Walnut Short-breads (p. 223) are a good replacement for this tart.

FOR THE PASTRY

1 cup + 2 tablespoons (140 g) flour (half white and half whole wheat)

Pinch salt

1/2 cup (110 g) cold butter, cut into pieces

3 tablespoons (50 mL) cold water

FOR THE FILLING

1 tablespoon (15 mL) butter

1 tablespoon (15 mL) olive oil

1 red or yellow onion, sliced

Salt and pepper

2/3 cup (70 g) chopped, lightly toasted walnuts

A handful of chopped fresh parsley

2 1/2 ounces (70 g) crumbled blue cheese, such as Roquefort

3 eggs

1 cup (250 mL) milk

For the pastry, put the flour, salt, and butter in a food processor and pulse to fine crumbs. Add the water and pulse for a few seconds, just until the mixture pulls together. Pat into a disk, roll flat, then line a 10-inch (25 cm) tart shell. Trim the edges. Wrap in plastic and refrigerate until you need it.

Heat the oven to 375°F (190°C). Melt the butter with the oil in a sauté pan. Add the onions, season with salt and pepper, and gently fry until very soft, about 15 minutes. (At the same time you can toast the walnuts.) Spread the onions in the pastry shell. Scatter over the parsley, cheese, and nuts.

Beat the eggs, whisk in the milk, and season with salt and pepper. Pour over the filling. Bake the tart until set, about 30 minutes. Serve warm or at room temperature.

FAUX DUCK CONFIT WITH FRESH THYME

MAKES: 4 SERVINGS

This is a bit like duck confit, only a fast version for when you want to make a small quantity to eat right away. Really it's just slow-roasted duck legs, with crisp skin and meat that falls from the bone. This is a French menu, so I use thyme. If you want to be more exotic, use Chinese five-spice powder instead—you'll need 1 to 2 tablespoons (15 to 30 mL). It's not necessary, but for slightly more depth of flavor, if you have the time, season the duck legs with salt and pepper, coat them with chopped thyme leaves (or five-spice), wrap, and refrigerate overnight before cooking. Don't get too hung up about the thyme, though; this is above all about soft, juicy duck and crisp skin.

4 duck legs

2 garlic cloves, halved

Salt and pepper

1/4 cup (30 g) duck fat, cut into pieces

8 sprigs fresh thyme

Cut around the end of the duck legs (an action not unlike cutting around the wrapper at the top of a bottle of wine), going through the tendon so that the legs will self-French during cooking. Rub the legs well with garlic, and season with salt and pepper.

Heat the oven to 300°F (150°C). Lay the duck legs fat side down in a large frying pan. Scatter the duck fat around them, and tuck in the thyme sprigs. Turn the heat to medium and render the fat on the legs, up to 15 minutes.

Once the fat is a pool around the duck, turn the legs skin side up. Cover the pan with a lid or foil, sealing tightly, and transfer to the oven. Bake 2 1/2 hours, until the meat falls from the bone. Remove the legs from the fat and lay skin side up on a baking sheet.

Turn the oven to broil, but leave the rack in the middle of the oven. Broil the legs until the skin is golden and crisp, about 5 minutes. Serve immediately.

Pork Belly with Five-Spice

Here is another rich and delicious confit-like creation.

2 pounds (900 g) pork belly, skin on
Salt and pepper
2 tablespoons (30 mL) grapeseed oil
1 onion, chopped
2 tablespoons (30 mL) apple cider vinegar
1 tablespoon (15 mL) sugar
2 tablespoons (30 mL) five-spice powder
2 cups (500 mL) hard cider

Heat the oven to 325°F (160°C). Score the skin side of the meat without cutting through to the flesh. Season the pork belly with salt and pepper on both sides. Heat the oil in a casserole large enough to hold the meat flat, and brown the pork belly, about 3 minutes each side. Remove from the pan.

Add the onions to the hot oil and brown lightly, about 7 minutes. Deglaze with the apple cider vinegar, then stir in the sugar. Rub the browned pork belly all over with the five-spice powder and lay it on top of the onions. Pour in the cider, cover, transfer to the oven, and braise until the meat is fork-tender, 2 to 2 1/2 hours.

Remove the meat from the pot and set it skin side up on a foil-lined baking sheet. Move the oven rack to the top and turn the oven to broil. Broil the belly until the skin is crisp, about 4 minutes, but keep an eye on it because it can burn easily. Slice to serve.

It's not necessary, but if you'd like a *jus* with the pork, simply set the pot of cooking liquid on the stovetop and boil it down to sauce consistency.

LENTILS BRAISED IN RED WINE WITH RED PEPPER, BACON, AND BEET GREENS

MAKES: 6 SERVINGS

With the beet greens (or chard, if that's easier to get) and red pepper, this dish is colorful, and the wine adds a gentle acidity that I like here. You can leave out the bacon if you want (and you will if, for example, you're serving this with the pork belly), but it does add its *je ne sais quoi* to the duck ensemble.

FOR THE LENTILS

1 pound (450 g) du Puy lentils

2 garlic cloves, halved

2 bay leaves

2 sprigs fresh thyme

4 cups (1 L) chicken stock

1 cup (250 mL) red wine

FOR THE GARNISH

6 ounces (170 g) bacon, cut into lardons

A few splashes of olive oil

2 shallots, minced

1 red pepper, very finely diced

Leaves from 1 bunch beet greens
  (or chard leaves, stems removed)

Salt and pepper

A splash of sherry vinegar (optional)

Put the lentils in a pot with the garlic, bay leaves, thyme, stock, and wine. Bring to a simmer, cover, and cook gently until al dente, about 40 minutes.

Meanwhile, prepare the garnish. Fry the bacon until cooked but not crisp, then set aside. Add a small splash of olive oil to the same pan and fry the shallots. Remove and add to the bacon. Next, adding olive oil if needed, fry the red pepper until soft. Remove and add to the bacon. Finally put the beet greens in the pan with a splash of water, cover, and cook until wilted, about 3 minutes. Remove, squeeze dry, chop, and add to the bacon.

When the lentils are done, pluck out the garlic, bay leaves, and thyme. If there is any liquid remaining, drain and return lentils to the pan. Stir in the bacon mixture. Season with salt and pepper, and add vinegar and perhaps a little more oil if you like. Serve warm as a base for the duck.

Endive Braised in Orange Juice

This is a flavorful alternative if you're going a lighter route than lentils. For four people, you'll need about 6 large endives, halved lengthwise. Heat a tablespoon (15 mL) each of oil and butter in a large frying pan. Sprinkle over 2 teaspoons (10 mL) sugar. Lay the endives in the pan cut side down and cook until golden on the underside. Season with salt and pepper. Turn the endives over, then pour over about 1/2 cup (125 mL) orange juice. Cover and cook until soft, 5 to 7 minutes. Remove the endives, add a teaspoon (5 mL) balsamic vinegar, and boil the juice down to syrup, about a minute. Pour over the endives and serve.

Sautéed Thyme Potatoes

MAKES: 4 SERVINGS

If you're serving the tart for the first course, you probably don't want to serve potatoes on the side of the duck. If you skip a first course, however, or make something that isn't starchy, then crisp potatoes are classic on the side: the softness of the confit meat is nicely foiled by the potatoes' crispness. If diced potatoes aren't winning you over geometrically, then you can do slices, which is how the French usually do them, also cooking them in duck fat instead of butter and oil.

1 1/2 pounds (675 g) waxy potatoes
3 tablespoons (50 mL) butter
1 tablespoon (15 mL) olive oil
Salt and pepper
A small handful of chopped fresh thyme

Peel and dice the potatoes. In a large frying pan on medium heat, melt the butter in the oil. Add the potatoes, season with salt and pepper, and add the thyme. Fry, stirring occasionally, until tender inside and very crisp and golden on the outside, 30 to 40 minutes. Serve immediately.

PRUNES AND FIGS IN ARMAGNAC SYRUP

MAKES: 4 SERVINGS

Once when I had friends for dinner and told them dessert was prunes, I could feel the air in the room suddenly stiffen. Don't you hate it when you make something divine and nobody believes you? The fruit looked positively glorious, glistening in a big bowl, so when I set it on the table, thankfully an eyebrow went up. Kerry, who I think was the most skeptical of the lot, took one bite of his and, after a pause, declared, "This is like an old friend telling you a new secret! It's familiar, but it's new. It's delicious!" This is a dessert neither to advertise nor defend: it will speak for itself, and then everyone else will speak for it too. Serve whipped crème fraîche on top, or slightly sweetened whipped cream with a few tablespoons of Greek yogurt folded in.

1/2 cup (95 g) sugar
1 piece orange rind, white pith removed
6 ounces (170 g) each dried prunes and dried figs
1/4 cup (60 mL) Armagnac or Cognac
Whipped crème fraîche or whipped cream with yogurt, for serving

Put the sugar and orange rind in a saucepan; add 1 1/2 cups (375 mL) water. Bring to a boil and add the fruit. Reduce the heat and simmer until the fruit is plump, 10 to 15 minutes. Transfer to a serving bowl, pour over the Armagnac, and let cool. Serve at room temperature, passing a bowl of cream for the topping.

Orange Jelly with Chantilly Cream (p. 249)

A Light but Satisfying Winter Dinner

THIS MAY BE THE WEIRDEST-SOUNDING MENU IN THE BOOK. I'M LOOKING AT IT NOW, holding the page away from my eyeballs at the end of my right arm, and I'm tempted to turn it upside down for another perspective. It's not that it sounds unappetizing, but neither is it what anyone would expect to get for dinner in the average, modern-day home on Friday night, which is why you absolutely must whip it up the first chance you get. Good surprises are one of the marvels of life, and this menu is full of them.

One of the interesting things about following an unknown menu to the letter is that it's like going out to dinner yourself: you have no idea what's going to land in front of you; you just order and hope for the best. That gives a whole new dimension to home cooking that I quite like: we get to be as surprised as our guests. (At least if we make something for the first time we do, and I'm all for that risky business.)

I did have a vegetarian at table once who pointed out that, strictly speaking, he shouldn't be eating the gelatin dessert because gelatin is derived from cattle. He ate it anyway, but if you have a die-hard on your hands, section an orange for them and put the sections in a nice coupe with (or without) a splash of booze.

Perhaps this is the place to bring up the issue of picky eaters. I don't know many, so I usually just keep my mouth shut and accommodate them should the occasion arise, but I do feel strongly that if people cannot eat something, or won't, they should let their host know well in advance. If someone is

BEEF CARPACCIO

MAKES: 4 SERVINGS

Unless you have a slicer, get the butcher to slice the meat for you, although it's possible with a sharp knife, too. (I once had a butcher slice mine *too* thinly, which makes the whole thing a bit tasteless and textureless, so you may prefer your own hand anyway.) The trick is to get the meat very, very cold first, preferably without having to freeze it (30 minutes in the freezer, say, and then out). I usually slice the meat to the thickness of thin bacon and then pound the slices a little thinner between plastic wrap with a mallet. The pounding doesn't just flatten it more, it also opens the fibers so the dressing can be absorbed better. In any case, the slices should stay between plastic wrap until serving to preserve the nice red color. If you don't feel up to thin slicing, then you can always finely chop the meat and toss it with the dressing to make tartare.

Overall, I admit, this starter is a bit restaurantish, but it's so simple it couldn't be pretentious if it wanted. Besides, everything else on the menu is served in a very home-style way, so one plated thing isn't going to offend. If you object to individually served dishes at home, as I as a rule do too, simply arrange the beef on a big platter and let people help themselves. Serve a little salad on the side, mâche or arugula lightly tossed in olive oil and a few drops of rich balsamic vinegar.

7 ounces (200 g) beef tenderloin or sirloin, thinly sliced and pounded

1 pink shallot, minced

Zest and juice of 1 lemon

2 handfuls of chopped fresh parsley

2 tablespoons (30 mL) capers, drained

High-quality extra virgin olive oil

Freshly cracked pepper and fleur de sel

Have the beef ready between sheets of plastic wrap and in the fridge.

For the sauce, put the minced shallot in a small bowl and add the lemon juice. In another bowl, stir together the lemon zest, parsley, capers, olive oil, and salt and pepper.

Arrange 5 to 7 slices of beef on each of 4 salad plates. Spoon over a bit of the parsley sauce. Drain the shallot, discarding the lemon juice, and scatter the shallot over the slices of beef.

HERBED DUMPLINGS

MAKES: ABOUT 24 DUMPLINGS, SERVING 4

These adorable dumplings call for ricotta cheese, which you can make at home instead of buying, if you like, although it does require tanks of milk. A friend of mine has a pot of ricotta on the go in her fridge at all times, and being somewhat of a thrift she refuses to throw out the whey, which she keeps in bottles in the fridge and uses in baking. You can use the cheese for stuffings or pasta dishes, or simply eat it with honey and fruit for breakfast. Or you can make a *classic Italian dessert* from it by mixing sugar, honey, or agave into the cheese, spooning it into serving bowls, and sprinkling over instant espresso granules or cocoa. My friend's recipe for *ricotta cheese* will make about 2 cups (500 mL):

Line a big colander with several layers of wet cheesecloth and set it in the sink. Pour 4 cups (1 L) milk and 2 cups (500 mL) buttermilk into a saucepan, and heat until the curds and whey separate. Remove from the heat. Ladle the whey into the sieve, leaving the curds behind, then ladle in the curds. Lift the cloth to help it drain, but do not press. When the draining has slowed down, lift out the cheesecloth and hang it from the tap until the cheese stops draining, up to an hour. Transfer to a container, cover, and refrigerate. It will keep a week.

1 pound (450 g) spinach, trimmed and washed
1 cup (250 mL) ricotta cheese
2 cups (80 g) finely grated Parmesan cheese
Salt and pepper
Pinch nutmeg
2 egg whites, kept separate and lightly whisked

Steam the spinach, drain well, wrap in a clean tea towel and squeeze dry, then finely chop. You should have 1 1/2 cups (375 mL). Mix with the cheeses, and season with salt (not too much, as the Parmesan is salty), pepper, and nutmeg. Stir through 1 egg white, then add only as much of the second to bind, without letting the mixture become too loose. Chill 30 minutes to firm slightly. Using 2 dessertspoons, shape into 1-tablespoon (15 mL) ovals. Set on a baking sheet lined with plastic wrap, cover, and refrigerate until cooking.

To cook the dumplings, line the bases of two 10-inch (25 cm) steaming baskets with rounds of parchment paper or with lettuce, beet, or chard leaves. Carefully lay the dumplings in the baskets. Stack the baskets in a wok with water at the bottom, and steam until very light and set, about 30 minutes. (If they feel heavy when you pick them up, they need a bit longer.) Arrange on a warm platter and carry to the table to serve on the vegetable ragoût.

ROOT VEGETABLE RAGOÛT

MAKES: 4 SERVINGS

This is a recipe from a vegetarian friend who is a skilled and imaginative cook, and a great dresser. She's always on the lookout for interesting dishes that are both filling and stylish, and when she discovers anything that sounds outlandish, she's always the first to try it. Good thing, because this is the kind of recipe that most of the rest of us would walk past, maybe even give a dismissive glance toward as we went by, and we would miss out.

Keep this ragoût on the front burner of your brain at all times as a potential side dish. It's delicious with roasted chicken or pork, and so fast and effortless to prepare you'll be quite astounded. It's the method that's interesting: high speed and low maintenance. You can vary the vegetables—just take care to cut them roughly the same size so that all the pieces reach the cooked state simultaneously. You won't always want chives and tarragon on them. It depends on what they're partnering and on what other flavors you've added. If one fine day you choose to use coconut cream with curry stirred in in place of crème fraîche, then coriander would be best. If you use sour cream, perhaps try dill.

2 tablespoons (30 mL) butter

3/4 pound (340 g) carrots (about 6 medium), halved lengthwise

3/4 pound (340 g) parsnips (about 6 medium), halved lengthwise

3/4 pound (340 g) rutabaga (about 1/2 a medium), cut into pieces

1/2 cup (125 mL) vegetable stock

Salt and pepper

1 pound (450 g) assorted mushrooms, halved

3/4 cup (175 mL) crème fraîche

Lemon juice, to taste (optional)

A very generous handful of chopped fresh chives

A very generous handful of chopped fresh tarragon

Put half the butter and all the vegetables except the mushrooms in a large pot. Add the stock. Season with salt and pepper, cover, and cook over medium heat until tender, about 30 minutes, depending on the size of the vegetables. Meanwhile, fry the mushrooms in the remaining butter until golden.

When the root vegetables are tender, stir in the fried mushrooms and crème fraîche. Taste, adding a squeeze of lemon if you like, and check the salt and pepper. Serve in a big warm bowl or straight from the pot, sprinkled with the chives and tarragon.

ORANGE JELLY WITH CHANTILLY CREAM

MAKES: 6 SERVINGS

This jelly is especially appealing to me because it's sexy and wobbly, not stiff, at the same time as being fresh tasting, almost salad-like. You could throw some orange sections into the jelly if you wanted, or serve orange slices or sections with the jelly on the side, but I like the purity of the dessert served plain with cream. The dessert is not too sweet, and the contrast between cold, jiggling citrus jelly and smooth vanilla cream is heaven.

I'd love to be more exotic in my cooking, but the fact of the matter is I'm usually trying to put dinner together with whatever I have at hand. From my current geographical standpoint, oranges are easier to find than blood oranges, so they're what I usually use. If you want to try a blood orange version, perhaps add a couple of tablespoons (30 mL) of Campari to the mix for depth and color. You could put liqueur in with the regular orange rendition, too, I suppose, but I rather like it tasting purely of fruit.

I have made this using orange juice from a carton. It's good, although not quite as fabulous as when you make it with fresh, and not as vibrantly orange (bought juice is more yellow). Finally, if you like a very soft jelly for spooning into serving dishes, use only 1 tablespoon (15 mL)—1 envelope—gelatin to set the mix. If you are molding the dish to turn out and slice, as below, you need the extra teaspoon (5 mL) of gelatin to set it properly.

4 teaspoons (20 mL) gelatin (1 20-g envelope + 1 teaspoon/5 mL)
1/4 cup (55 g) sugar
2 1/2 cups (625 mL) freshly squeezed orange juice (from 6 to 8 oranges)
Slightly sweetened vanilla-scented whipped cream, for serving

Line a 3-cup (750 mL) bowl or mold with plastic wrap.

Put 1/4 cup (60 mL) water in a small glass bowl, scatter over the gelatin, and set aside to soften. Put the sugar in 1/4 cup (60 mL) water and boil for about 3 minutes to dissolve. In a bowl, combine the sugar syrup and the orange juice. Set the ramekin of gelatin in a small saucepan of just boiled water, off the heat, for a few minutes and stir to melt it to liquid. When it's fluid and translucent, whisk it into the orange juice mixture. Strain into the mold and refrigerate until set, about 4 hours.

To unmold the jelly, set the pan for a few seconds in a larger pan of very hot water. Flip onto a plate and serve in wedges with slightly sweetened whipped cream.

Sticky Coconut Cakes

MAKES: ABOUT 14 TINY CAKES

This recipe landed in my lap just in the nick of time because I had this very dinner menu on the go one night and discovered, last minute, it *would* have to be a birthday party and I had no cake. All this was happening at a friend's house, by chance, and his Portuguese housekeeper came by early in the day. I'd not met her before, but she breezed in and out of the kitchen a few times over the course of the morning and eventually, across cultures and language barriers, we got talking recipes. She contributed this dainty number, which I whipped up on the spot, stacked onto a plate, pyramid style, speared with sparklers, and called "birthday cake." They're not like cake at all, really, more softish and macaroony, but they're nice with the orange jelly.

1 cup (100 g) unsweetened coconut
1 cup (200 g) sugar
3 eggs

Heat the oven to 375°F (190°C). Mix everything well with a fork, and spoon into mini paper baking cups. Arrange on a baking sheet and bake until cooked through and slightly golden on top, 15 to 20 minutes.

Coconut Macaroons
MAKES: ABOUT 20 MACAROONS

This recipe comes from my American cooking friend Nancy, who apropos of nothing quite openly calls herself "a cougar" and spent many a summer's day regaling me with tales that made my ears steam! (My lips, however, remain sealed.) One day, watching me attempt traditional macaroons, she declared she had a far better recipe. I had never made macaroons before, and frankly didn't have any interest in them, but for some reason I grew obsessed and was suddenly seeing macaroons everywhere I looked, a bit like those phases you go through when every woman you lay eyes on seems to be pregnant. Anyway, I finished my latest macaroon attempt, then "the cougar" made hers. Fortuitously, three children who were summering down the lane showed up, and we put them to a taste test. They polished off the whole lot, but Nancy's recipe was the unanimous winner. I bowed to the victor, and crumpled up my recipe and threw it in the bin. Here's hers.

1 tin (10 ounces / 300 mL) sweetened condensed milk
A generous 3 cups (300 g) unsweetened coconut
1/2 teaspoon (2 mL) vanilla
1/4 teaspoon (1 mL) almond extract
Pinch salt

Heat the oven to 350°F (180°C). Empty the condensed milk into a bowl and stir in the coconut, vanilla, almond extract, and salt. The mixture should be stiff enough to hold up in a mound, so if it's on the runny side, add more coconut. Line a baking sheet with parchment paper, and spoon about 20 macaroon mounds onto it. Bake until cooked through and lightly golden, about 20 minutes.

CLOCKWISE FROM BOTTOM LEFT:
LAMB CURRY (P. 257); SCENTED BASMATI RICE (P. 259); CUMIN ROASTED EGGPLANT (P. 262);
RAITA (P. 265); SPICED CAULIFLOWER WITH POTATOES AND PEAS (P. 261);
PAPPADAMS (P. 262); FRESH CORIANDER (FOR FINISHING);
MANGO CHUTNEY (P. 264)

Nostalgia and Exotica

*I*N MY EARLY TWENTIES, IT SEEMED A VERY COOL THING TO DO TO GO TO INDIA. I remember calling a friend in Canada from a phone booth in Barcelona and saying, "Meet me in London. Let's go!" And we did. We got six-month visas, landed in Delhi, ran around the country for six *weeks,* and then got homesick and flew back.

However challenging the trip, it must have had an impact because I have strong memories of it. One day we got a guide and a few camels and went out in the desert where we slept under the stars after a meal cooked over a camel-dung fire. We ate lemon pancakes in a restaurant in Dharamsala with the peace of the mountains all around us, and I remember we talked about what we should make of our lives once we got home. "We'll tell each other all the things we like to do and are good at," I proposed over pancakes, "and then one will tell the other what she should become." Lisa went first with her long list of skills and desires, and I declared she should become a journalist, which, in fact, she did. Then I gave my list and asked what I should become. She thought for a moment and then helpfully offered: "Rich man's wife." (Thanks a lot.)

There was a point on that trip when we were really desperate to eat something familiar. Indian cuisine is remarkable, but like any food that's not part of your regular diet, it can get to be too much and you crave a break. No more curry! No more flatbread! No different from how you occasionally need a break from your regular routine back home, I suppose (No more boiled potatoes! No more chicken soup!), which is why I've gone a little exotic, for me, anyway, with this menu.

Because there are a number of dishes involved, I often serve it buffet style (or "catch and kill your own," as my friend Mollie puts it), which requires, of course, a buffet. When I lived in a small apartment, I used to drag the console from beside the front door into the dining room, position it near the table, and throw a cloth over it. The dishes were lined up on that and everyone helped themselves before sitting down. It certainly takes the pressure off a busy host. In fact, my cooking teacher in France used to serve every meal like this at her country house. There was a side table that had warming trays on it, and the routine was always that guests served themselves from there—and got up and helped themselves to seconds whenever they pleased. I like that approach: it keeps everyone independent, and it means conversation isn't constantly interrupted by circulating dishes and enquires as to "Who'd like more cauliflower? Anyone?" (I say all this assuming that, like me, you're not surrounded by oodles of household serving staff, but what do I know?)

The lamb curry is best made a day ahead. Have the pomegranate dressing made well in advance, and you can even cook the eggplant early on. Get the dessert cream in the fridge early in the day. The nuts you do right before guests arrive, so they're warm. The cauliflower, rice, and pappadams happen as the curry is being reheated and the whole buffet laid out. The pineapple must be grilled at the last minute, unless of course you prefer to serve it sliced fresh.

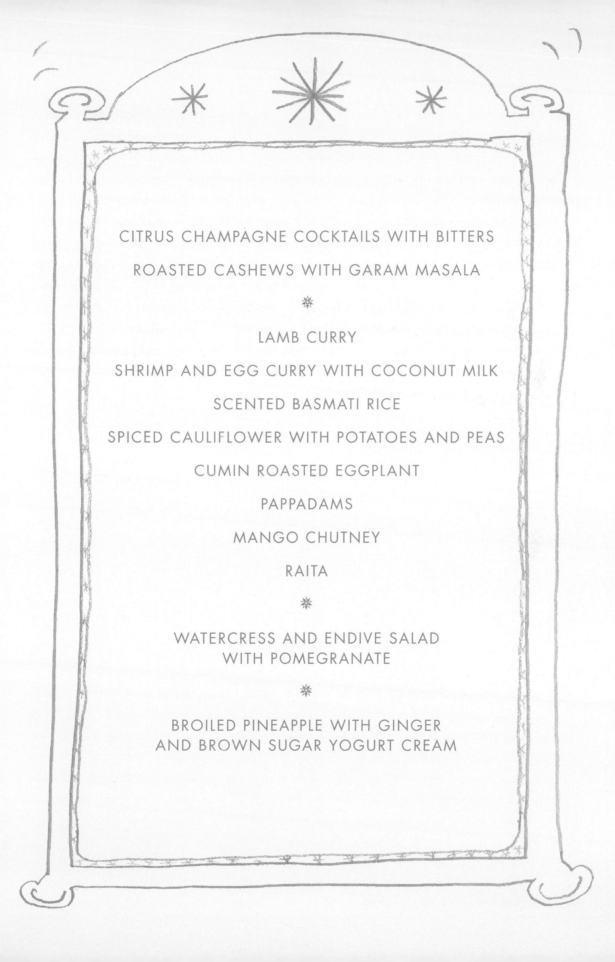

CITRUS CHAMPAGNE COCKTAILS WITH BITTERS

ROASTED CASHEWS WITH GARAM MASALA

✳

LAMB CURRY

SHRIMP AND EGG CURRY WITH COCONUT MILK

SCENTED BASMATI RICE

SPICED CAULIFLOWER WITH POTATOES AND PEAS

CUMIN ROASTED EGGPLANT

PAPPADAMS

MANGO CHUTNEY

RAITA

✳

WATERCRESS AND ENDIVE SALAD
WITH POMEGRANATE

✳

BROILED PINEAPPLE WITH GINGER
AND BROWN SUGAR YOGURT CREAM

CITRUS CHAMPAGNE COCKTAILS WITH BITTERS

Aperitif food is not my forte. I find it fussy and have neither the dexterity nor the patience to pull it off. However, a bowl of cashews and a cocktail drink I can muster. By cocktail I usually mean a glass of Champagne or wine, but if that sounds too lazy, there is an easy way to embellish.

Often, I've teamed up with my friend Bill for hosting dinner parties. His house has theatrical decor, which is always a good backdrop for colorful personalities, and he has an entire room dedicated to cocktails and music (grand piano, bar, staggering collection of vinyl recordings . . .). I do the cooking; Bill looks after music and Champagne cocktails. Here, in his own words, is his concoction, which he adamantly serves in Toulouse-Lautrec-style coupes instead of flutes:

"Put a lump of sugar in the glass, douse it with several drops of Angostura bitters, remove a coil of orange peel with the right zester tool and add it to the glass (this must be fresh, so that your nose gets a treat). Pour in the Champagne." I should add here that lemon zest in place of orange is also excellent. And by "right zester tool" he means the kind that really gouges out a nice thick coil.

Soda and Bitters

If you have any nondrinkers in the house, such as on-duty medics or pilots with a flight ahead, you can make them a nice cocktail like so: splash some bitters onto ice in a glass, pour over soda, and add a slice of lime.

ROASTED CASHEWS WITH GARAM MASALA

Normally with fizzy drinks I just set out a bowl of salted, roasted cashew nuts. With just a little more effort, however, you can make your guests feel slightly more spoiled: spread 2 cups (280 g) unsalted, unroasted cashews on a baking sheet. Roast at 300°F (150°C) until golden and sending a nice perfume into the air, 15 to 20 minutes. Remove from the oven and immediately toss with 1 teaspoon (5 mL) sugar, 1 teaspoon (5 mL) salt, and 1 tablespoon (15 mL) garam masala, which is an Indian spice mixture. I can't remember where I found that idea, but it's good, and it's a class act if the nuts are still slightly warm when you serve them.

LAMB CURRY

MAKES: 8 SERVINGS

The trick is to make this curry a day ahead so the flavors have time to mellow. All the better, I say, because it's that much less to worry about on the day of dinner. I learned this recipe leaning over the shoulder of a Norwegian sea captain with a booming voice and a love of strong flavors in food. Curry night at Tor's always involves at least five different curries, all plunked onto the table at once for ladling into at random. It's fun eating that way: curry night and bedlam go hand in hand.

Look for the spice Kashmiri mirch in South Asian markets.

About 1/4 cup (60 mL) clarified butter or vegetable oil

4 pounds (1.8 kg) boned lamb or stewing beef, cut into pieces

A 2-inch (5 cm) piece fresh ginger, peeled and chopped

8 garlic cloves, chopped

1 large onion, chopped

10 green cardamom pods, crushed

2 bay leaves

6 cloves

10 peppercorns

1 stick cinnamon

4 teaspoons (20 mL) ground cumin

4 teaspoons (20 mL) bright red paprika or Kashmiri mirch

2 teaspoons (10 mL) ground coriander

1 1/2 teaspoons (7 mL) salt

1/2 teaspoon (2 mL) garam masala

1/4 to 1 teaspoon (1 to 5 mL) cayenne pepper, to taste

6 tablespoons (90 mL) Greek yogurt

Black pepper

Roughly chopped fresh coriander

Heat half the clarified butter in a stew pot and, working in batches, brown the meat on all sides, removing the meat to a plate as you go and adding the remaining clarified butter as you need it. Meanwhile, put the ginger and garlic with 1/4 cup (60 mL) water in a food processor and blend to a paste.

Once all the meat has been browned, gently fry the onions until soft. Stir in the cardamom, bay leaves, cloves, peppercorns, cinnamon stick, and the ginger paste. Next stir in the cumin, paprika, coriander, salt, garam masala, and cayenne. Add the meat and any juices that have accumulated. Stir in the yogurt to coat. Pour over 2 cups (500 mL) water, cover, and simmer until the meat is very tender, about 1 1/2 hours, depending on the size of the pieces of meat.

Cool the dish completely and refrigerate overnight. Reheat, and serve garnished with a grinding of black pepper and chopped coriander.

SHRIMP AND EGG CURRY WITH COCONUT MILK

MAKES: 4 GENEROUS SERVINGS

I always feel curry night should be a real feast, and leftovers are always welcome, hence this recipe as well. Besides, if you have non-meat eaters in the mix, it's thoughtful to have an alternative for them that, for once, isn't a grilled Portobello mushroom. Feel free to serve this as a main course in and of itself. It's good on rice with peas and green onions (p. 260), only in that case omit the butter and mint from the rice dish. If you don't have curry powder, use instead 2 teaspoons (10 mL) ground coriander, 2 teaspoons (10 mL) ground cumin, 1/2 teaspoon (2 mL) garam masala, 1/2 teaspoon (2 mL) turmeric, and 1/2 teaspoon (2 mL) chili powder (more to taste, depending on how much heat you like). Finally, if you're not an experienced egg boiler, see p. 134.

1 to 2 tablespoons (15 to 30 mL) clarified
   butter or grapeseed oil

1 large onion, thinly sliced

3 garlic cloves, peeled

A 1- to 2-inch (2.5 to 5 cm) piece fresh ginger,
   peeled and grated

1 medium tomato, cut into rough chunks
   (optional)

1 green chili pepper

1 tablespoon (15 mL) curry powder or paste,
   more to taste

Salt

1 cup (250 mL) coconut milk

1/2 cup (125 mL) chicken stock

1 pound (450 g) shrimp, blanched, peeled,
   and deveined

4 peeled hard-boiled eggs

Shredded coriander or basil

Heat the clarified butter in a pot and gently fry the onions until very soft, adding the garlic and ginger for the last minute or two (do not let the garlic brown). Put the onion mixture in a food processor and add the tomato (if using) and chili; process to a paste. Return to the pot, add the curry powder and salt, and cook gently for 5 minutes. Stir in the coconut milk and stock. Bring to a simmer. Add the shrimp and eggs and heat through. Serve with the coriander strewn over.

SCENTED BASMATI RICE

MAKES: 8 SERVINGS

A friend of mine throws half a squeezed lemon into his rice pot while it cooks (the same guy who threw mint into his potato pot on p. 85). Rice isn't something I make that often, for no reason whatsoever, but when I do, just like when I go to the theater, I think, "There should be more of this in my life." This recipe is exceptionally fragrant.

2 cups (380 g) basmati rice

2 teaspoons (10 mL) salt

2 garlic cloves, minced

2 bay leaves

8 cloves

3 green cardamom pods

Rinse the rice several times in cold water. Drain, then place in a pot, add 4 cups (1 L) cold water, and leave to soak for half an hour. Add the salt, garlic, bay leaves, cloves, and cardamom. Bring to a boil, turn the heat to low, and simmer, partly covered, until the rice is tender and all the water is absorbed, about 15 minutes. Remove the pan from the heat, cover, and leave 10 minutes longer.

Rice with Peas, Green Onions, and Mint
MAKES: 4 SERVINGS

You're obviously not going to make this rice for this menu (unless you forgo the cauliflower and peas), but basmati got me thinking about rice in general, so I pass on this side dish for another time and place. The peas and green onions make boring old rice very colorful and inviting. If serving this with a dish that has sauce (such as the shrimp and egg curry, p. 258), omit the butter. You may also use shredded basil or coriander in place of mint, depending on what the rice is to accompany.

1 cup (200 g) basmati rice
Salt
1 tablespoon (15 mL) butter
2 green onions, thinly sliced
1 cup (125 g) cooked peas
A handful of chopped fresh mint

Rinse the rice several times in cold water. Drain. Put the rice in a pot with 1 3/4 cups (425 mL) water. Salt it. Cover, bring to a simmer, and cook until all the water has been absorbed, about 12 minutes. Remove from the heat and set aside, covered, 5 minutes. Stir through the butter, green onions, peas, and mint.

SPICED CAULIFLOWER WITH POTATOES AND PEAS

This is a wonderfully flavorful and mildly exotic dish that you can whip up in a hurry. I even make it on weeknights as a side dish to chicken or meat, and it's very satisfying. The textural contrast between the soft potatoes and the pop of peas is particularly nice, and it's very pretty.

3 tablespoons (50 mL) grapeseed oil

2 tablespoons (30 mL) ground coriander

1 tablespoon (15 mL) ground cumin

2 teaspoons (10 mL) cumin seeds

1 teaspoon (5 mL) turmeric

1/2 teaspoon (2 mL) cayenne pepper

4 teaspoons (20 mL) salt

1 medium cauliflower, about 2 pounds (900 g), cut into large florets

2 pounds (900 g) large waxy yellow potatoes, peeled and cut into chunks

1 tin (14 ounces/398 mL) diced tomatoes

2 cups (250 g) fresh or frozen peas

Heat the oil in a large pot. Stir in the coriander, cumin, cumin seeds, turmeric, and cayenne; fry for a few minutes until fragrant. Stir in the salt. Add the cauliflower and potatoes. Pour over the tomatoes and 3 cups (750 mL) water. Bring to a boil, then reduce the heat and simmer, covered, until the vegetables are tender, about 15 minutes, depending on their size. Five minutes before they're done, stir in the peas.

CUMIN ROASTED EGGPLANT

I have discovered that it is worth salting eggplant, because it gets rid of bitterness, prevents the eggplant from discoloring, and keeps it firmer during cooking. For this menu, I use 2 medium-large eggplants. Slice them into 1/2-inch (1 cm) rounds and sprinkle with salt. Put them in a colander in the sink for 30 minutes. Rinse, drain, and thoroughly pat dry.

Brush both sides of the slices very generously with grapeseed or olive oil and season them with salt and pepper. Heat a dry frying pan to very hot, and, working in batches, fry the eggplant, turning once, until nicely golden, about 2 minutes per side, adding extra oil if needed. (This step may seem superfluous, but it does make the eggplant nice and crisp, as it would be if you did the whole job in the oven.) You can do all this in advance and finish just before serving. To finish, heat the oven to 375°F (190°C). Lay the eggplant slices in a single layer on a baking sheet. Sprinkle judiciously with ground cumin, and bake until the eggplant begins to crispen at the edges, about 15 minutes.

PAPPADAMS

It's nice to have a big bowlful of crisp disks to snap through with the soft curry. It's one of the few things I don't make on my own: I buy a packet from the grocery store or specialty shop. My friend Anne does them one at a time in the microwave and then piles them high in a bowl. They need 38 to 41 seconds each, according to Anne, which is awfully precise, but she's a lawyer so I'd expect nothing less exacting from her. If you don't have a microwave (I don't) and aren't one to worry about fat (I'm not), then a more traditional method is to fry the wafers. Heat peanut or grapeseed oil in a frying pan until smoking, then drop in a pappadam for a few seconds until it crispens. Remove it before it turns brown and drain on paper towels.

MANGO CHUTNEY

MAKES: ABOUT 4 CUPS (1 L)

The other thing I do on curry nights is add a jar of mango chutney to the table. You can buy that, or make your own if you want to show off a bit. Most recipes call for green mangoes, but it's actually nicer, I think, using mangoes slightly riper than that. You don't want them soft, but neither do you want them green.

2 slightly under-ripe mangoes

2 cups (500 mL) malt vinegar

2 tablespoons (30 mL) tamarind paste

1/2 cup (125 mL) preserved ginger in syrup (p. 318) or a 3-inch (7.5 cm) piece fresh ginger, peeled and thinly sliced

1/2 large red onion, coarsely chopped

2 cups (390 g) sugar

4 garlic cloves, minced

Peel the mangoes, cut the flesh from them, and cut it into pieces; set aside. Put the pits, which will still have some flesh clinging to them, in a saucepan and pour over the vinegar. Bring to a boil, lower the heat, and simmer 30 minutes. Discard the pits.

Whisk the tamarind paste into the liquid. If you're using preserved ginger, add it now. If you're using fresh ginger, add it and simmer 30 minutes. Add the onion, sugar, garlic, and mango. Simmer, uncovered and stirring occasionally, 45 minutes. The liquid should now be lightly syrupy around the mango and onion. If it isn't, remove the mango, onion, and ginger with a slotted spoon and boil down the liquid to the right consistency before stirring the solids back in. Cool and transfer to a bowl. Store leftovers in sterilized jars in the fridge.

RAITA

It's not a bad idea, when you serve spicy food, to have an edible fire extinguisher handy. A cooling bowl of raita is just the trick and it takes about 1 minute to make. Chop or grate half a peeled and seeded cucumber, pat dry with a clean tea towel. Stir it into 2 cups (500 mL) Greek or Balkan yogurt, along with a few handfuls of chopped fresh mint and a little salt. *Voilà*—condiment number two.

WATERCRESS AND ENDIVE SALAD WITH POMEGRANATE

MAKES: 8 SERVINGS

I realize that this salad may make you feel a bit as if you'd just got off the plane from Delhi for a stop-over in Beirut. However, I couldn't help myself. After a substantial main course, I crave the fresh, raw, scrumptious crunch of greens, which is palate cleansing and refreshing. The glamorous tangle of watercress and endive studded with juicy, ruby pomegranate gems is just the right touch after the mellow and spicy curried lamb, and it holds its own as far as exoticism is concerned. The good thing about salad served after the main course, too, is that it somehow perks up the appetite again, which is a good thing, not because the light and simple dessert that follows requires much space, but because it is so fabulously good you'll eat twice as much as you intended.

You can buy pomegranate syrup and pomegranate molasses instead of making your own. If you have some on hand, use 2 tablespoons (30 mL), omit the sugar, skip the boiling step, and simply mix the dressing as described below. Use only enough dressing for the greens as you need: there's nothing worse than salad soup.

2 large pomegranates

2 tablespoons (30 mL) sugar

1 teaspoon (5 mL) balsamic vinegar or red wine vinegar (especially if syrup is very sweet)

About 1/2 cup (125 mL) olive oil

A squeeze of lemon juice (optional)

Salt and freshly ground black pepper

2 bunches watercress, trimmed

2 small endives, thinly sliced lengthwise

To make the pomegranate syrup, halve the pomegranates. Fill a large bowl with cold water, plunge in each half, and, working with your fingers, extract the seeds from their honeycomb membranes. In the water, the seeds will sink to the bottom and the yellow bits will rise to the top. Scoop out and discard the latter. Drain the seeds, set aside 1/2 cup (80 g) of them, and purée the rest in a blender. Strain the purée into a saucepan. Add the sugar, bring to a boil, and simmer to syrup consistency, about 30 minutes. Cool. Whisk in the vinegar and just enough olive oil to make a dressing. If you need a squeeze of lemon juice, add it, and season with salt and plenty of pepper.

Put the watercress and endives in a serving dish. Scatter over the reserved pomegranate seeds, and toss with some of the dressing.

BROILED PINEAPPLE WITH GINGER AND BROWN SUGAR YOGURT CREAM

MAKES: 8 SERVINGS

Thick, smooth mouthfuls of tangy-sweet cream collapsing over bright, fruity rounds of warm candied-ginger-strewn pineapple: that's what this dessert is. There's nothing Indian about it as far as I know. That said, pineapple, tangy and tropical as it is, does remind me of days on that India trip when I lolled around for a couple of weeks on the beaches of Kerala. Local women dressed in patterned cotton fabrics to rival tropical birds would come around to sell mango, papaya, and pineapple from woven baskets balanced on their heads.

Similar recipes usually tell you just to sprinkle sugar on yogurt, but when I have tried this I've not been impressed because the result is too heavy and cloying. The secret to reaching nirvana is the addition of whipped cream. In fact it's the principal ingredient, but a nearly invisible one. The cream lightens everything up, while still allowing the tanginess of the yogurt to ping through, all giving a dreamy texture to the fudgy brown sugar, which, by the time you serve dessert, will have melted into a dark, caramel pool over top of those satiny dairy drifts and dribbled decadently over the edges.

2 cups (500 mL) heavy cream
3/4 cup (175 mL) full-fat Greek yogurt, more to taste
1/2 cup (110 g) dark brown sugar
1 large pineapple, peeled
Grapeseed oil, for brushing
About 8 chunks of preserved ginger, cut into slivers

Whip the cream to stiff peaks and fold in the yogurt. Spread the mixture in a shallow serving dish and sprinkle the sugar evenly over. Cover and refrigerate at least 4 hours. The sugar will melt into a dark pool on top.

Slice the pineapple into rings a pinkie finger thick, and lay on a baking sheet. Brush the tops lightly with oil. Scatter the slivers of candied ginger over the rings. Broil for about 5 minutes, until the pineapple is hot and the edges are golden. Serve with the yogurt cream.

Spiced Red Lentil Stew with Spinach and Lemon (p. 273)

An Easy Vegetarian Menu
with Color and Spice

I T USED TO BE A REAL TREAT TO DINE IN A RESTAURANT. NOT ANYMORE. EVERYBODY'S in them all the time, not uncommonly twice a day, and the result is that the experience has become downright ho-hum. Special, on the other hand, has become an invitation to dine at someone's house. That's where you get to taste things that are out of the ordinary or that you wouldn't have thought of making yourself, and, in my experience, that's where you have all the fun.

It's the meals you share with friends in their houses (or yours) that you tend not to forget, either. I may be alone in this, but for me it's rare to remember a meal I ate in a restaurant. I'm racking my brain right now and I can't think of a single one, except for the time a friend ordered brains and the waiters came out carrying a long board of about 10 lamb skulls for the whole table, then scooped the brains straight out of the skulls onto our plates. That and the time I was nearly poisoned to death by bad oysters (and charged for it after I complained!) are by and large the extent of my restaurant memories. Otherwise, virtually all the times I've eaten out are a blur. Seems such a waste, because some of those meals were superb.

On the other hand I'll never forget the dinner in Muskoka at which someone stood up and read "The Men Who Won't Fit In" by Robert Service; or the dinner in Burgundy when my Australian friend leapt onto the table after dinner with a rose between her teeth; or the feasts I made with university friends in "the buttery" of our student residence in London. And I'll always remember the night my yoga friend Nancy was about to leave a dinner party when Mollie piped up and said, "Oh wait, Nancy! I don't suppose before you leave you could do for us one of your lovely contortions?"

Because I entertain constantly, it sometimes slips my mind that everyone's not doing it. When I first moved to Toronto and didn't know many people, the way I made friends was by inviting people over and feeding them. The first time my friends Anne and Ian came to dine, Ian said, "We've been in Toronto for six years and before this we were invited to eat in homes only three times . . . and those dinners were all catered." (Shriek!)

Anne and Ian were neighbors, and we soon got in the habit of eating together quite often. Not dinner parties proper, just dinner—a bowl of pasta, a quick sauté . . . nothing grand, just good food and conversation that made us feel connected. I was at their place just the other night, in fact, and Ian was still in his workout clothes when I arrived. "I'm in the worst shape of my life," he complained. The kitchen counter was covered in cookbooks and the fridge was brimming with fresh things from the market. "I've been eating in restaurants way too much. We're turning over a new leaf."

We can all get stuck in the restaurant trap, I guess. A quick way out is to find a few dishes you can make practically blindfolded, so that when you get home from work and are too exhausted to think straight, your hands can kick into gear for you. The lentil dish of this menu, for example, is one of my top weeknight meals. (In fact, I just emailed it to Anne and Ian in support of their cause).

Prepare the pears to the point of baking as a first step. Make the lentil stew next, but cook the spinach part at the last minute. The slaw you can toss more or less before you serve. The pears you can pop in the oven during the main course so they come to the table warm and fragrant.

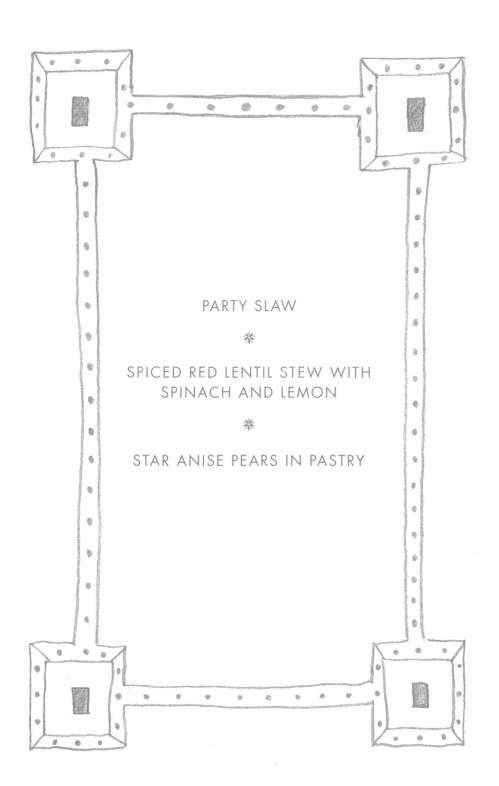

PARTY SLAW

❋

SPICED RED LENTIL STEW WITH
SPINACH AND LEMON

❋

STAR ANISE PEARS IN PASTRY

PARTY SLAW

MAKES: 4 SERVINGS

This is one of my favorite new discoveries. It is gorgeous to look at and full of surprising and delightful fresh tastes, which the body so craves in winter. A big bowl of this colorful confetti on the table as a first course is very festive indeed, and versatile. Odd as it may sound, this is fantastic with avocado sauce (p. 18) on the side. If you're turning it into lunch, feel free to add some crumbled feta cheese.

1 1/2 cups (140 g) grated carrots
1 1/2 cups (140 g) very thinly sliced red cabbage, large ribs removed
1 1/2 cups (140 g) thinly sliced fennel
A handful of broccoli sprouts, pulled apart so as not to clump
1/4 cup (60 mL) olive oil, more to taste
1 tablespoon (15 mL) lime or lemon juice, more to taste
1 to 2 teaspoons (5 to 10 mL) sesame oil
1 teaspoon (5 mL) soy sauce, more to taste
2 generous handfuls of shredded fresh mint
Salt and pepper
3 green onions, thinly sliced
1/2 cup (60 g) roasted, salted cashews, chopped

Put the carrots, cabbage, and fennel in a large bowl. Scatter over the sprouts and toss. Just before serving, add the olive oil, lime juice, sesame oil, soy sauce, and mint. Season with salt and pepper, and toss to combine thoroughly. Scatter over the green onions and cashews, and serve.

SPICED RED LENTIL STEW
WITH SPINACH AND LEMON

MAKES: 4 SERVINGS

Please do not overlook this recipe, because it's fast, delicious, and extremely healthy, an excellent supper when friends drop in at the last minute, or even if no one drops in at all. I probably make it once a week myself, and never tire of it. A friend who works for the UN World Food Programme taught it to me. She has been stationed in many far-off countries over the years, often with minimal access to ingredients, but this she could make anywhere (Swaziland, for example, which is where I picked it up).

The dish is not too spicy; it has just enough heat under the surface, and the spice mixture is actually very mellow, so it's congenial for a crowd. It is also gorgeous to behold: an orange-red thick lentil dal with a bright tangle of steamed spinach on top, and some lemon wedges for squirting. The price is right, too, but you needn't mention that to your guests. I am asked for this recipe time and time again, which is the best flattery any recipe can hope for.

2 tablespoons (30 mL) olive oil

4 garlic cloves, minced

1 peperoncino, crushed

2 teaspoons (10 mL) ground cumin

1 teaspoon (5 mL) ground coriander

1 teaspoon (5 mL) curry powder

Pinch turmeric

1 cup (200 g) red lentils

1 tin (14 ounces/398 mL) diced tomatoes

4 cups (1 L) vegetable or chicken stock

Salt and pepper

8 ounces (225 g) large spinach, stems trimmed

Lemon wedges, for serving

Heat the oil in a large saucepan over medium heat. Add the garlic, peperoncino, and spices, stirring until the garlic is light brown, about a minute. Add the lentils, tomatoes, and stock. Cover and simmer, stirring occasionally, until the lentils turn to purée, about 20 minutes. Season with salt and pepper.

Wash the spinach and put it in a large pot with the water still clinging to the leaves. Cover and steam over medium-high heat, turning once or twice with tongs to make sure it doesn't stick to the bottom of the pan, until wilted, about 3 minutes. Serve the thick lentil stew in warmed shallow bowls with spinach on top. Pass lemon wedges for squeezing over.

STAR ANISE PEARS IN PASTRY

MAKES: 4 SERVINGS

Anyone who invites me to dinner is in serious danger of having their recipe collection raided. I'm positively shameless about this, because I'm not one who develops recipes in lab-like conditions. My passion is for recipes that come from real people and that have stories and memories attached. Poor Jennifer McLagan, who is a cookbook author in her own right, has had her files pillaged by me over the years. Lucky for her, she comes up with an amazing new recipe every day, so she's fairly nonchalant about letting me have any she won't be "using," which is how I got my paws on these tarts. They're the cutest things! The pear halves are wrapped snugly in pastry so the golden, buttery cut sides peek out like happy faces from a bonnet. I suppose you could try it sometime with apples, too.

FOR THE PASTRY

1 cup (125 g) flour

Pinch of salt

1/3 cup (70 g) cold butter, cut into pieces

2 tablespoons (30 mL) ice-cold water

FOR THE PEARS

2 firm but ripe pears

4 whole star anise

6 tablespoons (75 g) sugar

4 1/2 tablespoons (65 g) butter

Slightly sweetened whipped cream, for serving

For the pastry, put the flour, salt and butter in a food processor and pulse to crumbs. Add the water, then pulse just long enough for the ingredients to come together in clumps. Pat into a disk, wrap in plastic, and chill 1 hour. On a lightly floured surface, roll out the dough and divide into 4 even pieces.

Heat the oven to 400°F (200°C). Peel and halve the pears, and core them using a melon-baller. Place a star anise in each cavity and press so it stays in place. Set each half hump side up on the counter and drape over a quarter of the pastry. Press around the pear to seal, then trim with a knife so that the pastry covers the backs of the pears where the skin was. I give a little twist at the top, too, for a pastry stem.

In an ovenproof frying pan over medium heat, melt the sugar to a golden caramel, then whisk in the butter. Lay the pears in cut side down and cook 5 minutes. Transfer to the oven and bake until the pears are tender and the pastry is golden, about 20 minutes. Serve cut side up with whipped cream.

John's Clove Pears

I know it's not every day we're in a pastry-making mood, so another approach to pears is to peel, core, and quarter 4 firm but ripe Bartletts, then poach them in a syrup made from 4 cups (1 L) water, 1 cup (225 g) brown sugar, a strip of orange peel, and 1/2 teaspoon (2 mL) whole cloves, until the pears are tender. The timing will depend on how ripe the pears are, anywhere from 15 to 40 minutes, so just keep testing with a knife. You want them soft, but not mooshy. Use a slotted spoon to hoist the pears from the syrup into a nice glass bowl. Boil the liquid down to syrup consistency, then pour it over the fruit. This sauce is wonderfully peppery and unusual. A bowl of fresh, creamy homemade Vanilla Ice Cream (p. 280) on the table at the same time will take this dessert (and you) right over the edge. Devonshire or double cream is also a dreamy, and perhaps less competitive, garnish.

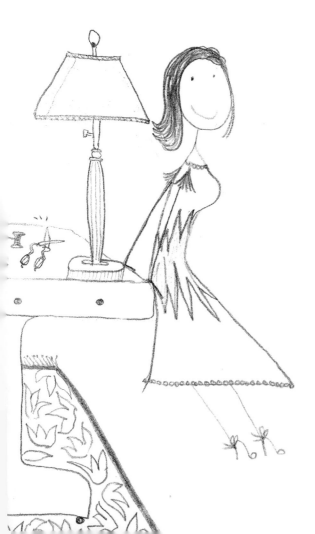

Pineapple Upside-Down Cake

MAKES: 8 SERVINGS

I just about made myself insane one summer trying to find a good recipe for pineapple upside-down cake. I'd been served a delicious one on a holiday in Muskoka, where I stayed in a spacious old stone house overlooking the water that had three enviable pantries (pantry, scullery, larder, to be precise) off the country kitchen, and a sauna down by the lake . . . ahh. That cake was made with peaches, and the hostess made it by smearing butter in the bottom of her pan, then generously sprinkling over brown sugar, laying in peeled peach halves, and finally pouring cake batter over top. It was cake from a mix, which, however yummy, got me yearning for a recipe of my own. I must have tried six different versions before I gave up.

A week or so after my decision to abort the search, I was invited to dine *chez* my friends Ivy and Kerry. They're both involved in food professionally, so I knew I'd be dining well, but what I didn't expect was that dessert would be the *ne plus ultra* of upside-down cakes. Kerry made it with plums, and the recipe that follows is his, except where I have pineapple, he had two each of green, yellow, and red plums and he had orange juice where I use pineapple juice. (Try his version sometime too!) To serve, he cut out rounds with a cutter and slapped them with a heaping spoonful of whipped cream to which he had added a little sour cream, lemon juice, and brandy. For pineapple cake, I might opt for rum instead.

FOR THE TOPPING

1/2 cup (95 g) white or brown sugar

2 tablespoons (30 mL) butter

1 tin (14 ounces/398 mL) unsweetened pineapple chunks, drained, juice reserved

FOR THE CAKE

3/4 cup (95 g) all-purpose or cake-and-pastry flour

1 teaspoon (5 mL) baking powder

Pinch salt

1/2 cup (125 mL) milk

1 tablespoon (15 mL) butter, melted

1 teaspoon (5 mL) orange zest

1 teaspoon (5 mL) vanilla

2 large egg yolks + 4 egg whites

1/2 cup (95 g) sugar

Heat the oven to 350°F (180°C).

For the topping, in a 9-inch (23 cm) cast-iron pan or cake pan, combine the sugar, butter, and 3 tablespoons (50 mL) of the pineapple juice (save the rest for another purpose). Stir over medium heat until melted and combined. Remove from the heat and scatter the pineapple chunks evenly over. Set aside.

For the cake, sift the flour, baking powder, and salt into a large bowl. Add the milk, melted butter, orange zest, vanilla, and egg yolks; beat smooth. In another bowl, whisk the egg whites to stiff peaks, then beat in the sugar a spoonful at a time. Stir a large spoonful of whites into the batter to loosen it up, then gently fold in the remaining whites. Pour the batter over the fruit in the pan. Bake until cooked through, about 45 minutes. Cool 5 minutes in the pan before inverting onto a plate. Warm in the oven before serving with rum-whipped cream, into which you've stirred a bit of sour cream or crème fraîche.

Vanilla Ice Cream

MAKES: ABOUT 4 CUPS (1 L)

I like ice cream as I like so many other things: rich and old-fashioned, tasting as if Anne of Green Gables had just churned the batch for a Sunday school picnic. The best ice creams I've ever eaten have been in Bologna, the university town in northern Italy. That town has way more than its fair share of superb, artisan ice cream shops, and as a student there I used to spend afternoons on pilgrimages to the best, each of which had a unique offering of flavors and its own signature style. My favorite was a firm-textured pumpkin ice cream from a parlor cum café down an otherwise ho-hum street. God, if I could have that right now . . .

Anyway, we forget how incredibly good ice cream can be because we eat too much bought fluff. We don't know what we're missing! I remember during my first week at cooking school in France being served this ice cream (it's my former teacher Anne Willan's perfect recipe) with orange-flower water and candied orange in it on crêpes Suzette. I just about passed out, it was so good. If you're using vanilla extract instead of a bean, add it after the custard is done.

2 cups (500 mL) whole milk

1 vanilla bean, split lengthwise

5 egg yolks

2/3 cup (140 g) sugar

1 cup (250 mL) heavy cream, whipped

Put the milk in a saucepan. Scrape the seeds into it from the vanilla bean, then drop in the pod. Bring just to a boil, then cover and set aside to infuse 15 minutes.

Beat the yolks and sugar until pale and thick. Gradually whisk in the milk. Set a strainer over a metal bowl and have it ready beside the stove. Return the custard to the saucepan and cook over gentle heat, stirring constantly with a wooden spoon, until slightly thickened. The custard will go from sounding splashy like milk to sounding more like stirred paint. Do not boil or it will curdle. It's ready when you run your finger across the back of the spoon and it leaves a clear trail through the custard. Pour through the sieve into the bowl. Cool completely, then cover and chill thoroughly, preferably overnight.

Begin churning the mixture in an ice-cream maker. When it is partially set, add the whipped cream and continue churning according to your machine's instructions.

Vanilla Milk Ice

If you are in the mood for something whiter and less rich-tasing, you can make an ice cream without yolks. Put 1 cup (200 g) sugar in a saucepan with 1/2 cup (125 mL) whole milk, and heat, stirring, to dissolve the sugar. Remove from the heat and add another cup (250 mL) milk, 3 cups (750 mL) heavy cream, and 1 1/2 teaspoons (7 mL) vanilla. Cool, chill (preferably overnight), then churn in an ice-cream maker. This will get very hard when you freeze it, so take it out a good 10 minutes before you serve it.

Mushroom Cups (p. 287)

Good Food Fast

I ALWAYS LOVE THE AFTER-DINNER SCENES IN PERIOD FILMS OF THE JANE AUSTEN ILK where people are sitting around a drawing room engaged in various parlory activities: a young girl with ringlets playing the piano; a couple of giggly teenagers at tiddlywinks; a gentleman with worries and a whisky leaning against the mantel with a furrowed brow; a grandmother doing needlepoint and looking disapprovingly over the top of her specs at a suspicious tête-à-tête. If she could hear what the conspirators were saying, it would be something like, "I say, Tilly, would you care to take a turn about the room?" That's when you know some juicy mischief is coming right up to tangle the plot.

Someone told me once that "boudoir" comes from the French *bouder,* which means "to sulk." In other words, you withdrew to your boudoir when you needed to be alone with your dark thoughts. "Parlor" (quite the opposite) comes from the French *parler,* "to talk," which is why in my mind there's no place for electronic devices, except for perhaps those that play music, in the room. (Apart from anything else, you might trip on them when you go to take your "turn" around the periphery.)

The nice thing about parlor games is that conversation so nicely spins out while you play them. I remember staying up very late one night in Paris with friends, all of us sitting around with names taped to our foreheads. I forget what the game is called, but the idea is that you go around and around in a circle asking yes-no questions, trying to narrow down what name is on your own head. Example: "Am I a man?" (yes), "Am I alive?" (no), "Was I a military genius?" (yes), and so on until you nail it: Julius Caesar! Actually, I think I ended up being Céline Dion that night, which was a stretch. It was 3 a.m. before I figured it out. (I blame the digestifs.)

Charades is obvious; Dictionary is perhaps not quite so obvious. We used to play that on New Year's Eve, and it was good for a laugh. Limbo is definitely not the first thing to spring to mind, but I remember playing that after an al fresco lunch on a lawn behind a château once. I wonder whose idea that was. I seem to remember it involved a broom and that there was a lot of falling over. I wouldn't try it in a salon, if I were you.

Even if you're not a games player, it can be fun to throw the odd bit of fortune telling into dinnertime. My friend Johanna has Chinese fortune sticks, and it's quite a hoot when everyone draws one, especially when you add "in bed" to the end of every fortune, as recommend by our friend Dugald. Example: "Your natural wit will be your fortune . . . in bed"; "A long-delayed package of value will come to you . . . in bed." (etc.). Once that gets tired you can sit around guessing one another's star signs or playing "Where will you be in five years?" With all that to do, you'd better get the eating over with fast and scurry into the living room for the after-party. This menu is good for that, not being a long-drawn-out one.

The cookies you can make a few days before. Prepare the granita about 2 hours before dinner. It doesn't matter whether you prepare the filling for the mushroom cups or the salmon next. Stick both in the fridge until you're ready to assemble (but bring them to room temperature before using). The vegetables, and obviously the Negronis, are last minute.

NEGRONI

MUSHROOM CUPS

❋

PARMESAN SALMON

CREAMED SPINACH

SAUTÉED CARROTS

❋

COFFEE GRANITA

HONEY HEARTS

NEGRONI

A friend of mine makes this as his specialty pre-dinner drink, and I love it for its appetizing bitter edge. I'm told that traditionally the Negroni consists of equal parts Campari, gin, and sweet (as in red) vermouth, with a generous strip of orange zest and an ice cube essential in each glass. But then my friend decided that grapefruit peel is even better. If you're several wanting Negronis, mix up a batch in a small glass jug (without the ice and zest), for sharing. And finally, if you have a minimalist bar, know that sweet vermouth on ice with lemon juice squeezed in is another delicious aperitif and just as festive. I'm having one right now!

MUSHROOM CUPS

MAKES: ABOUT 24

There is an expression a Moroccan friend of mine living in Italy used to use all the time: *l'arte d'arrangiarsi* (*l'art de s'arranger*, in French). It basically means the art of finding clever and unconventional ways to get what you need or want when there's no obvious solution before you. For example, say you're desperate for a reservation at a famous restaurant in Copenhagen, as was another friend, Kevin. He could get the flight, he could get the time off, he just couldn't get a table and had no connections to help him out. What did he do? He demonstrated one of the finest examples of *l'arte d'arrangiarsi* I've ever witnessed in my life: he wrote a letter to the chef begging for a table and offering to pay for the entire meal in gold nuggets from a mine in the Yukon. He taped a tiny nugget to the letter of request and wrote, "Here's my first installment."

I think it actually took two such letters, but it worked, and I happen to know about it because on his way back from Denmark he stopped off and we cooked a dinner party together. (I even got a gold nugget myself, which now hangs daintily from the thinnest possible chain around my neck as a reminder of "where there's a will, there's a way.") At that same party he gave me an idea for an hors d'oeuvre that to me is worth its weight in gold too. These mushroom-stuffed crisp pastry shells have all sorts of hidden surprises: a little truffle oil, a pinch of goat cheese, a feathery hint of lemon zest. Earthiness and fruitiness all at once, and they won't spoil your appetite. (For a summertime version, try chopped tomato, seasoned, with a pinch of pesto hidden underneath.)

I buy croustades, which are thin pastry cups about an inch (2.5 cm) across. You could also use mini pastry shells, but I prefer the lightness and crackery crispness of croustades.

8 ounces (225 g) cremini mushrooms, stems discarded	Zest of 1 lemon
A drizzling of olive oil	A squirt of lemon juice, to taste
Salt and pepper	1 to 2 tablespoons (15 to 30 mL) fresh goat cheese
A handful of finely chopped fresh parsley	24 baked aperitif shells
A few drops of truffle oil	

Heat the oven to 400°F (200°C). Spread the mushrooms on a baking sheet. Toss with a drizzle of olive oil and season with salt and pepper. Roast to intensify their taste somewhat, about 10 minutes. Finely chop. Toss with the parsley, a few drops of truffle oil, some lemon zest, and a squeeze of lemon juice. Check the seasonings.

Put the very tiniest pinch of goat cheese in the bottom of each croustade and top with the mushrooms. Serve.

Katherine's Chick-peanuts

MAKES: 1 CUP (180 G)

"Chick-peanuts" is a good name for these because that's a bit what they're like. They're crunchy, salty beads made lively with fresh mint, all very weird and wonderful. (They came to me via Katherine, sister of *l'arte d'arrangiarsi* Kevin.) Tinned chickpeas will not yield good results, so only bother with the recipe if you've planned ahead and have soaked and cooked some dried chickpeas (see p. 197). You can do these in a 400°F (200°C) oven also, but I find they get a bit too hard that way, and nobody wants to eat pebbles. I have also heard about deep-frying them, which I have an inkling may be the best way of all, but I've yet to test the hypothesis.

1 cup (200 g) cooked chickpeas (not tinned)
1/4 cup (60 mL) peanut oil
Salt
A handful of finely chopped fresh mint

Dry the chickpeas well in a tea towel. Heat the oil in a sauté pan over medium-high heat, then fry the chickpeas, stirring frequently, until they achieve a nut-like crunch and are beginning to turn golden. Remove to paper towels and immediately season with salt and toss in the mint.

PARMESAN SALMON

MAKES: 6 SERVINGS

One weekend in the French countryside, my friend Nathalie taught me how to slice the neck off a Champagne bottle using the base of a Champagne glass. It's an impressive trick, and given the number of dead soldiers we counted at the end of the weekend we got a lot of practice. This recipe is one she made during that visit. It's a pinch to throw together and very tasty, bound to become one of your weeknight specialties. I give measurements, but personally I wouldn't bother getting out the scales: the idea is simply equal amounts of grated Parmesan, bread crumbs, and chopped parsley packed onto the top of each salmon piece to make a crust. Don't be tempted to substitute olive oil for the butter, because it's the butter that takes the crunchy topping to its highest heights.

6 skinless salmon fillets, 5 ounces (140 g) each
Salt and pepper
3 ounces (85 g) fresh white bread crumbs
2 ounces (60 g) finely grated Parmesan cheese
Leaves from 1 large bunch parsley, finely chopped
1/3 cup (70 g) butter, melted

Heat the oven to 400°F (200°C). Lightly oil a baking sheet and lay the salmon on it. Season with salt and pepper. Combine the bread crumbs, cheese, and parsley and pack on top of the salmon. Drizzle the melted butter evenly over top. Bake until the salmon is just cooked, about 8 minutes.

CREAMED SPINACH

MAKES: 6 SERVINGS

There are actually two ways to cream spinach. One is the lazy way (below), which is just to pour cream onto cooked spinach and warm it up, which will give you a bit of a pale green pool in the plate around the vegetables. The other way, which will keep things more amalgamated, is to blanch the trimmed spinach briefly in salted boiling water just to wilt, then rinse it in cold water. Drain and squeeze dry. Next, heat a tablespoon (15 mL) butter in a pan, whisk in a tablespoon (15 mL) flour for a minute, then whisk in 3/4 cup (175 mL) milk until smooth. Stir through the spinach to reheat and season as below. If it needs thinning out, do so with heavy cream. Both versions are good, so take your pick, but in either case please don't use packaged baby spinach leaves, as they have no taste. You want the hearty stuff, preferably from a farmers' market.

1 1/2 pounds (675 g) large spinach leaves, trimmed
1/2 cup (125 mL) heavy cream
Salt and pepper
Nutmeg (optional)

Wash the trimmed spinach leaves and put them in a large pot with the water still clinging to them. Cover and set over medium-high heat to steam, turning once or twice with tongs to make sure it doesn't stick to the bottom of the pan. It will have wilted in about 3 minutes. Drain away any excess liquid, pressing down on the spinach to squeeze it as dry as possible. Add the cream and reheat, stirring. Season with salt and pepper and a scrape of nutmeg if you like it, and serve.

SAUTÉED CARROTS

MAKES: 6 GENEROUS SERVINGS

This sounds almost idiotically simple, and I suppose it is, but the result of frying carrots, slowly and with intent, is exquisite: they get tender with a sweet, golden edge on all sides.

2 pounds (900 g) carrots
1/4 cup (55 g) butter
Salt and pepper

Slice the carrots into coins. Melt the butter in a sauté pan over medium heat. Add the carrots, season with salt and pepper, and cook, stirring occasionally, until golden on all sides and tender in the middle, about 15 minutes, depending on their thickness.

COFFEE GRANITA

MAKES: 6 SERVINGS

Coffee granita may well be the ideal dessert: light, palate-cleansing, flavorful, and it eliminates the need to serve coffee. Here's the pain in the neck about it: if you don't have a timer, you'll forget your granita in the freezer and it will become a solid, mud-brown ice rink. It once took me four days to make granita (I had no timer). Every time I put it in the freezer, it became as out-of-sight-out-of-mind as pine nuts toasting (read: burning to cinders) in the oven, so I'd have to take it out, melt it down, and start over. Until the last time, when I'd seriously had it, and put the whole frozen lot in the food processor and pressed "whiz." The result was a strangely amalgamated coffee ice, a bit like slushy sorbet. It was not bad, I suppose, but a proper granita, scraped into flaky crystals, is certainly better and more interesting. Texturally, it's like eating fireworks if they were made of ice.

Because ices melt so quickly, it's not a bad idea to chill the serving dishes first in the freezer, the way some people do with beer steins. That way the granita will survive longer once it's served: spoon the crystals into the cold coupes, top with whipped cream (I'm told Sambuca-flavored is a treat, if you have any of that in the cupboard), and that's it. Or, for an exciting textural juxtaposition, try it spooned onto Vanilla Ice Cream (p. 280).

Incidentally, how much sugar you want in granita is a matter of personal preference. I have seen recipes using as little as 1/4 cup (55 g) and others using 1 1/2 cups (300 g) for this amount of coffee. Stir in a lesser amount if you're not sure, taste the warm coffee, and then decide if you want more sugar.

4 cups (1 L) warm strong top-quality coffee or espresso
About 1 cup (200 g) sugar

Stir together the coffee and sugar until the sugar is dissolved. Pour into a shallow dish and freeze for 1 hour. Stir with a fork to break up the frozen parts, moving the edges in toward the center. Repeat this every half hour until you have a dish full of fine coffee crystals, about 2 hours in total. (If you forget it and it freezes too hard, take it out of the freezer until you can stir it again, then put it back in and carry on.)

HONEY HEARTS

MAKES: ABOUT 2 DOZEN COOKIES

The taste of these cookies, which happen to be my favorite on earth, is mysterious. They have only the faintest hint of cinnamon, which will have even professional cooks asking what it is; also, the honey works magic because its taste matures the longer the cookies sit around, making the flavor mellow and deepen even more. Texturally, Honey Hearts snap happily in the mouth (there's no egg to soften them), but at the same time they're very buttery rich and remind me vaguely of toffee. I promise you, tea has never had a more perfect companion. This recipe comes from my Danish-born sister-in-law and is her family's top Christmas cookie. I'm so in love with them that I make them all year long, which is cheating, I know, but don't rat on me.

3/4 cup + 2 tablespoons (200 g) butter, slightly softened
3/4 cup + 2 tablespoons (185 g) sugar
3 tablespoons (50 mL) unpasteurized honey
1 teaspoon (5 mL) cinnamon
1 1/4 teaspoons (6 mL) baking powder
2 cups (250 g) flour

Heat the oven to 350°F (180°C). Lightly grease a baking sheet. Cream the butter and sugar together until smooth. Add the honey and stir until thoroughly combined. Mix the cinnamon and baking powder into the flour, then work into the butter mixture until you have a smooth dough. Divide into 2 balls and flatten into disks.

Working in batches, on a lightly floured surface roll out the dough about 1/4 inch (5 mm) thick. Cut into hearts with a cookie cutter and arrange on the baking sheet. Bake until the cookies turn a dark gingery color, about 10 minutes. Carefully (because they are soft and delicate when still hot) transfer to racks to cool. They will quickly harden. Store in an airtight container.

LETTUCE AND CUCUMBER SOUP WITH RYE CROUTONS AND LUMPFISH CAVIAR (P. 299)

A Proper Sunday Lunch

FASHION HAS ALWAYS BAFFLED ME A BIT, AND THE OLDER I GET THE MORE I FEEL I have one or two looks I feel good in and that's the end of it. Even though I don't consider myself skilled at getting dressed, I do think dressing well matters. The world has gone slack in this department (straight downhill along with good manners), and I don't believe it has done any of us any good. Fortunately, it seems pretty much the current etiquette to dress up at least a little a bit for dinner parties. Some we obviously dress up for more than others, but I'd say no matter what the occasion, the extreme "casual Friday" look is out of the question. You may find this ridiculously precious of me, but I'll explain what sold me so firmly on this school of thought.

I was at a birthday party in Paris with a lot of Americans once, and I'd come straight from some physical activity or other, which meant I was not put together as smartly as I ought to have been. I don't know what the other guests' excuses were, but for some reason they were looking rather scruffy too. The doorbell rang and a Frenchwoman entered looking as if she'd just walked off the set from hosting a game show. I mean, seriously glamorous. The rest of us shifted in our seats. "Wow!" said the birthday boy to her. "You look . . . fabulous!" She said, humbly, *"C'est pour toi"*—"It's for you." Seeing it in that light, suddenly the rest of us were ashamed of ourselves. It was as if we'd all shown up without presents and she'd walked in with a big box beautifully wrapped and tied with a bow.

Having been brought up in a place and time in which notions of jackets for men and dresses for women were being abandoned in favor of jeans and T-shirts all round, the idea that spending time getting dolled up to face the world could get drummed into the brain as being a bit frivolous. But my time in France, and in particular this incident with that Frenchwoman, reinforced the opposite message.

Her upbringing had obviously taught her this: when you go out in public, other people have to look at you, so it's only socially decent to make sure you're as easy on their eyes as possible.

It's a question of respect, but it's also a cultural value that holds beauty for beauty's sake as something the soul needs. We must admit it's much nicer to walk into a room where everyone looks good rather than like a pack of slobs. Besides, we feel much better about ourselves, and behave better out in the world, when we look delightful. I suppose all this seems like rather a digression, but I had to get it off my chest before sitting you down to a proper Sunday lunch, didn't I?

I know this menu looks a bit long, but in fact it's simplicity itself. You see, the great thing about Sunday lunch is that you tell people that's what they're getting, so they don't gear up for crab cakes topped with threads of deep-fried ginger, followed by chops encased in phyllo pastry and assaulted by several squirt bottles of sauce, etc. No, with this Sunday lunch, guests know it's a comforting granny's-house sort of thing that they're coming round for, and they'll look forward to it being exactly that. In other words, this is a great dinner for setting expectations and knowing you'll meet them every time: perfectly cooked beef; thick, flavorful gravy; crisp golden potatoes; leafy sprouts; and creamy puréed squash. It's colorful, healthy, and I'd even say bonding for the people who eat it together. I recommend a brisk autumn walk afterward.

Make the trifle first and stick it in the fridge. Next the soup, so it's ready to reheat, and have the croutons ready. Open the oysters not too long before serving and keep them in the fridge. Get the potatoes ready to roast. While the meat is in the oven, prepare the purée and make the sprouts. Pop the potatoes in the oven as soon as the meat is out and resting, and make the gravy. (If you have two ovens, start the potatoes in the second oven about half an hour before the beef is finished roasting.)

OYSTERS WITH HORSERADISH

✻

LETTUCE AND CUCUMBER SOUP WITH
RYE CROUTONS AND LUMPFISH CAVIAR

✻

SLOW ROAST OF BEEF WITH GRAVY

SHAGGY CRISP POTATOES

BUTTERED BRUSSELS SPROUTS

SQUASH PURÉE

✻

TRIFLE

OYSTERS WITH HORSERADISH

Either grate peeled fresh horseradish into a bowl or serve bought horseradish (less desirable) with a spoon in it alongside the oysters. Three oysters per person is enough in a substantial menu like this, and that's not too much hassle for the shucker.

I have to slip in another recipe here because it is quite simply *the most delicious oyster sauce I have ever eaten* in my life. It comes from "The Dude," a burly Norwegian oyster raiser with a very colorful vocabulary and a uniform of rubber boots, jeans, knitted Norwegian sweater, and blue bandana. He told me this recipe on the pier one day, with all the nonchalance of one discussing the weather. Later, he showed up at the house where I was staying with a sack of oysters (extra smalls) and a jar of the sauce he'd made himself to demonstrate his method.

The recipe, which he handed to me neatly written on a paper napkin, goes like this: 1/2 cup (125 mL) ponzu soy sauce (which is a citrus-flavored type); 1 to 2 teaspoons (5 to 10 mL) mirin; the zest of half a lemon, half a lime, and half an orange; and about a tablespoon (15 mL) each of lemon, lime, and orange juice. He insisted on letting this concoction sit for the flavors to meld before we could eat it, so be sure to make it, say, an hour ahead.

He then opened the oysters, loosening the tendon from the shell, and rinsed the oysters under the cold tap. I shrieked, "You throw away the juice?" And he said, "Do you want to go down and take a sip out of the ocean?" I'd never thought of it that way before, but he has a point. Rinsing, he informed me, also gets rid of any grittiness from the shell, so I may be a convert. Besides, once you rinse the water from the shells, the oysters will squirt out a new pool anyway, and the fresh one will be *sans* grit. The Dude insists on oysters served on a bed of ice because they must be eaten very cold. He spooned a scant teaspoon of the sauce onto each one and topped it with very daintily sliced green onion. They were gorgeous, and the taste, utterly out of this world.

LETTUCE AND CUCUMBER SOUP WITH RYE CROUTONS AND LUMPFISH CAVIAR

MAKES: 6 TO 8 SERVINGS

Nobody gets excited when you tell them the first course is lettuce and cucumber soup, but they sure perk up when you set it in front of them because it is quite stunning in appearance. The soup is an earthy green with surprisingly deep flavor, accessorized with a garnish of teensy-weensy rye bread croutons, a scattering of dill, a spoonful of crème fraîche, and a dollop of gem-like lumpfish caviar on top. I like it because it is light and healthy (a puréed salad, nutritionally speaking, only warm), and it is a fine example of how humble ingredients can quickly be transformed into something eccentric and regal. This is a course to add to lunch if you really want to stretch it out. If you leave it out, however, the menu won't suffer.

FOR THE SOUP

2 tablespoons (30 mL) butter

1 large onion, thinly sliced

1 tablespoon (15 mL) flour

8 ounces (225 g) lettuce, such as romaine, shredded

1/2 English cucumber, peeled and thinly sliced

4 cups (1 L) vegetable or chicken stock

Salt and pepper

1/2 cup (125 mL) heavy cream

FOR THE GARNISH

3 tablespoons (50 mL) butter

2 slices dark rye bread, crusts removed, diced very small (about the size of an eraser on the end of a pencil)

1 teaspoon (5 mL) per serving of crème fraîche or sour cream

A handful of roughly chopped fresh dill

1 teaspoon (5 mL) per serving of lumpfish caviar

For the soup, melt the butter in a large pot. Add the onions and cook very gently, stirring occasionally, until soft and translucent, about 7 minutes. Sprinkle over the flour and cook, stirring, for 1 minute, then add the lettuce, cucumber, and stock. Season with salt and pepper, then cover and simmer until the vegetables are very tender, about 15 minutes. Working in batches, purée in a blender, and return to the pot. Check the seasonings.

For the crouton garnish, melt the butter in a frying pan over medium-high heat. Add the diced bread and toss to coat. Fry until crisp, a matter of minutes. Remove to paper towels.

Stir the heavy cream into the soup and gently reheat until piping hot. Ladle soup into warmed soup plates. Garnish with a spoonful of crème fraîche, a scattering of dill and croutons, and a spoonful of the red caviar.

Bongo Bongo Soup

Instead of oysters followed by lettuce soup, you could make Bongo Bongo Soup, which more or less puts the two together. Bongo Bongo Soup is another recipe from my friend John, who raved on about it for months, indeed *bragged* about it, remembering how he'd eaten it in private clubs over forty years ago and how he had finally learned to make it on his own and improve it. It's a good use for large oysters, which, personally, I can't enjoy raw on the half-shell and so prefer to cook anyway. What you do is cook 1 pound (450 g) spinach (stems removed first), drain it, squeeze the liquid out, and put it in a blender. Add 2 tablespoons (30 mL) melted butter, 2 chopped garlic cloves, a teaspoon (5 mL) HP or A1 sauce, 10 shucked oysters with their liquid, a cup (250 mL) filled half with cream and half with milk, and salt and pepper. Whiz it up, then, when you're ready to eat it, heat it very gently. It should be piping hot, but don't boil it. Ladle it into warm bowls, which you've arranged on a baking sheet, top with a generous spoonful of whipped cream, and broil for a minute to brown the cream slightly. "That's the touch," John would say. I don't think I've ever seen anyone more proud of a recipe than John with his Bongo Bongo Soup. It is, for him, a true signature dish and, as he promises, silky and memorable.

SLOW ROAST OF BEEF WITH GRAVY

MAKES: 8 TO 10 SERVINGS

For something so straightforward, it's astounding how no two recipes for roast beef are alike. Somewhere, I read a suggestion to cook a prime rib at 500°F (260°C) for half an hour and then turn off the heat and leave it in the oven with the door closed, like a meringue, until done. (I was too chicken to try that myself, having paid $130 for the roast.) Others say to cook roasts, cake-like, at 325°F (160°C) or 350°F (180°C) straight through until done. Certain versions start with high heat, then go low, others recommend the exact opposite, and yet others swear instead by searing the meat on the stovetop first, which I do. Then there are the debates about cut. A friend swears by prime rib with the bone in from the small end, but you practically have to mortgage your house to get one of those. Sirloin tip, eye of round, chuck, or blade roast are less expensive alternatives and they've never left me wanting. Well . . . except that boneless cuts seem to mean the gravy looks more turkey-like, whereas with a bone-in expensive cut, you get a gravy that's a bit richer, darker, and more luxurious. That's easily solved by using some of the money you've saved on the roast to buy a seriously decent beef stock from a fancy butcher, one that's wobbly, gelatinous, and the color of mahogany. Browning a few aromatics in the base of the pan first and using them as a perch for the roast helps enrich the gravy as well.

FOR THE ROAST

Roughly a 4-pound (1.8 kg) sirloin tip, chuck,
   eye, or blade roast

About 4 garlic cloves, thinly sliced lengthwise

Olive oil, for rubbing

Salt and pepper

1 onion, thickly sliced

1 large carrot, halved lengthwise

1/2 celery rib, cut in two

FOR THE GRAVY

2 tablespoons (30 mL) flour

About 1 cup (250 mL) rich beef stock

About 1 cup (250 mL) squash cooking water
   (see p. 307), more as needed

1 teaspoon (5 mL) tomato paste (optional)

Bring the beef to room temperature for about an hour before cooking. Heat the oven to 250°F (120°C).

Slide the tip of a sharp knife into the roast in several places and slip a sliver of garlic into each incision. Rub the meat lightly with olive oil and season with salt and pepper. Set a suitable roasting pan on the stovetop and heat over medium-high. Lay the meat in, fat side down, and brown it all over, 3 to 4 minutes per side.

Lift the roast out. Add the onions, carrot, and celery and fry until deep golden. Set the roast, fat side up, on top on the vegetables and transfer the pan to the oven. Roast the meat to an internal temperature of 125°F (50°C), about 1 1/2 hours for medium-rare. (Cheaper cuts are best cooked on the rare side, but prime rib, at least for me, is preferable cooked to medium, about 135°F/58°C.) Remove the roast from the roasting pan, wrap in foil, and let rest at least 30 minutes. (Up to an hour is also fine. The meat will stay hot.)

While the meat rests, make the gravy. (And put the potatoes in the oven!) Discard the vegetables from the roasting pan. Tilt the pan and skim off all but a few tablespoons of fat from the pan juices. (Most of the time, you won't have to remove any fat at all, so don't worry too much about this step.) Set the pan on the stovetop over medium-high heat. When the juices sizzle, sprinkle over the flour and cook, whisking, for 1 minute. Whisk in the stock, vegetable water, and tomato paste (if using) until smooth, and boil down until you have a rich, thick, brown gravy, about 10 minutes. Keep warm.

Open the foil around the meat and pour the dark juices into the gravy, whisking them in. Carve the meat thinly (I cannot abide thickly sliced roasts) and arrange on a serving platter. Pour the hot gravy into a warm sauceboat to serve alongside.

SHAGGY CRISP POTATOES

MAKES: 8 TO 10 SERVINGS

I was going to call these Slater's Taters, because British food writer Nigel Slater's books are what put me on to them, but then I started to realize that there's barely a British cookbook on the market without a recipe for these. Goose fat or duck fat can be worth seeking out to use in place of butter and oil.

I should add that potato fanatics love having two different types of potatoes at these Sunday lunch affairs. If you're a member of that cult, prepare John's Minty Potatoes (p. 85), using new potatoes, as well as these.

4 pounds (1.8 kg) floury potatoes, such as russets (about 8)

2 to 3 tablespoons (30 to 50 mL) semolina or fine cornmeal

3 tablespoons (50 mL) butter

3 tablespoons (50 mL) olive oil

Salt and pepper

Heat the oven to 400°F (200°C). Peel the potatoes and cut them in three. Put the chunks in a large pot, cover with cold water, and bring to a boil. Salt the water and boil the potatoes 5 minutes. Drain, sprinkle over the semolina, then put the lid on the pan and give it a few good shakes to fluff up the edges of the potatoes.

Melt the butter in the oil in a pan large enough to hold the potatoes. Add the potatoes and turn gently to coat. Season with salt and pepper. Bake, turning once or twice, until golden and very crisp, 45 minutes to an hour.

TRIFLE

MAKES: 8 SERVINGS

I grew up with trifles that relied on pound-cake cubes instead of ladyfingers for the base, so that's how I still approach the dessert, only I use sponge cake now, which is lighter. I particularly love the delicate texture of this cake, with its faint wisps of lemon and orange. The custard takes no time, so definitely don't use the kind made from powder. This is proper trifle and deserves only the best. Which reminds me that you must be sure to serve it as flatteringly as possible (trifle being one of those slightly frumpy-looking English puddings that needs a bit of help in the beauty department). For example, at home we always ate trifle out of thin-lipped pink Champagne coupes, topped with whipped cream and toasted almond slivers. Thus dolled up, it looked very glamorous indeed.

Another way to simplify the menu, if you must, is to forgo trifle and instead make *Victoria Sponge:* Steal the cake part of the trifle, bake in two 7-inch (18 cm) pans, and sandwich the layers with raspberry jam and slightly sweetened, vanilla-scented whipped cream. *Voilà!* To fancy up the top, dust with icing sugar before serving, possibly laying a doily or paper cut-out on top first so you leave a dusty pattern behind. It's less celebratory than trifle, so I wouldn't automatically take this shortcut, but I couldn't hold back from telling you about the cake because it makes divine tea-party fare and is ideal for a little girl's birthday cake. In fact, it's so easy that little girls can make it themselves and be very proud.

A word about the cake. If the butter is not extremely soft when it goes in you'll end up with clumpy batter, which it turn will lead to a cake full of holes with grease running out and all over it. Make sure the butter is at super-soft room temperature, but not melting, before you use it.

FOR THE CUSTARD

1 cup (250 mL) whole milk

1/2 cup (125 mL) heavy cream

4 egg yolks

1/4 cup (55 g) sugar

FOR THE SPONGE CAKE

3/4 cup + 2 tablespoons (110 g) flour

1 1/2 teaspoons (7 mL) baking powder

1/2 cup (110 g) *very soft* room-temperature
   butter

1/2 cup + 1 tablespoon (110 g) sugar

2 large eggs

1/4 cup (60 mL) milk

A few drops of vanilla

Zest of 1/2 lemon and 1/2 orange

FOR THE TRIFLE

2 to 3 tablespoons (30 to 50 mL) dry sherry

1 cup (250 mL) drained crushed pineapple

1 cup (250 mL) crushed strawberries (about
   10 ounces/280 g, mashed with 1 tablespoon/
   15 mL sugar)

1 to 2 bananas, sliced

FOR THE GARNISH

1 cup (250 mL) heavy cream

2 teaspoons (10 mL) sugar

A few drops of vanilla

1/2 cup (40 g) toasted slivered almonds

For the custard, heat the milk and cream in a saucepan. In a bowl, beat the yolks and sugar until pale and thick. When the milk mixture is hot, gradually whisk it into the egg mixture, then pour it back into the saucepan. Stir with a wooden spoon over medium heat until thickened enough to coat the back of a spoon, about 10 minutes. Strain into a bowl, cool, cover, and chill.

For the cake, heat the oven to 325°F (160°C). Grease two 7-inch (18 cm) cake pans and line the bottoms with parchment paper. Sift the flour and baking powder into a bowl. Add all the other ingredients and mix with an electric beater just until the batter is smooth, light, and drops easily from a spoon, about 3 minutes—do not over-beat or the cake will be rubbery. Pour into the pans and bake until a toothpick inserted in the center comes out clean, about 30 minutes. Cool completely. Turn the cakes out of the pans; cut into roughly 1-inch (2.5 cm) cubes.

To assemble the trifle, put a spoonful or two of custard in the bottom of a glass serving bowl. Make a layer of cake cubes in the base and up the sides of the bowl. Sprinkle with some sherry, then layer in half of each of the three fruits. Pour over half the custard. Arrange a layer of cake cubes on top and repeat the process, finishing with the custard. Cover and refrigerate overnight or all day.

Before serving, whip the cream with the sugar and vanilla. Bring the serving bowl to the table and spoon the trifle into pretty dessert dishes. Top each serving with a spoonful of whipped cream and a scattering of toasted almonds.

ENDIVE SPOONS (P. 314)

Just Plain Good

HOUSES HAVE ALWAYS FASCINATED ME. AS A CHILD, I USED TO SPEND HOURS DRAWING floor plans—not facades and picket fences, but actual floor plans like you see in builders' magazines—and I used to march through my parents' house, standing in doorways trying to imagine how things could be improved, desperate to understand *why* if a room didn't work.

My friend John, mentor in so many matters of daily life, gave me a classic book on towns and houses called *A Pattern Language.* He told me he has read at it for a lifetime, and indeed it is a book you tend to read "at" rather than actually read: a series of short essays that follow various pronouncements, such as, "Rooms without a view are prisons for the people who have to stay in them . . . ," or "Bedrooms make no sense . . . ," or "Make a place in the home, perhaps only a few feet square, which is kept locked and secret; a place which is virtually impossible to discover . . ." Reading the book, I started looking differently at everything in the houses I entered, analyzing every aspect, from the presence or lack of windowsills to the length of kitchen countertops, to the configuration of salon furnishings . . . which eventually led me around to an obsession with dining tables.

Jackie Kennedy was much praised for introducing round tables seating 8 to 10 to the White House, and I have given that some thought. It certainly beats a horseshoe and it avoids the refectory effect of a roomful of rectangles, but round tables are not without their hitches. Three round tables of my life come to mind right now and, I think, illustrate the pros and cons. The first was seriously enormous, seating something like 30. It was in the common room of an inn where I stayed for a week with a television crew, and we all ate at it. That table worked, *I guess,* because nobody knew each other anyway and didn't care about talking. Good thing, because to try to talk across that table was like shouting across a lake, so you were stuck with whomever you had left and right. The rest you could only admire from afar.

More recently, I dined with friends at a round table that seated 12 and, shockingly, it did not work. For whatever spatial reasons, that table allowed for only one conversation to take place at a time; in other words, everyone at the table had to sit and pay attention while one person barked out a story for the whole crowd. To break off into smaller, more intimate, conversations, which would have been easy in rectangular or oval form, felt at this round table somehow rude.

The third round table in my mind wins the prize: it was mahogany, placed in a bit of a far-off corner of a drawing room, and it seated four. Perfect! A round table for just a few people has a certain magic, because it really does put you *tête-à-tête*—and much gets revealed in what feels like a natural "cone of silence." I can imagine it's possible to seat six at a round table with equal success, but personally with any number higher than that I'd go rectangle or oval. Once you're up to eight people at a dinner party, conversation must be allowed to split; that's the bottom line. It's not that you never come together on one topic, but there is freedom to break off now and again, to get close to the people on your right and left and directly across the table. (It also makes serving easier.)

I don't know why I'm yakking on about this now when you have an apple pie to get at, but I suppose these are the sorts of things that come to gnaw on the brain while one is caught up in the meditative rhythms of stirring and chopping. So, think on these matters as you go make your pie. Then prepare the fillings for the "spoons," but assemble them just before eating. The main course is also last minute, but it's very unfussy, so don't stress.

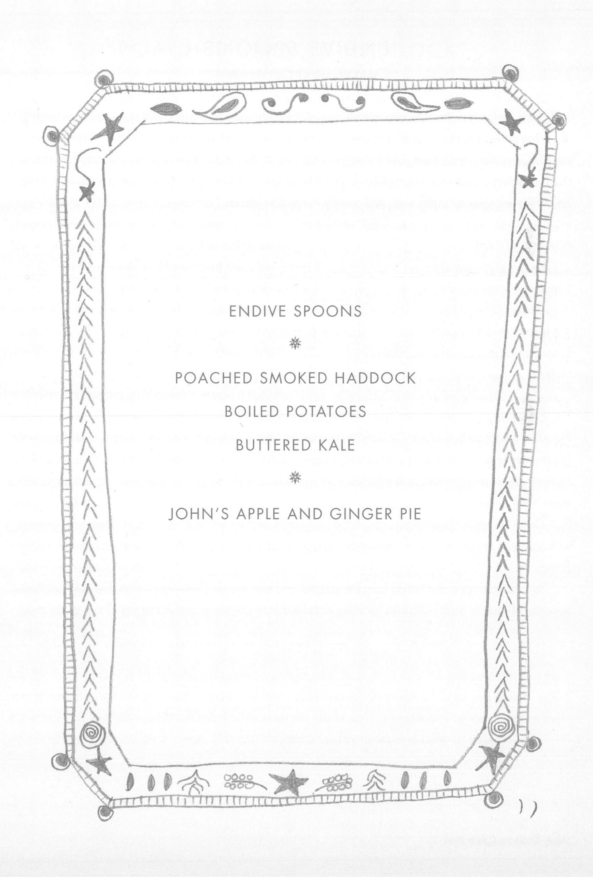

ENDIVE SPOONS

❋

POACHED SMOKED HADDOCK

BOILED POTATOES

BUTTERED KALE

❋

JOHN'S APPLE AND GINGER PIE

Pear and Ginger Tart

MAKES: 8 SERVINGS

I'm sure this is fine without preserved ginger, if you don't have any. It's extremely tasty and foolproof no matter what, and very German. It reminds me of the *Kuchen* in German coffee houses, places empty from lunch until about four o'clock, when they suddenly bulge with people coming in to eat slabs of cake the size of doorstops. I'm sure Quark cheese was the original before cream cheese in this recipe, but either way it's easy and impressive.

FOR THE CRUST

1 cup (250 g) flour

1/2 cup (110 g) cold butter, cut into pieces

1/3 cup sugar (70 g) sugar

1/4 cup (15 g) sliced almonds

FOR THE FILLING

4 ounces (110 g) cream cheese, at room
  temperature

1/2 cup (95 g) sugar

2 eggs

2 tablespoons (30 mL) chopped preserved ginger

1/2 cup (125 mL) heavy cream

1/2 teaspoon (2 mL) vanilla

3 to 4 firm but ripe pears, peeled, cored,
  and sliced

Heat the oven to 400°F (200°C). Lightly grease a 9-inch (23 cm) tart pan. Put the crust ingredients in a food processor and pulse to crumbs. Press into the bottom and sides of the tart pan. Bake until just starting to turn golden, about 15 minutes. Remove from the oven. Reduce the heat to 350°F (180°C).

While the crust bakes, make the filling. In a large bowl, cream the cream cheese and sugar, then beat in the eggs, ginger, cream, and vanilla until smooth. When the shell comes out of the oven, arrange the pear slices in concentric circles in the bottom, then pour over the custard. Bake until the pears are tender and the filling golden, 30 to 40 minutes. Serve warm or at room temperature.

Chicken Pot Pie for Perfectionists (p. 327)

A Comforting "Family" Dinner

A SCRIPTWRITER ONCE TOLD ME THAT EVERY SITCOM IS ULTIMATELY ABOUT FAMILY, even if it's not about family. *Friends* was about "family," *Sex and the City* was about "family," *Gilligan's Island* goes without saying. I mean, real family is real family, I know, and it's irreplaceable, for better or for worse, but the general concept of family is actually quite fluid, and I think because of our need for it we try to recreate it no matter where we are or who we have around us.

Which is how I ended up among a bunch of strangers who meet at a local pub every Friday at five o'clock. I had been out of town at a dinner party and met a man who asked me how I liked living in my newly adopted city. (This was not long after I'd moved there and knew no one.) Not being one to mince words, or so I'm told, I responded, "I hate it! It's ugly and I have no friends." "Good God!" exclaimed the man. "Well, you'd better meet *my* friends." No sooner was I back in town than my voicemail introduced me to Mollie, who invited me to meet the group at a specified pub on Friday. There I met a collection of people who over time became not just friends but much more like relatives.

Before long, in addition to pub nights, we started dining together about once a week. This went on all year until I got busy at something and couldn't entertain for a while. A pub night came along on an evening when you could really feel the change of season (this was early fall). The air was cool and it had threatened rain all day; in fact, it was the first night we moved from the pub terrace to the dark indoors and declared it our last night of the "summer pub," agreeing next week to switch back to our winter location.

Everyone had shown up that night, which isn't always the case, and for some reason we all seemed to be lingering longer than usual, reluctant to part ways. I said it first: "God, I've missed you guys!" Heads nodded. We'd been sticking to our pub routine, but somehow it hadn't been enough. I suddenly realized what was wrong. "It's because we haven't eaten together," I gasped. "We haven't eaten together!" they chimed back in a minor key, with all the horror in their voices of a chorus declaring the sky was about to fall. We fixed a date for Sunday and all went home breathing sighs of relief.

That must have been the first time I became fully aware of the necessity of breaking bread with family, however one might define the term at any given time. Something unusual happens when you eat with people, different from when you go jogging with them, or build a stone wall with them, or see a concert. It has to do with a sense of personal security and of knowing your place in the world. Dinner with family (or "family") is anchoring, in the way other activities can't be, and it's part of what gives us the confidence to go out into the world afterward and take risks.

This has everything to do with chicken pot pie, of course. If, when we sit down with people to share a meal, whoever they may be, we become "family," then family food is not only appropriate for dinner guests, it's a huge part of what everyone is craving. It's also, in the case of this menu, a bit of a project, and you would only want to serve a labor of love like that to worthy souls.

Have the pie assembled well ahead of time and waiting in the fridge to bake. Prepare the salad components and assemble those too just before eating (unless you're axing the first course and just serving watercress alongside the pie). The cherries you can have already done and ready to reheat and flame just before serving.

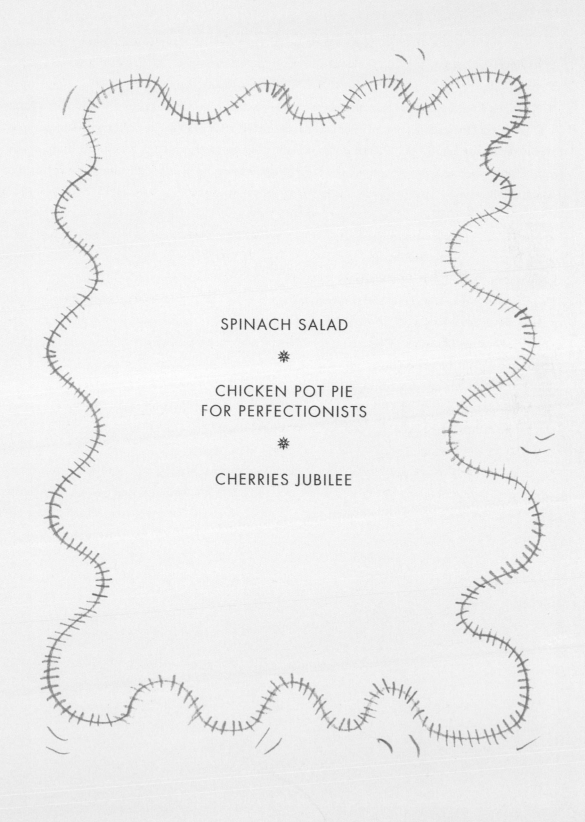

SPINACH SALAD

✳

CHICKEN POT PIE
FOR PERFECTIONISTS

✳

CHERRIES JUBILEE

SPINACH SALAD

MAKES: 4 SERVINGS

When I was living in France, there wasn't a whole lot of food from home I missed, but a good spinach salad was one of them when the mood struck. If you'd rather something more exotic, serve watercress, endive, and pomegranate salad (p. 266) instead as a first. Or forgo a first course altogether and just serve watercress or perhaps mâche, lightly dressed, alongside any of the pies that follow.

About 6 ounces (170 g) spinach leaves, trimmed (roughly 8 handfuls)

4 slices bacon, cut into lardons

1 tablespoon (15 mL) red wine vinegar

1/2 teaspoon (2 mL) Dijon mustard, more to taste

1 garlic clove, crushed

About 1/4 cup (60 mL) olive oil (or less, depending on amount of bacon fat)

2 handfuls of minced red onion or pink shallot

About 12 button mushrooms, thinly sliced

Salt and pepper

2 to 3 hard-boiled eggs, sliced (optional)

Put the spinach in a large bowl. Fry the bacon until crisp, drain on paper towels, and set aside. Whisk the vinegar, mustard, and garlic into the warm bacon fat, adding as much olive oil as needed to make a dressing. Add the onion and mushrooms and cook for 1 minute, then pour the dressing over the spinach and toss. Season with salt and pepper. Arrange on a serving platter with the egg slices on top (if using) and the bacon scattered over. Serve.

CHICKEN POT PIE FOR PERFECTIONISTS

MAKES: 2 PIES, FOR 8 TO 10 SERVINGS IN ALL

I wish I could think of an adequate translation for the French word *aboutir*. *Bout* refers to the tip of something, so the verb *aboutir* is, I suppose, a coming to an end, but in the sense of peaking, which is positive. A chef I once knew in Paris used the word when he was talking to me about a recipe he was working on. "It good," he said of his dish, mind all a-tinkering, "but it is not yet *abouti*." How well I know that feeling, knowing a recipe is *almost* perfect, but still needs a little . . . something before it's "finished."

Such was the case with my chicken pot pie, and it always bugged me. I mean, it's pretty difficult to make a *bad* one, but at the same time all too easy to make one that's mediocre. One of my television directors always used to say, "Good is the enemy of great," and every time I made chicken pot pie those words rang in my ears. I tried various tricks: using leeks in place of or in addition to onions, omitting mushrooms (I find them oddly rubbery in chicken pie and too close texturally and in taste to the chicken itself), adding a small handful of dried herbs, sneaking a teaspoon each of soy sauce, tomato paste, and chicken stock powder into the stock to enrich it . . . Those were all useful ideas, but the *key* to greatness in a chicken pot pie I didn't discover until I made one using leftovers from a roasted bird. That was it! I had always poached chicken in stock to make pot pie, which works, but what a difference when you make stock from a roasted carcass that has some color and caramelization. This to explain why I'm putting you through roasting a small chicken before you get to make the pie. (By all means use leftovers from a larger roasted bird.) The other consideration is that pan size matters for all pot pies: the ratio of pastry to filling must be balanced, which it isn't, really, if you make one enormous casserole (not enough crust) or if you make miniature pies (too much crust). Ah, the 9-inch (23 cm) pie plate, what a perfect invention! You'll need two here.

Lard Pastry

Lard pastry is the only way to go for savory pies, I've been convinced. It takes longer to brown than butter pastry, so you'll notice high temperatures in the recipes here and longer baking times. Also, on meat pies it's nice to have a bit of a thick crust, so don't roll it too, too thinly. Once a pie is covered, you can use any scraps to cut out decorative shapes, such as leaves, and lay them on top. This is the pastry I use for all of the pies that follow. (I use this same crust in a sweet version for the apple pie on p. 318, just so you know it's not limited to savory.)

3 cups (375 g) flour
1 cup (225 g) cold lard, cut into pieces
1 teaspoon (5 mL) salt
1/2 cup (125 mL) ice-cold water
Egg wash
Fleur de sel, for garnish

Put the flour, lard, and salt in a food processor and pulse to crumbs. Add the water, and pulse until the dough just comes together. Remove, pat into a disk, wrap in plastic, and chill until you're ready to roll it out. Once it's on the pies and just before baking, cut a few steam vents, brush all over with egg wash and strew over fleur de sel. The pastry will emerge beautifully golden and flecked with the crunchy crystals.

Rough Puff Pastry

MAKES: 2 DISKS, TO COVER TWO 9-INCH (23 CM) PIES

A buttery, puffy pastry variation for when you're in that kind of mood. I'm rather obsessed with lard crust at the moment, but a bit of poof isn't bad either now and again.

2 cups (250 g) flour
1 cup + 2 tablespoons (255 g) cold unsalted butter, cut into pieces
3/4 teaspoon (4 mL) salt
1/2 cup (125 mL) ice-cold water
Egg wash
Fleur de sel, for garnish

Put the flour, butter, and salt in a food processor and pulse to crumbs. Add the water and pulse just until the dough holds together. Remove to a floured board and roll into a rectangle about 16 x 8 inches (40 x 20 cm).

Working from the short sides, fold up the rectangle like a business letter. Give the whole a quarter turn and roll flat again. Fold in the ends again. Wrap in plastic and refrigerate 30 minutes. Repeat the entire double folding and rolling process a second time. Wrap and refrigerate the dough at least 30 minutes longer or until ready to roll out.

Divide the pastry in half and roll each piece to about 1/4- inch (5 mm) thickness to fit your pie plates. Put in the filling, drape the crust over top, trim, brush with egg wash, and strew with fleur de sel.

Bamfield Beef and Kidney Pie with Guinness and Oysters

MAKES: 2 DEEP PIES, FOR 8 SERVINGS EACH

Not to be sexist, but this is definitely boy food: a hearty, mahogany-dark pie of fork-tender stewed beef, slightly gamey-tasting kidneys, and salty oysters, all held together with glossy Guinness gravy and topped with a crisp, golden lard pastry. It's yet another John recipe, and I love how it perfectly articulates place in his life: oysters from his current ocean-side home in Bamfield, B.C., and otherwise traditional British pub pie ingredients from his native England. A heap of green salad such as watercress or mâche on the table at the same time is the only accompaniment you need, although peas or green beans are also nice. This recipe makes a lot of pie, but you can always freeze one for another time if you're not feeding a crowd.

FOR THE FILLING

3 pounds (1.3 kg) boneless rump or bottom round, cut into 1/2-inch (1 cm) cubes

Salt and pepper

4 tablespoons (60 mL) grapeseed oil, more as needed

1/4 cup (55 g) butter, more as needed

1/4 cup (30 g) flour

1 cup (250 mL) rich beef stock

2 medium onions, chopped

6 garlic cloves, minced

1 tablespoon (15 mL) tomato paste

1 teaspoon (5 mL) dry mustard

1 teaspoon (5 mL) Worcestershire sauce

1 teaspoon (5 mL) summer savory or dried thyme, more to taste

2 bay leaves

2 1/2 cups (625 mL) Guinness (about 2 1/2 cans, which leaves a sip for you)

3/4 pound (340 g) veal kidneys, peeled, trimmed of fat and membrane

8 ounces (225 g) mushrooms, sliced

12 fresh medium oysters, cut in half or thirds

A handful of chopped fresh parsley

TO FINISH

Egg wash

Fleur de sel

FOR THE CRUST

Lard pastry (p. 330)

Season the meat with salt and pepper. Heat a couple of tablespoons (30 mL) each of oil and butter in a heavy casserole and, working in batches, brown the beef cubes until deeply caramelized, removing to a bowl as you go and the leaving the fat behind. Add the flour and cook, whisking, 1 minute. Add the stock, whisking until smooth, and pour over the meat.

Add a tablespoon or two (15 to 30 mL) each of oil and butter to the same pan. Fry the onions until soft but not colored. Add the garlic and cook 1 minute. Stir in the tomato paste, mustard, and Worcestershire sauce. Add the savory and bay leaves. Return the meat and any juices to the pot, stir in the beer, and simmer very gently, partly covered, until the meat is fork-tender, about 2 hours. (You can also do this for the same amount of time in a 350°F/180°C oven.) At this point, the liquid should be reduced to thick gravy. If it isn't, remove the meat and boil the sauce down to that consistency. Discard the bay leaves, then put the meat back in. Taste and adjust the seasonings.

While the beef cooks, soak the kidneys in salted water for 30 minutes to an hour. Drain, rinse, pat dry, and slice. Cover and refrigerate until ready to use. Heat 1 tablespoon (15 mL) each of oil and butter in a frying pan and sauté the mushrooms until tender and colored, 7 to 10 minutes.

When the meat is ready and the sauce reduced, stir in the kidneys and mushrooms. Cool completely. Just before assembling the pies, stir in the oysters and parsley.

Put a baking sheet on the bottom rack to catch any drippings, and heat the oven to 425°F (220°C). Divide the mixture between 2 deep 9-inch (23 cm) pie plates. Roll out 2 disks of pastry and cover the pies. Trim the edges and pinch to seal. Brush with egg wash, sprinkle with fleur de sel, and make 3 slits in the top of each to let steam escape. Bake the pies 25 minutes. Reduce the heat to 350°F (180°C) and continue baking until the filling is hot and the crust is crisp and golden, about 20 minutes longer. Serve warm (although some, I'm told, prefer it cold).

Million-Dollar Fish Pie

MAKES: 8 SERVINGS

I'm just being honest. If you live on the coast and can reach your hand into the ocean and haul out all your fish and seafood for free, great. If you live in a city inland, then I recommend you cash a few bonds before you make this pie. Mind you, at least you can rest assured that with this recipe none of your pennies are wasted: it is positively regal, while at the same time being completely unpretentious. Of course, you can adjust the fish and seafood types to suit your budget (not to mention your audience).

Traditional English fish pies, at least all those I'd seen until recently, are made more like shepherd's pie, which is to say with a mashed-potato top. The filling underneath is usually flavored with parsley instead of dill, the fish combination often involves a mixture of fresh and smoked, occasionally hard-boiled eggs are added (a way to add extra protein cheaply, although I'm not a fan of the texture against the fish), and I've sometimes seen grated Cheddar cheese in the potato topping. No matter what the fiddling, they've all been, in my experience, bland and uninteresting. I made one of these English pies for a dinner party once, adding my own ideas of extra flavor hoping to make it more interesting. It looked magnificent and I set it on the table with pride, but one bite and I was crestfallen. I asked everyone else what they thought and there was a lot of shifting in seats and mumbling. The next day I called my friend on the West Coast who fancies himself a fish-pie expert, and he announced, "I heard about your pie last night." "Oh," said I, "what did you hear?" "Mine's much better," he said smugly.

Next time he came to visit, obviously I insisted on being taught the secrets. We went to the market together and launched into an afternoon of pie-making. Meanwhile, I invited the same fish-pie crowd as before, assuring them that all sins were going to be rectified that night. And they were! (Well, all culinary sins, anyway . . .) Fish pie, done right, can be made into the life of the party. Don't be put off by the long ingredients list or by the multiple steps. Trust me, this is all easy. You just have to get your elements organized before assembly, that's all.

FOR THE FILLING

1 small lobster

6 large prawns or shrimp

1 celery rib, chopped

2 cups (500 mL) milk

1 bay leaf

1 pound (450 g) cod fillets, skinned, boned,
    and cut into pieces

8 ounces (225 g) haddock fillets, skinned,
    boned, and cut into pieces

5 ounces (140 g) sole fillets, skinned, boned,
    and cut into pieces

6 large scallops, cut in half or thirds

1 tin (14 ounces/390 g) crabmeat

1/2 cup (110 g) + 1 tablespoon (15 mL) butter

1 tablespoon (15 mL) grapeseed oil

1 medium onion, sliced

1 large shallot, minced

2 garlic cloves, minced

1/2 cup (125 mL) dry vermouth or white wine

1/2 cup (60 g) flour

Salt and pepper

A squirt of lemon juice (optional)

2 very generous handfuls of chopped dill

2 tablespoons (30 mL) capers

FOR THE CRUST

2 disks lard pastry (p. 330)

TO FINISH

1 egg, lightly beaten

Fleur de sel

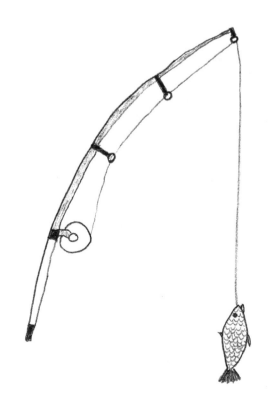

Butter an 8 x 12-inch (20 x 30 cm) casserole or two 9-inch (23 cm) pie plates and set aside.

Bring about 2 cups (500 mL) water to a boil in a pot large enough to hold the lobster. Drop it in, head first, cover, and steam 5 minutes. Remove the lobster. Add the prawns and cook 1 minute, then remove them. Turn off the heat while you remove the lobster and prawn meat from the shells. Throw the shells back into the pot of liquid along with the celery. Return to a boil to start reducing it. Cut the lobster meat into pieces and slice the prawns in half lengthwise. Put these in a large bowl.

Put the milk and bay leaf in a pan and bring to a simmer. Add the fish and scallop pieces and poach 5 minutes. Strain, reserving the milk, and pluck out the bay leaf. Add the fish pieces to the lobster mixture, along with the crab.

Melt 1 tablespoon (15 mL) of the butter with the oil in a frying pan and gently fry the onions and shallots until soft. Add the garlic and fry 1 minute. Add to the fish mixture. Deglaze the pan with the vermouth, boiling it down somewhat, then add it to the boiling cooking liquid in the lobster pot. Boil this down to 1 cup (250 mL). Strain and set aside.

Melt the remaining 1/2 cup (110 g) butter in a large saucepan. When the foam subsides, whisk in the flour and cook, whisking, 1 minute. Whisk in the strained lobster cooking liquid and the strained milk and bring to a boil, whisking, to thicken. Remove from the heat immediately and season with salt and pepper. (You may want a squirt of lemon juice, too.) Stir in the dill and capers. Pour over the fish, and mix gently so as not to break up the seafood. Tumble the whole business into the casserole or pie plates.

Roll out the pastry and lay it over the pie. Trim the edges and pinch to the edge of the pie plate to seal. Brush the top with egg wash, scatter over fleur de sel, and make 2 or 3 slashes in the top to allow steam to escape. You can wrap the pie and refrigerate at this stage until just before dinner.

Heat the oven to 425°F (220°C). Bake the pie until it's bubbling hot and the crust is crisp and golden, about 45 minutes. Serve hot.

CHERRIES JUBILEE

MAKES: 8 SERVINGS

My friend Bill, who plays lovely jazz piano and knows how to fix your every computer problem, is, along with the rest of it, somewhat of a kitchen-equipment junkie. He has a meat slicer, for example, just so he can slice his own bacon. He has one of those fancy coffee machines that looks as if you could attach wheels to it and drive it smoothly down the boulevard. But the real pièce de résistance in his vast collection is a copper chafing dish on its own stand. You can set it tableside and make impressive pyromaniacal displays of dessert. Dramatic, yes, but easy with something simple like Cherries Jubilee.

It's a bit of a cheat, using tinned cherries, but that is how I've always been served this classic. If you have fresh cherries at hand, then naturally use those (you want about 2 pounds/900 g, pitted). I sauté them briefly in butter, scatter over the sugar, then mix the cornstarch with a spoonful of the juices before stirring it in. Either way, this kingly concoction belongs over scoops of Vanilla Ice Cream (p. 280).

2 tins (each 15 ounces/425 g) pitted dark sweet cherries
1/4 cup (55 g) sugar
1 teaspoon (5 mL) cornstarch
1/4 cup (60 mL) warm kirsch

Drain the cherries. Pour 1 cup (250 mL) of the juice into a sauté pan (or chafing dish) and set over medium heat. Mix the sugar and cornstarch, stir in a spoonful of the juice to make a slurry, and return to the juice in the pan. Bring to a boil and cook, stirring, until thickened. Add the cherries to heat through. Pour over the kirsch, stand back, and ignite. Serve the flaming cherries over vanilla ice cream.

Acknowledgments

Bill Hutchison is the number one man I have to thank for making this book possible. In his superbly equipped kitchen, a huge percentage of these menus were born, and at his dining room table much of the text was written. I couldn't have done it without him.

John Evans is another who repeatedly shared his kitchen with me. I spent weeks ransacking his cupboards, dirtying his dishes, depleting his flour and sugar supply, and copying down scores of his best recipes, which he so generously shared.

Many other friends, family members, and acquaintances shared recipes for this book also, and because of their presence the book is extra special to me. I open its cover like a living-room door and there they all are inside: Keith Froggett, Sinclair Stewart, Beth and Barb Fullerton, Bob Blumer, Kirsten Hanson, Bridget and Nancy Oland, Ruth Jewkes, Henry Less, Freeman Patterson, Andrea and Poppy Butler, John and Doris Calder, Kenny Skarland, Peter Fiala, Jennifer McLagan, Oliver Evans, Judith Phillips, Donnalu Wigmore, Kerry and Ivy Knight, Nancy Sherry, Luisa Golino, Kevin Mooney, Katherine Mooney, Chris Mooney and family, Johanna Eliot, Alison Calder, Nathalie Findlay, Tor Bordevik, Christopher Keiser, Cathy Grant, Pamela Brickenden, Tiffany MacKay, Deborah Madison, Grace Bostwick, Erin Donovan, Malcolm Jolley, Ian Tuck, Anne Fitzgerald, Patti Hetherington, and Anne Willan.

Many thanks to photographer James Ingram, as well as to food and props stylist Patti Hetherington, for making the pictures in this book so elegant. (Thanks also to Patti for recipe tests at the eleventh hour!) Thanks to Greg Campbell, food assistant; Alison Beckett, photography assistant; and to Johanna Eliot for letting me use her glorious sunlit kitchen for the shoot location. For the cover we worked with Kathryn Hollinrake and her assistant Mark Luciani. Thanks to them both for a gorgeous result.

Once again I had the honor of working with my editor and friend Kirsten Hanson at Harper-Collins Canada, without whose sensibilities, sensitivity, and sense of humor the writing in this book (not to mention the kooky drawings) would never have seen print. Thanks also to copy editor Shaun Oakey for his close eye on the final text and exquisite polishing skills, as well as to Alan Jones for the fine design of the book.

Thanks to my literary agent, Bruce Westwood, not least of all for encouraging me to step out from behind the recipes and reveal a little more life in writing. Also thanks to Carolyn Forde at Westwood Creative Artists.

Finally, a big thank you to my family (and "the family") for their constant encouragement and support. To them and the many friends who shared both recipes and the experience of these dinners with me: endless love and gratitude. You're what gives my cooking meaning.

INDEX